Thirty Days of Forex Trading

Founded in 1807, John Wiley & Sons is the oldest independent publishing company in the United States. With offices in North America, Europe, Australia, and Asia, Wiley is globally committed to developing and marketing print and electronic products and services for our customers' professional and personal knowledge and understanding.

The Wiley Trading series features books by traders who have survived the market's ever changing temperament and have prospered—some by reinventing systems, others by getting back to basics. Whether a novice trader, professional, or somewhere in-between, these books will provide the advice and strategies needed to prosper today and well into the future.

For a list of available titles, visit our web site at www.WileyFinance.com.

Thirty Days of Forex Trading

Trades, Tactics, and Techniques

RAGHEE HORNER

WILEY

John Wiley & Sons, Inc.

Published by John Wiley & Sons, Inc., Hoboken, New Jersey.
Published simultaneously in Canada.

eSignal charts used with permission of eSignal, www.esignal.com.

Designations used by companies to distinguish their products are often claimed as trademarks. In all instances where John Wiley & Sons, Inc., is aware of a claim, the product names appear in initial capital or all capital letters. Readers, however, should contact the appropriate companies for more complete information regarding trademarks and registration.

For general information on our other products and services or for technical support, please contact our Customer Care Department within the United States at (800) 762-2974, outside the United States at (317) 572-3993, or fax (317) 572-4002.

Wiley also publishes its books in a variety of electronic formats. Some content that appears in print may not be available in electronic books. For more information about Wiley products, visit our web site at www.wiley.com.

Library of Congress Cataloging-in-Publication Data:

Horner, Raghee.
   Thirty days of forex trading : trades, tactics, and techniques / Raghee Horner.
      p. cm.
   Includes index.
   ISBN-13 978-0-471-93441-7 (cloth/cd-rom)
   ISBN-10 0-471-93441-0 (cloth/cd-rom)
   1. Foreign exchange market. 2. Foreign exchange futures. 3. Speculation.
 I. Title.
 HG3851.H674 2006
 332.4'50973—dc22   2006014052

Printed in the United States of America.

10 9 8 7 6 5 4 3 2 1

Contents

Acknowledgments

There are people who are set on this earth to make all things they touch better than they found them. Some of us can walk the earth all our lives and not find a single one of these special people. I have been lucky enough to have found one, and she's my sister Nila. Nila, you're the best person I know.

I love adventure, and I know life, like trading, can be risky. But loving someone is the biggest and most rewarding risk of all. To my best friend Herbie, I love you more than yesterday and will love you more tomorrow.

I want to be the person you think I can become, Ma.

Special thanks:

To my unsung hero, Chris Kyrza, as brilliant as he is an all-around good guy. You always humor me when I ask, "Chris, can we do this with the charts?" And somehow, no matter how impossible it may seem, you figure it out, buddy!

To my friends at eSignal, Raphel Finelli and Marisa Arnold . . . and that Quotrek that I can't seem to get enough of. I love brainstorming with you, Raphel! I'm always smarter after one of our chats. (I need to call you soon!) And it's great to have you back, Marisa!

To my good friend Robert Ruiz, the never-tiring supporter of "The Raghee Way" . . . my ambassador of verisimilitude.

To my friends at Gain Capital, Todd Gordon, Samantha Roady, Elissa Fulop, and Glenn Stevens. Did I mention I am the founder of the Todd Gordon Fan Club?

To Jayanthi Gopalakrishnan and *Stocks & Commodities* magazine.

To Tim Bourquin and the Forex Trading Expo.

To the Body for Life team and champs. Thanks, Porter, Marc, Jerry, and Gregg.

To Jeff Gibby at Metastock.

To Derek Gehl and the staff at the Internet Marketing Center.

To my friends over at one of the coolest sites on the Internet, Forex TV. Hey, Julie, Sara, and Jason—we've got to go out again when I get to New York City!

And to my "trading partner" of nine years, my puppy dog, Shana. I miss your fuzzy little face.

RAGHEE HORNER

The Mechanics of Trading

NO ONE IS BORN KNOWING HOW TO TRADE

Thanks for joining me for these next 30 days. You and I are going to be sitting down together and examining foreign exchange (forex) setups on a number of time frames. In the trading day chapters themselves I assume that you know a little about charting and execution and also the way I analyze the markets; however, if you need a refresher on trend lines, support, resistance, and so on, I do have free video available at my Raghee.com web site. So the first part of this book is what I endearingly have called "the brain dump." Here I discuss all the ideas that you will see carried through into the trading days: the trades, tactics, and techniques. I also have to mention that while you are reading this and whenever you may decide to put this information to use, use it *as is*. Don't add or subtract anything from it. I haven't left anything out; there is no secret indicator I have kept from you. Just use the tools and rules I explain and try not to change them, if for no other reason than before you can make something better, you first must have a foundation. You can't change something for the better unless you already know it. *Please play and win by the rules before you go about changing the rules.*

This entire book is part instruction, part trading journal. The main focus is on forex, but I want to get across one message if nothing else: *I trade all markets with these tools. I trade momentum and swing setups the same way regardless of whether that setup is on forex, futures, or the stock market.*

The time frames may differ as well as the "hot zones" that move the particular market. In the end, though, it's the same "Three Classic Tools to a Three-Step Setup," and that doesn't change. Recently I was interviewed for an article about my trading approach. I spent a good 20 minutes explaining to the author that I was a chartist and that meant that I relied on price and not on fundamental data or news. I thought I got my point across well until I read what was printed in the article.

Raghee Horner, a currency trader and author, prefers to ignore the news alto-gether and stare at charts instead. She plans trades based on the movement of currency charts. If a news item triggered the movement, Horner said, she usually finds out after the fact.

"A chartist like myself feels that all the economic data are represented in the price," Horner said.

Thank God they put my quote in the article! Maybe I am being too sensitive, but I hated the reference to my "staring" at charts and the suggestion that if news triggered a movement I find out only after the fact. Then I started thinking about it. I guess that's how chartists or technical traders are perceived, aren't we? *We need better PR!* I think there is a lot of misinformation out there about the way chartists process the fear and greed of the market. In the end, that's all that fundamental data represents. Chartists and technical traders, at least the ones I know, don't "ignore" news and fundamentals! We just don't base our entries and exits on them. I want you to remember that fact re-gardless of whether you are trading forex, futures, or stocks. Never be ignorant of the news, but at the same time it has no place in deciding the price at which you will enter or exit a trade. The use of news is more of a timing element (aka "hot zones") than a price element (support, resistance, trend lines). If you keep that distinction in mind you will be able to utilize fundamental releases to your advantage.

Hot zones are the minutes leading up to and during and one minute after the release of economic reports and scheduled fundamental data. The increased volatility that accom-panies these scheduled releases is based on the way market participants feel the actual data relates to the consensus data that has already been discounted into the market. Be-fore any scheduled data is released, in the days and weeks leading up to the release, a certain consensus of what the result may be is factored, or discounted, into the market. Think of this as the impetus for "buying the rumor and selling the news."

So why do I want to stress how I use fundamentals and why you should trade multi-ple markets so much, you may ask? Well, we trade. Period. We are traders of any mar-ket. We look for any market that has good execution and liquidity. That's it. So if it comes in the form of a euro/U.S. dollar trade or in the form of a sugar trade, we should be equally open to the potential.

Let's talk about some specifics, though. I don't want you thinking that you have to be glued to multiple charts all day long. I certainly am not! I trade mainly the six "ma-jors" of forex on one of five time frames and am done by noon eastern standard time (EST). The majors are the pairs that make up over 80 percent of daily trading activity. They are pairs that involve the U.S. dollar. The main ones are the EUR/USD, GBP/USD, AUD/USD, USD/CHF, USD/JPY, and USD/CAD. If I decide to trade the E-mini S&P or

NASDAQ-100 futures contract, I do that only from the 9:30 A.M. open until about 11:30 to 11:30 A.M. When I set up commodity futures or stock trades, I do so on end-of-day charts and do that homework in the afternoon; it takes 30 to 45 minutes. If you restrict your trading pursuit to only one market, you are limiting yourself in a number of ways. First, you are missing out on opportunities in other markets. Did you know that around the same time the crude oil market was climbing so was the coffee market? And coffee was coming up off all-time historical lows!

If you limit yourself, you will also find yourself trying to squeeze too much out of your trades since they are all you have. You'll inevitably try to get those few extra pips or half a point out of a trade. (A pip is the smallest increment of price. It is similar to a tick in the stock market.)

I speak from experience, my own and watching dozens of traders over the years do the same thing. It was especially clear in the late 1990s. Some traders had switched from stocks to E-mini futures after a mandatory $25,000 account requirement for day trading stocks was put into effect. The S&P 500 and NASDAQ-100 E-minis required much less capital. Because these traders, who were used to scanning through dozens of stocks, were now basically watching one or maybe two markets—the "spooz" and the "naz," as they are nicknamed—they had very little to watch. There was more squeezing going on than at the lemonade stand. Traders would try to get that extra quarter or half point and give back much more than that because the desire to increase their profits overrode the fact that the trade had reached its profit target. This may be an extreme example, but the psychology works across any market. Don't limit yourself. The fatal mistake that these traders made was to lose sight of one thing:

Your vocation in life should in some way contribute to who you are and who you may become. In some way it should make you a better person!

In fact, if you've met me or seen me present live at eSignal online chats, at Trade-DirectFX presentations, or at the Forex Trading Expos, you know that I mention a philosophy of mine in regard to my pursuit of trading. I don't want to be chained to my computer. I wanted to become a trader for the freedom I think this career represents. And yes! It is a career. I think we all hit a time of our life when we realize that we have become proficient at a certain skill and it's what we know. I am a trader. I've spent so much of my life now in pursuit of that goal that it's a part of who I am, the way I think, and the way I present myself to the world.

The freedom that trading provides is unlike what one can experience in any other career or business. I have the freedom to trade at almost any hour of the day. I can trade for a few hours or I can trade all day long and well into the early morning of the next day! (By the way, if the latter describes you too often, get a hobby!) I can take a day off or a week off. It's the freedom of trading that attracted me to this pursuit, not just the goal of making money. Now before you start rolling your eyes at me, hear me out. There are tons of ways to make a living in this world. Many of them are easier than trading, and certainly there are many that can afford you a higher income. If you are trading with the sole interest of making money, you will burn hot, burn up, and burn out. Listen to me now, believe me later.

Early in my own pursuit of becoming a trader I heard the following statement: "Trading is the hardest way to make an easy living." It stuck with me. There is a certain percentage of the population that thinks trading is easy, that chart reading is something you can pick up in a weekend seminar, or in a two-hour video, or in a piece of software that tells you when to get in and out of the market.

If you've been to a trading seminar that whetted your appetite to begin trading forex, futures, stocks, whatever, and you later found out that you were presented with only a fraction of what you really need to know, do not necessarily be angry or feel duped. Simply thank them—whoever they may be—for the introduction and know that you now have the knowledge to seek out more knowledge! I speak from experience. We've all been there. We all fall into the same traps in this pursuit. No one is born knowing how to trade.

YOU'LL LEARN ONLY WHEN YOU DON'T THINK YOU KNOW IT ALL ALREADY

I was instilled with a love for learning early in my life. I can thank my ma for it. She was as relentless as all good mothers are. Education and respect for your teachers was always a biggie in my home growing up. I think we all take our motivation from things we heard, saw, and experienced early in life. My parents were both born and raised in India. My mother was born with the most indomitable (and stubborn) spirit given to a woman this side of Calcutta. My father was a brilliant man and two feet smarter than I can ever hope to be in this life. I think he would have enjoyed seeing his eldest daughter do well and write books, but I will never be able to experience that because he passed away shortly after my 15th birthday.

You don't realize how little you know about your parents until they are gone. Needless to say, at just over 15 years of age, I hadn't gotten to know my dad as much as I wish I could have. Not long after he passed away, my ma told us a story of how he came to this country. To say my father was poor growing up is an understatement. What is considered poor here in the States is nothing compared the gut-wrenching poverty in developing nations or third world countries. And while India is the largest democracy in the world (by population) and has one of the best educational systems on the planet, producing some of the best engineering and medical minds, it is also in many areas still very poor. Education is therefore of vital importance, as it is widely held that your mind and education can infinitely better your lot in life.

Through a solid education, my dad was able to attend university in London on full scholarship. He went to school with John Lennon. He traveled to Venice during one of the floods and helped the citizens there for a time. He did well enough in London to be invited to the United States to work for an engineering firm in Boston and then got a job at IBM, which, for those of you who remember, was quite a prestigious gig to have! Who would have thought that education would take this man, my father, so far? Who would have thought his daughters would have the opportunities they have now in this country? My father grew up sleeping under the staircase of his childhood home because there was nowhere else to sleep, and my grandmother would place little pieces of food by his feet while he slept so the rats wouldn't bite his toes. Yes, I believe in education. No one ever knows it all. If you think you have figured the markets out, set your watch because you can predict the time until you blow your account up.

So even after I had been trading for years, when Dave, a student of mine, had an idea about some moving averages set upon Fibonacci numbers, I was all ears. (Fibonacci numbers are a sequence of numbers in which each successive number is the sum of the two previous numbers: 1, 1, 2, 3, 5, 8, 13, 21, 34, 55, 89, 144, etc.) I don't ever feel like I know it all. That doesn't mean that I do not stick to a certain set of tools and rules—more is not better!—but I am open to new ideas or at least hearing what other people have to say. If I hadn't been open to the idea my student was curious about, I never would have discovered, tested, and adopted the Wave into my trading. The Wave in its beautiful simplicity improved my trading in ways I never thought possible. So let's talk about the Wave and why it is the first tool that you will use to analyze any market and why it must become a permanent resident on all your charts.

Trading in the mid to late 1990s was defined by specifically stock trading. People were trading stocks and trading mutual funds. The market was skyrocketing and everyone thought they had what it took to be a trader! In fact, most people didn't even call themselves traders. They thought they were investing, which made the situation all the more dire when the market reversed in early 2000. You see, traders and trading rules are defined by price action moves. Investing, however, adopts ideas of market capitalization, product introduction and innovation, and ownership most often via dollar cost averaging (investing a fixed amount of dollars in a specific market such as equities or futures at regular set intervals over a period of time, thereby averaging the cost paid per share). There is little thought given to stop-loss orders. In fact, I think the first time the public at large was introduced to the term *stop-loss* was during the trials and tribulations of the Martha Stewart witch hunt. Since most people thought they were investing in the mid to late 1990s, most or all of the market corrections were opportunities to buy more of, well, frankly, everything.

So when the market actually stopped ascending toward the clouds and actually reversed, these investors hardly knew the difference and dollar cost averaged their accounts into oblivion. And this story gets written over and over again. The market may change, but the last chapter holds no mystery. Venturing into any market without the proper education will, in the end, result in disappointment. I can already see the writing on the wall for those folks who have wandered into the newest bull market, real estate. While this is not new advice, it does seem to be frequently forgotten advice: Don't confuse a bull market with a perceived notion of your investing (or trading) genius.

I am not making light of all the money that individual investors lost during the crash, and I am certainly not hoping that this real estate bubble is going to burst. But it doesn't take Nostradamus to figure it out. All markets have their ebb and flow. There is no exception. Like the Borg recite in unison: "Resistance is futile." (Yes, I'm a bit of a

Trekkie.) Playing the market is a skill, and the traders with any longevity know that a bull market does not make or preserve a career. A few good trades or lucky picks do not mean you should quit your job and try to trade full-time. I most often liken trying to become a full-time trader to attempting to be a professional golfer.

Part-time trading is perfect for most people. Being part-time doesn't make the person any less a trader! It just means they have other things going on their lives that produce an income. There's nothing wrong with that! Forex is a part-time trader's dream market.

I love playing golf. To me it's the sport that is most akin to trading. Around my second year trading full-time I realized I had to get out of the house and away from the markets at least once a week. I was a die-hard futures trader then, getting streaming quotes from the satellite dish mounted on my roof. This was pre-Internet, and that dish was high-tech. I figured I would take up golf again. (I had played on and off since the age of 7 when I got my first junior golf set. I'm quite certain that my dad had aspirations for me to be the next Nancy Lopez.) I used to hang out occasionally at the local cigar shop because my friend Manny, the owner, made the most incredible espresso and a good cup of coffee, too! The guys would golf once or twice a week. We'd go to the humidor in the shop, pick out one to two cigars each, and then go to the golf course. It was fun, it was an escape, and it had nothing to do with trading. In other words, it was fairly stress-free—or as stress-free as playing golf can be.

But imagine yourself a *professional* golfer. No signing bonus. No long-term contract with a team. You get paid for results. Now that four-foot putt to make par isn't just among friends and a couple of cigars you light to keep the mosquitoes away. Now that putt is in front of the gallery and for the mortgage, car payment, insurance, electric bill, and groceries. The same thing is true for a person who is trying to become a full-time trader. When there is no other income to run your household, every trade is a four-foot putt in front of the gallery, for the mortgage, and so on.

And people wonder why they can't trade well! There's a reason why you will hear so many traders talk about trading psychology. So what's my point here? Well, first, give professional golfers credit. It's not easy! And if you are learning how to trade, don't make it the sole source of your income right away; don't just jump into it. It's not a skydive.

If you want to trade, full-time or part-time, use psychology in your favor. Do you think you're going to trade well when every trade has a bill with its name on it? Or do you think you will trade well knowing that it could provide that extra income or maybe replace a small percentage of your household income? Take the time to learn this new skill, test it out, and if or when your returns merit it, you can go full-time. Take it slow—the market is not going anywhere.

Case in point: I know the real estate market has been on fire for the past few years.

I don't know a thing about real estate investing, so I am not jumping in without any knowledge or experience. I pay people to teach me, and my husband Herbie is the one who is currently pursuing it. A forex trading student of mine is experienced in a niche of real estate investing through what he calls short selling, and I am learning those strategies from him since he is out there doing it full-time himself. *I'm always a student.*

As I said earlier, I am not making light of all the money that individual investors lost during the crash and I am certainly not hoping that this real estate bubble is going to burst. If the stock investors of the 1990s had known that they were in actuality speculating or trading, there would have been a set of rules that would have guided them more effectively. That brings us to the Wave. I'm sure many of you who read my first book, *Forex Trading for Maximum Profit* (John Wiley & Sons, 2004), already know of the Wave and hopefully are using it every day. For those of you who are new to it, here's how and why I use this tool. The Wave is made up of three 34-period exponential moving averages (EMAs)—one on the high, one on the low, and one on the close. An exponential (or exponentially weighted) moving average is calculated by applying a percentage of today's closing price to yesterday's moving average value; exponential moving averages place more weight on recent prices. The three lines of the Wave have a permanent place moving across all my charts. These three lines act as dynamic support and resistance. The question my student Dave asked me was why—since I was such a fan of Fibonacci numbers—did I not use these numbers as moving average periods? I couldn't come up with a reason not to, so I spent the next six months testing and using this idea, applying it to the high, low, and close of all the Fibonacci numbers up to 144. We chose 34 not only for its effectiveness in acting as support and resistance but also because the angle at which it traveled offered a unique market insight. The 34-period EMA, one on the high, one on the low, and one on the close, allowed me to accurately measure and identify market cycles.

This is not just semantics. Market cycles are the reason I learned to both swing and momentum trade. Although I have to say that 80 percent of my entries are momentum based, understanding when to use each increases the likelihood that you are entering the market at the right price and at the right time. The market typically follows a cycle—it will move sideways, then trend up or down, only to slow the trend and move sideways again. Trading sideways or choppy markets with tools better used for trending markets and vice versa will lead to low-percentage entries. Swing trading is a useful and powerful style of trading, as is my favorite, momentum trading. The distinction is in knowing that momentum entries are best applied to markets trading in ranges (sideways or choppy markets) and that swing trading is best done in established trends. This reminds me of something that I learned watching the Winter Olympics this weekend. The Turin, Italy, games have just begun and I am enjoying the almost 24-hour sports coverage immensely. I heard this weekend that in figure skating the jumps are actually given their names and are distinguished based on the way the skater takes off from the ice. That's exactly how trading works. The different trading styles are distinguished by how you decide at what price to enter, and that decision is based on the underlying market cycle.

Since I know that at any time the market is going to be either trending or moving side-ways, I must be able to (1) recognize which it is doing and (2) decide at what price to en-ter using either swing or momentum entry rules.

Recognizing market direction is as easy as looking at the Wave. Since the three lines of the Wave will be on every one of your charts, you can simply glance at the Wave to get a clock angle reading. Clock angle readings are the way we define market cycles using the Wave. Please don't try to complicate this. It is not difficult. Let's take a look at the chart of the daily (end-of-day) euro/U.S. dollar (EUR/USD) price action in Figure I.1.

In this chart I have drawn straight line segments that follow the middle line of the Wave for the sake of clarity. Notice how they compare to the twelve, three, and six o'clock angles? This is how we determine clock angles. If the Wave is traveling at be-tween twelve and two o'clock, then the market is in an uptrend. The closer to twelve it is traveling, the stronger and steeper the price movement is.

When the Wave is traveling downward between four and six o'clock we have a downtrend, and the closer to six it is traveling the stronger and steeper the price movement.

Now, look at the charts of the twelve to two o'clock Wave (Figure I.2) and the four

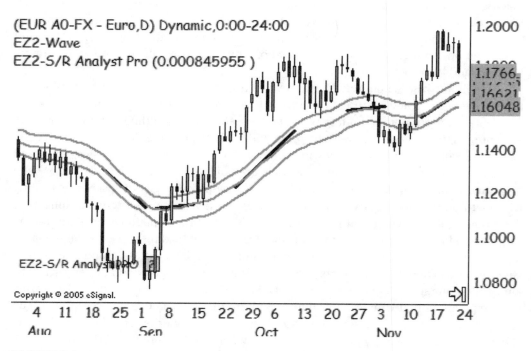

FIGURE I.1

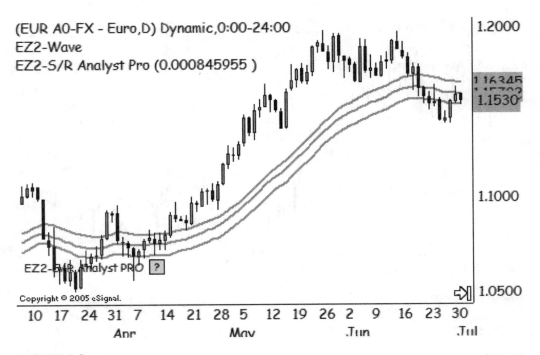

FIGURE I.2

to six o'clock Wave (Figure I.3). Burn these into your memory and train your eyes to notice the angles because these two charts show when—and only when!—you will be swing trading. Swing trading entries are used when you can identify an established trend. Trends are funny things, if you ask me. There are so many truisms out there in trading lore about the trend being your friend and trading with the trend and not trying to pick tops or bottoms in a trend. Now, I'm not saying that some of this advice isn't true! I'm just saying that some of this is easier said than done. None of these sayings ever really explain how to accomplish these feats! You're left on your own when it comes to figuring all this out. Take trends, for example. They are always crystal clear . . . in hindsight! They look great on the charts . . . after the fact! Do you see where I am going with this? Going long in an uptrend requires that you find a logical place to do so. The same goes for getting short in a downtrend. (You remember which clock angles those are, right?)

Swing trading is best defined by entering an established trend by waiting for bounces or pullbacks. A correction is a bounce or a pullback. In a downtrend it's a bounce and in an uptrend it's a pullback. When I am swing trading it is my job to enter on any bounce or pullback within the context of an established trend. But how do we measure what is a sufficient bounce or pullback? Well, glad you asked! That's where the charts come in. While we will get into more detail as the trading days progress, I use Fibonacci retracement and extension levels and the Wave to measure these corrections

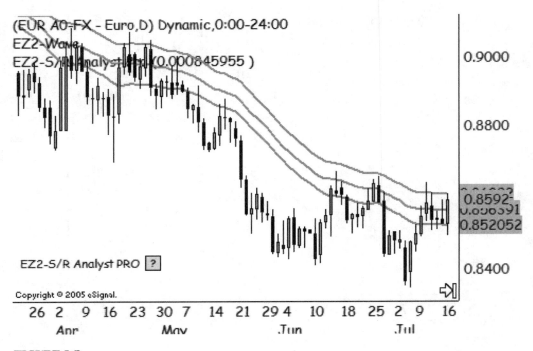

(EUR A0=FX - Euro,D) Dynamic,0:00-24:00
EZ2-Wave,
EZ2-S/R Analyst PRO (0.000845955)

0.9000

0.8800

0.8592
0.8583591
0.852052

EZ2-S/R Analyst PRO ?

0.8400

Copyright © 2005 eSignal.

| 26 | 2 | 9 | 16 | 23 | 30 | 7 | 14 | 21 | 29 | 4 | 10 | 18 | 25 | 2 | 9 | 16 |

Apr   May   Jun   Jul

FIGURE I.3

but only after I see the Wave traveling at either between twelve and two o'clock or between four and six o'clock. Both Fibonacci levels and the Wave offer a trader ways to find measured pullbacks and measured bounces.

It is at the measured pullbacks and measured bounces that I will enter a swing trade. So, for example, if the market is heading downward at the four to six o'clock angle, I will wait for a measured bounce. That bounce must be high enough to hit my predetermined Fibonacci level or even the Wave; I will then short the market at that predetermined price. What is a sufficient measured bounce is not one magical level. Your risk tolerance will dictate this to a certain degree. A basic rule of thumb in this scenario is the higher the bounce the smaller your risk. I use the Wave as the final determination of what is a correction versus a reversal. If the market trades beyond the Wave, then I know that the market has gone past just a correction and is reversing. No matter where you enter, the top line of the Wave must be where you place your stop-loss order, because in this short setup it represents the point beyond which the trade is no longer valid.

The stop-loss placement in any trade is the price beyond which the trade is no longer valid.

For swing trades the setup is fairly simple. Identify the clock angle of either twelve to two or four to six o'clock, wait for the correction and enter. The correction for the twelve to two o'clock Wave will be a pullback in which you will get long (buy). And as we just discussed, you will short a bounce in a four to six o'clock Wave, and your stop is going to be the top line of the Wave. Your stop will be the bottom line of the Wave for a buy in a twelve to two o'clock Wave. Again, in both those two scenarios, the line of the Wave that is furthest away represents the point beyond which the swing trade entry is no longer valid. If you decide to enter on a bounce or pullback to a Fibonacci level that is often closer to the price action than the Wave, you must still consider the line of the Wave that is furthest away your stop. For this reason, many of my students will enter swing trades only when prices correct back to the Wave and use the furthest-away line as their stop-loss. This will severely limit the number of swing setups you will see. Remember, since the Wave is made of three lines, you can use the bottom two lines as entry areas in a downtrend and you can use the top two lines as your entry area in uptrends.

> Swing entries and swing trade management rules are applicable only to twelve to two o'clock or four to six o'clock Waves. If the Wave levels out to between two and four o'clock, the market cycle has changed.

We will have examples of swing trades during the next month. Remember, though, that swing trading entries make up less than 20 percent of my trading. So let's talk about the other 80-plus percent.

Momentum trading is what you will see a lot of in the following days and pages—not so much because it's my favorite style, but because it is a high-percentage entry and affords a trader the opportunity to enter a fresh trend. In many ways swing trading or, more accurately, entering a trending market is like playing catch-up. The market has already broken out of its range (the sideways market cycle) and is now following through with higher lows (an uptrend) or lower highs (a downtrend). It puts a trader in a position of having to wait to enter the market on a correction of some sort, which, quite frankly, the market is not always obliging enough to give us.

Momentum trading, in contrast, is like waiting for a compressed coil to pop. It will—it's only a matter of time and knowing exactly when to get in. Support and resistance are what we use to gauge this pop, which I refer to as "breakouts" when prices break up through resistance and "breakdowns" when prices break down through support. Almost all momentum trades are characterized by two popular chart patterns: triangles and rectangles (also known as channels, which come in both the wide and the narrow variety). These two chart patterns are made up of some combination of support and resistance, whether they be uptrend or downtrend lines or horizontal support or resistance lines.

Chart patterns are great tools, especially for momentum traders. I, however, would much rather see you first draw all relevant support, resistance, and trend lines on the chart you are analyzing. Then and only then can you visually take a step back and see if those lines combined to form triangles or rectangles. If you've just read one of the many books on chart patterns you may be on the lookout for one of them. If you look hard enough your brain will find a way to "connect the dots" on your chart and find just about any chart pattern you want. Look up at the clouds—want to find a castle? Stare long enough and your brain will find it! Charts are the same way, so you must consciously guard against this.

With that in mind, I also encourage you to draw multiple uptrend and downtrend lines, as well as multiple horizontal support and resistance levels. The assumption that there is one right downtrend line or uptrend line is not only completely false, it is limiting! There are both minor and major lines and levels on almost any chart. Your goal is to first find and draw them, and then gauge their importance by four factors. When a trend line has three or more hits it is referred to as solid. When a horizontal support or resistance level has more than two hits at or very near the same price (i.e., within three to five pips), that level is considered solid. If there are two or more hits with wider variance in price, that level is considered soft.

The four factors are:

1. The number of hits or touch points on that line or level (the more touch points, the stronger or more solid the line or level is).

2. The distance between each hit or touch point.

3. How far back these touch points originated.

4. How close to current prices the line or level is (the closer the more relevant).

ORDER TYPES, ORDER EXECUTION, AND TRADEDIRECTFX.COM

Now I know there are going to be some of you thinking, "Oh, great, now she's telling me where to trade!" Nope. You're a grown-up. You don't sleep with the light on anymore. I'm not your mother or your babysitter. If you've read this far, then you also know I do not have any shortage of opinions. Opinions are like elbows—we have a couple of them. I execute my trades on the TradeDirectFX platform. TradeDirectFX is an introducing broker to the Gain Capital Group. Although I have tried some others, I have been executing trades through this platform since late spring 2000. At TradeDirectFX.com you will find dozens of multimedia online videos that cover everything from trading instruction to order execution demonstrations to charting strategies, free. When you trade through TradeDirectFX you will be eligible for specials and free offers like the Raghee Report, free charts, client-only online seminars, and special discounts.

While you are deciding whom to trade through, I just want you to keep a couple of things in mind. First off, execution platforms are for execution! I know that may sound obvious, but it seems that now brokerages are getting into the data provider and charting business. I don't know about you, but I would rather my broker execute my trades, spend time giving me better execution, provide more execution flexibility, and keep my order entry free of other information that could slow those processes down. My execution platform doesn't need to be nor should it be a Swiss Army knife.

Most platforms have user-friendly limit and market order capabilities; beyond that, though, my platform of choice must have equally user-friendly conditional order capabilities like one cancels the other (OCO) and if/then orders. If you are solely a stocks and/or commodity futures trader, then your typical choice of market, limit, and stop-loss orders will do the job just fine because mostly you will be able to manage your trades during waking and working hours. But if you are a forex trader, well, now, that's an entirely different set of trading hours. Forex doesn't so much have trading hours as it has a "trading week." This market is like New York City: It doesn't sleep! Being able to place conditional orders is not a luxury, *it is a necessity!*

Please don't fall into the trap of gravitating to a particular platform because of the bells and whistles. It seems that now platforms are competing to give you the features you can already get from established and reliable data providers like eSignal. It's no secret that I use eSignal for my charts. I have been for going on a decade. Some of you may also do so already. I won't say it's inexpensive, but I will say that if you are a craftsman, then you are only as good as your tools. If you are a trader, you are only as good as your data and execution. Did I forget to mention that TradeDirectFX offers you eSignal charts and data through eSignal forex charts? Well, it does and for free when you open an account of at least $1,000 and place five round-trips a month.

By the way, I wouldn't spend the time mentioning all of this if I didn't use it myself day in and day out. You'll be able to set up the Wave, use all the Fibonacci retracement and extension levels I do, as well as draw trend lines and use candlestick charts.

My husband has two tall Craftsman tool boxes in our garage and more tools than I even know what to do with. He always tells me with a big smile (usually after a visit to Sears to buy more tools) that you have to use the right tool for the right job. eSignal's sole job is to offer me reliable charts and clean data. TradeDirectFX's job is to execute my trades. When I see traders using a platform (and this goes for stocks and futures trading, too!) that combine charts and execution I tell them the same thing: It's like watching someone try to hammer in a nail with a screwdriver handle!

After I wrote *Forex Trading for Maximum Profit* I received many ideas, comments, suggestions, and reviews. One of the most common questions asked in some way related to how to execute trades. I have always thought that any confusion with the mechanics of executing a trade had more to do with not having a plan or not understanding why or when to enter or exit. I still believe that to be the case, but I cannot deny that when reading through scores of e-mails I realized that far too many traders do not understand order execution. Let's talk for a moment about order types and how I use them, since as we progress through the trading days you will need to understand how this all works.

Market Orders

Most traders are familiar with market orders. This is the most basic type of market entry. The order basically tells you broker to "get me in now" or "get me out now" and at whatever price the market is currently trading at. There are two things to consider. First, you are guaranteed an execution; market orders are a sure thing. Second, the market moves, and moves fast sometimes, and your broker may have different ways to handle your order. Since I trade with TradeDirectFX, I am guaranteed my fill at the price of the quoted bid or offer (depending on whether I am buying or selling, of course). We pay the spread in forex, so keep that in mind. **Pro:** You will get your fill. **Con:** There's really no con except that you are getting in and out at the market price, which can often move quickly before you are able to click your mouse button. *Welcome to the real world.*

You are probably familiar with the way most platforms show the prices at which you may execute your buy or sell order. (See Figure I.4.)

Click on the "Sell" or "Buy" price button of your choice and your order is placed for that price, which is really telling your broker, "Get me in now at this price that you are showing me is available." This is probably the most commonly used way to enter the market, long or short. And it's really well suited for that. I would rather see you use limit orders for profit targets and stop orders for protection (stop-losses). But for entries, if you are at your desk, market orders will do the job. TradeDirectFX has a no-slippage policy on stops and limits during normal trading hours, which is to say from 5:00 P.M. EST Sunday through 4:30 P.M. EST Friday. All guarantees are off during fundamental announcements, though. (Keep reading, because I show you how to handle trading during releases and how to place your stops during these volatile hot zones.) I use what I call a "60-second stop," a time-based stop used during economic releases, which I will discuss at length later. Frankly, I can count on one hand the times that this has affected my order. Most of it can be handled with some heads-up trading and good risk management.

Limit Orders

The other commonly known and used order is the limit order. (See Figure I.5.) I have to say that many people become upset when they place a limit order and don't get their fill.

FIGURE I.4
Source: Forex.com.

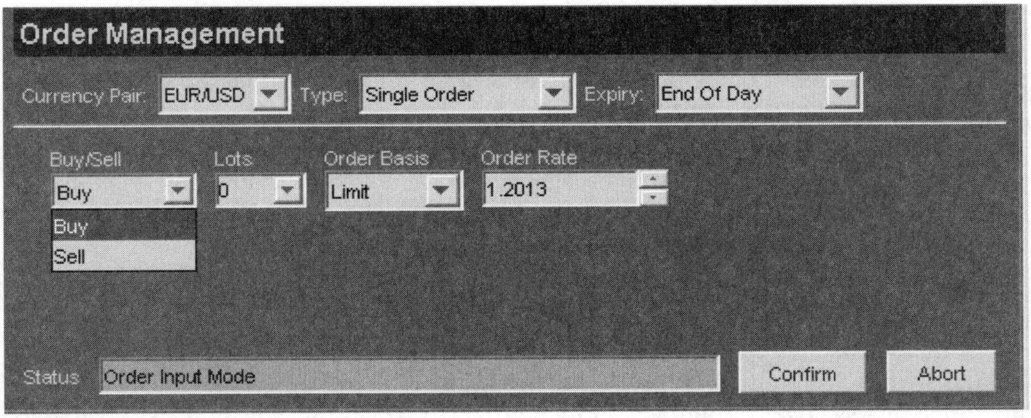

FIGURE 1.5
Source: Forex.com.

A good rule of thumb is only to expect your order to be filled if prices trade through your limit price. This is not always the case, but it is the best way to know you got your fill without worry. I think some of this confusion stems from the fact that some folks just don't understand how orders are filled when you are paying the spread. This is often a point of frustration with traders who are used to directing their own order flow.

Limit orders place a specific price at which you are telling your broker that you will expect a fill. You will accept a better price, which is why limit orders are also referred to as "or better" orders. Let's look at how this works. Let's say that the EUR/USD currency pair is trading at 1.1893 by 1.1896. That's a bid/ask spread. The first price represents the bid (the buyers), while the second price represents the ask or offer (the sellers). The spread is three pips. Since we pay the spread in forex trading, if I want to buy I will pay 1.1896 and if I want to sell or short I will receive 1.1893. It's simpler to understand if you picture a line of buyers starting at the highest price of 1.1893. There is also a line of sellers, and that line starts with the lowest price someone is willing to sell for, which in this example is 1.1896.

If I want to sell now, the easiest way is to go straight to the buyer and sell at their price.

If I want to buy right now, the easiest way is to go directly to the seller and give them their price.

Let's take these concepts to actual executions. Since we understand that buy orders get filled at the sell, also known as the ask or offer, and that sell orders get filled at the buy price, also known as the bid, how does this affect how our limit (and stop) orders are executed?

Imagine that you are long the GBP/USD at 1.7420. Prices are currently trading at 1.7430 and you would like to exit the market at your profit target of 1.7445 so you place a limit order to sell at 1.7445. This order is accepted by your execution platform and you now wait for your price to be hit. Since you want to sell your position at 1.7445, you will be going to the bid or buyers so you won't be filled until the bid reaches 1.7445. Again since we are talking about a limit order, just assume, to be safe, that you won't get your fill until prices trade *through* 1.7445.

That's precisely how this concept of paying the spread works. The earlier EUR/USD pair's spread of 1.1893 by 1.1896 is three pips, and I'm not going to lose any sleep over it. By the way, if your trading approach is made or broken by the spread, it's time to find a new trading approach. If I had a quarter for every time traders tell me that the spread is killing their trades and that they are losing money because of it, I could go buy my own island somewhere in the Caribbean.

Now that we understand how paying the spread works, we can begin to examine the mechanics of a limit order. And by the way, you don't pay the spread only when trading forex; unless you are routing your own orders, it works this way in the stock and futures markets too! Forex is just one of the few markets where the brokerages are open about it.

Limit orders will be used most frequently for profit targets. But I am getting a little ahead of myself. If you want to place a limit order to buy, remember that limit orders are also considered "or better" orders. If you want to buy on a limit and prices are lower than your limit price, then as soon as you place your order you will get filled at the current price. This is because you asked for your specific price *or better* and since prices were lower than your limit price, any system perceives this as price improvement. The same thing goes for situations where you want to go short. If prices are trading higher than your limit price, then as soon as you place your limit order you will get filled at the current price. Like I said earlier, this order type is best suited for profit targets because you are specifying to the market that you will pay a maximum price when buying or you will expect to receive a minimum price when selling or shorting. But also think about swing trades for a moment. A swing trade entry has a lot in common with profit target exits. Limit orders are perfect for swing trading entries because we want to see prices bounce to a certain price so that we can short or pull back to a certain price so we can buy.

Here are a couple of things to think about with limit orders. Because you are specifying a price and will accept no worse price, you are not guaranteed a fill. You can place the order for a day or good till canceled (GTC) or until the end of the day. **Pro:** You can place an order with price control. **Con:** You are not guaranteed a fill.

Stop or Stop-Loss Orders

The next order type we should discuss is the stop or stop-loss order. (See Figure I.6.) Stop orders are what I like to refer to as market orders with a price trigger. That means that the order waits until the order price is reached and then becomes a market order, filling the order at the order price. Most brokerages will guarantee the stop order price Monday through Friday under most market environments but there are exceptions, most notably during economic releases. Stops have been associated with the "stop-loss"

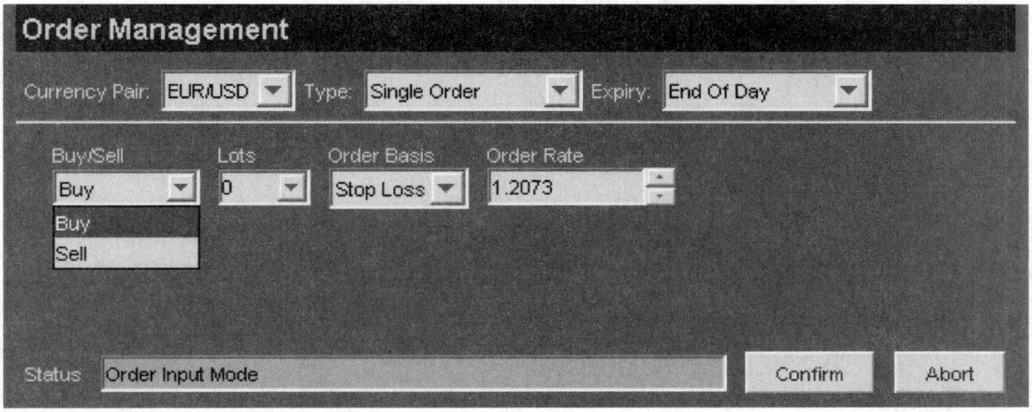

FIGURE I.6
Source: Forex.com.

order, which is simply a stop order. However, stop orders are an excellent way to enter the market as well. Once a stop price is hit, because the order becomes a market order, a fill is guaranteed, although, as mentioned earlier, the price of the fill is not necessarily guaranteed. TradeDirectFX will guarantee your stop order 5:00 P.M. EST Sunday through 4:30 P.M. EST Friday, although, as with any forex broker out there, all guarantees go out the window during fundamental announcements. But again, I can't think of the last time that this disclaimer burned me.

Limit orders, by contrast, are "or better" orders that designate that the order will be filled only once the limit price is reached and only at that price "or better." In other words, there is no risk of slippage and there is no guarantee of a fill because the order will accept only the limit order price. This is not an ideal order type for a stop-loss but rather is an excellent entry order, especially when swing trading.

Stop or stop-loss orders execute in a similar manner to limit orders. So if you place a buy stop, you will be filled on the ask or where the sellers are waiting. If you place a sell stop, you will be filled on the bid. Here's how it would work: You have specified your sell stop price and sent in your order. As soon as your sell stop price is at the bid, your order will be triggered and you will be filled. Because you are paying the spread, you are virtually guaranteed your price on the stop order. As mentioned, I think stop orders are great for entries a well. **Pro:** You can place an order with price control. **Pro:** You are guaranteed a fill after your price is triggered. **Con:** There's really no con here except for the fact that you want to be very aware of where you place your stop order. Make sure you are not placing it at a common, psychologically obvious level. *(Think psychological numbers!)* This is where to herd places their orders. You do not want to be in the same pool of orders as the herd. Get out before them if the herd's order pool will be potential resistance. Use the herd when you want to see prices move beyond support; you can surf their wave of orders after the psychological level. Always think of where the herd is most likely waiting (whole, round numbers) and then consider what their order flow is most likely to do. Will it create resistance or support or will it propel prices through resistance or support?

Conditional Orders

Now we are going to discuss conditional orders. These are powerful orders that allow you to step away from a 24-hour market and still manage your trades and risk. Conditional orders are not new order types; rather, they utilize stop and limit order types in combination. Without conditional orders I wouldn't even dream of trading the forex market. I have three types of conditional orders at my disposal on my platform:

1. One cancels the other (OCO) order.
2. If/then order.
3. If/then OCO order.

It's like having a trading autopilot. I can leave my active orders with the execution platform and it will wait and watch and then execute my wishes. *If only everything in life were that simple.*

I utilize one cancels the other (OCO) orders most frequently. (See Figure I.7.) These orders allow you to place (for example) a stop order and a limit order simultaneously, and if one order is executed, the other will automatically cancel. (You could place two stop orders or two limit orders as well.) OCO orders are very different from placing independent stop and limit orders, because independently placed orders do not communicate with one another the way contingent orders like OCOs do. This is the perfect order type to bracket and manage an entry. So imagine that you have entered a trade—it doesn't matter whether it's long or short. Now you are in risk/trade management mode. You want to place your stop for protection and also a limit order at your profit target. (You will continue to place a number of OCO orders on a single trade as prices move in your favor utilizing a trailing stop and a profit target. Initially, however, your first OCO order will place your stop-loss and your initial profit target order.) Even though an OCO is a single order entry, you are really placing two connected orders, one stop and one limit. When one is executed it automatically cancels the other so you don't have a live order waiting out there. Again, remember we're going to utilize the limit order to place our profit target and the stop order to place the protective stop-loss.

If/then orders are a little more involved, not in the sense that they are difficult to send, but because they involve a completely different mind-set from OCO orders. (See Figure I.8.) We now know that OCO orders place a live stop and a live limit order in the market (or two live stop orders or two live limit orders). If/then orders can place the same order combinations; however, if/then orders differ in the way they are executed. If/then orders dictate that *if* the first order is executed *then* the second order will become a live order. In situations where the "if" is not triggered, the "then" will remain dormant.

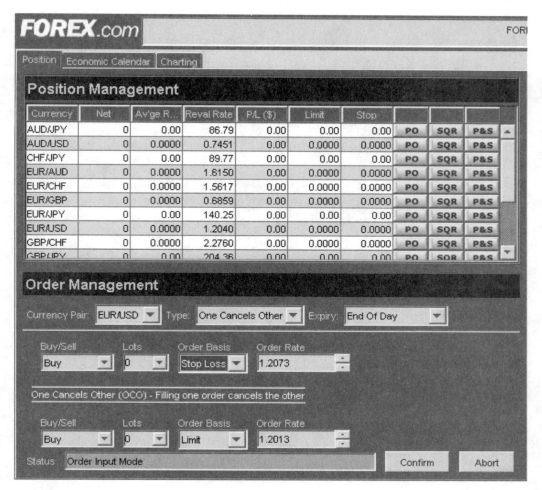

FIGURE 1.7
Source: Forex.com.

When would you utilize such an order? Again, all this takes a little planning like all conditional orders do. Because I know at exactly what price I want to enter the market and also where I want to place my protective stop and profit target order, I can input these prices into orders that will allow me to sit back and see my trading plan executed.

I will place if/then orders in situations where I may be in and out of my trading office or intermittently away from my PC or laptop. Life happens, and there are days when I know I will be multitasking. I know it's not an ideal way to trade, but if I told you that I lock myself away in my trading office and am able to shut out the rest of the world every day I would be lying to you. So that's where if/then orders can come in handy for me. Let me give you a number of scenarios where I have utilized if/then orders:

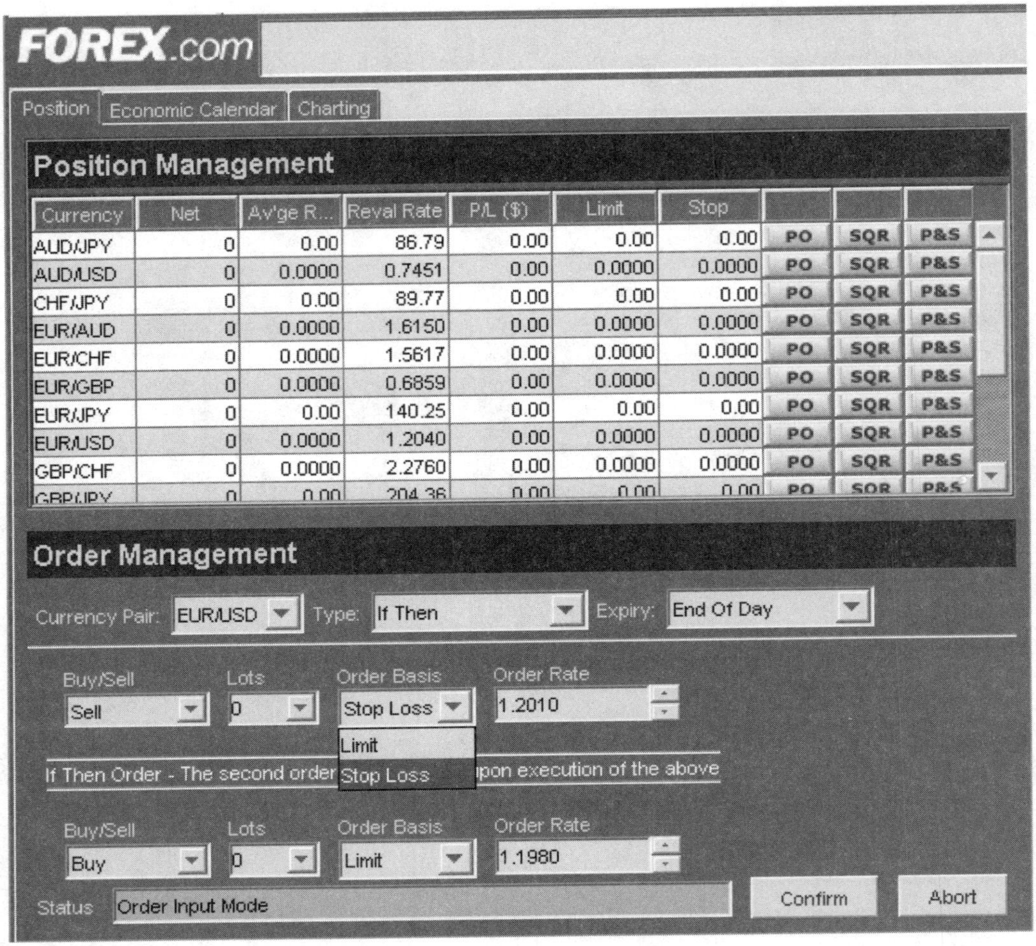

FIGURE I.8
Source: Forex.com.

If/then orders are like a bird of prey waiting to strike. They hover and wait and when the time is right they swoop in. Once I have set the prices at which I would like the orders to become activated, I just sit back and let my conditional orders handle the market. They also give me an autopilot. I can't always be at my desk, and by leaving an if/then order, I can autopilot an entry and a stop-loss. If I am managing profits I can park two exit orders. Conditional order types are like dominoes: One order execution will start the next, so everything is contingent upon the first order being triggered.

There is a lot of flexibility with if/then orders, but let's talk about an even more powerful conditional order type: the if/then OCO. (See Figure I.9.) If/then OCO orders add a whole other depth to putting your trades on autopilot. This order is simply utilizing both

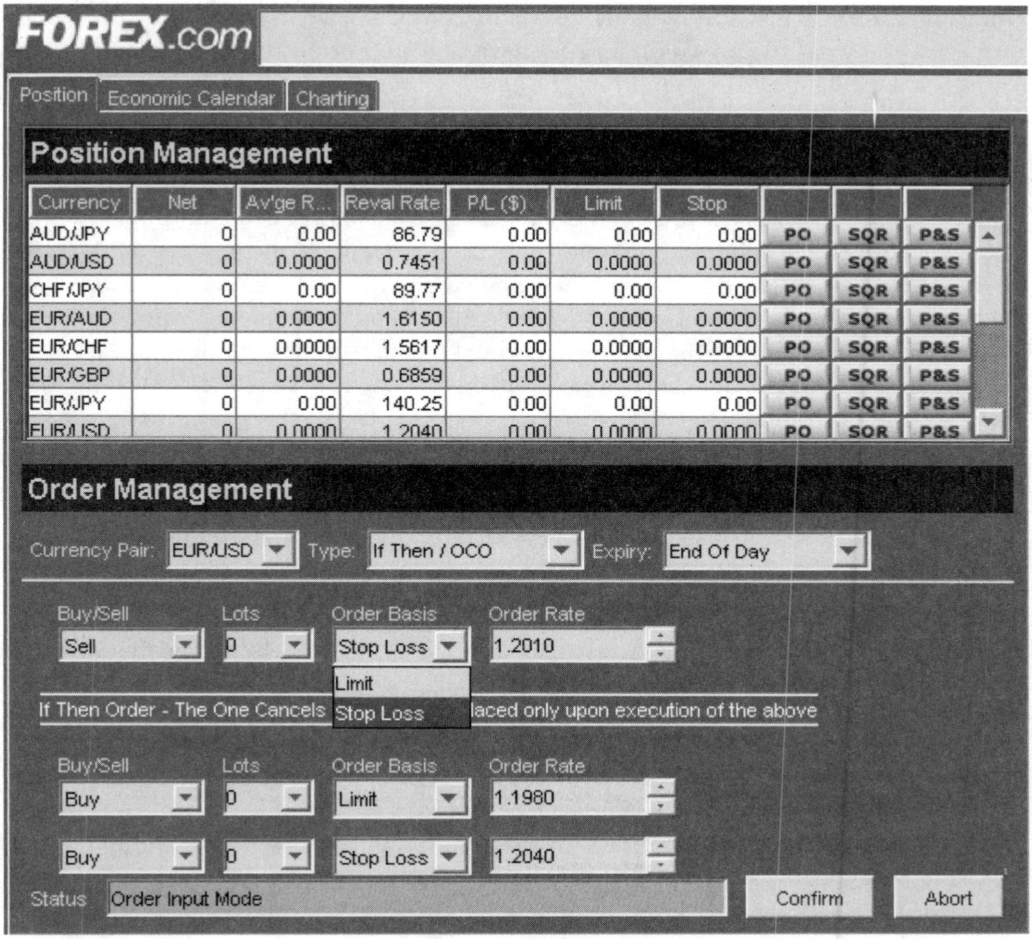

FIGURE I.9
Source: Forex.com.

the order types that we just finished discussing. Think of if/then OCO orders like this: You have placed an if/then order and the "if" leg of the trade is triggered; now your "then" is an OCO order. So in reality it is a total of three orders. Consider that the entire order will lie dormant until the "if" order is triggered. You would utilize this autopilot order by making your "if" order the entry order, and then once that is triggered and you are in the market, your OCO would bracket the position with a stop-loss and a limit (profit target) order.

Don't let these conditional autopilot order types intimidate you. They are just combinations of limit and stop orders that will react as you tell them to. Since you already know the prices at which you would like to enter or exit the market, these conditional orders just follow your instruction. You tell your order execution platform that you want to place a limit order here or a stop order there . . . and it does it. And it's not swayed at all by emotion. *Autopilot or conditional orders are often you, only better!*

As we wrap up this discussion of order types and order entry, let me address the most frequently asked question I get in regard to executing orders: *"Do I wait for the candle (or bar) to close before I enter the market?"* The answer is no, not ever. The reason is because I have confirmation tools (indicators) that allow me to enter on the price break. As soon as prices reach my predetermined entry price, I reference the appropriate confirmation tools for that entry type. Let's discuss momentum and swing trading in particular. In Figure I.10, you can see the breakout up through the resistance of the downtrend line. Note the moving average convergence/divergence (MACD) histogram is also above the zero line. This means that as soon as you get your price break, you can enter the trade. But remember, price comes first! You must wait for the actual breakout and then check the MACD histogram reading. For a long entry, the MACD histogram must be above the zero line. For a short entry, the MACD histogram must be below the zero line.

Swing trades are confirmed simply by the correction to the support level in a swing entry long or to the resistance level for a swing entry short. (See Figure I.11.) The support or resistance level that you will use to enter is decided by using the Wave or

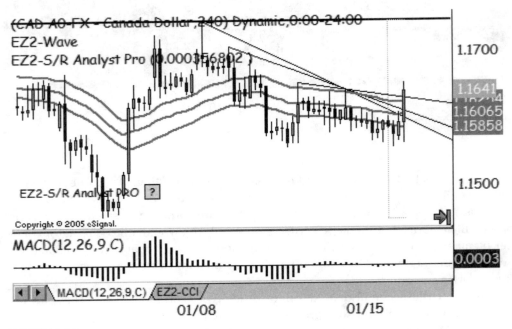

FIGURE I.10

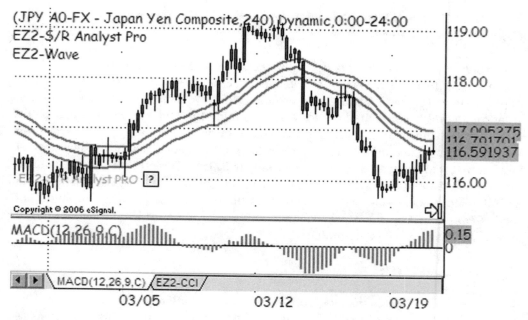

(JPY A0-FX - Japan Yen Composite,240) Dynamic,0:00-24:00
EZ2-$/R Analyst Pro
EZ2-Wave

FIGURE I.11

Fibonacci levels. The Wave is the more conservative of the two. Fibonacci levels give you much more flexibility to choose how deep a correction (retracement) you would like to see before entering a swing trade. The stop is easy, though. Swing trades are defined by a twelve to two o'clock or four to six o'clock Wave; therefore the support in the case of an uptrend or resistance in a downtrend are perfect places for stop placement. The point at which a long swing entry is no longer valid is three to five pips below the lowest line of the Wave. You don't have to use this level as your stop, but certainly keep this in mind when you place it. A swing entry short is no longer valid three to five pips above the top line of the Wave.

If you want to see online videos of how any of these orders are placed, go to www.tradedirectfx.com/orders.html and you will get to see the multimedia videos I have recorded that walk you through each of the orders. It's full video and audio, so you will see and hear exactly what I am doing as I walk you through the steps.

MY CHARTS: eSIGNAL AND eSIGNAL FOREX CHARTS (AKA eSIGNAL "LITE")

I like eSignal. I use eSignal every day without exception. Do you have to use it? Well, no. There are certainly other viable options. Metastock's a great alternative. (In fact, I am hoping to unveil some new tools with the help of Metastock in the very near future.) So what's my point here? Well, don't for a second think that you can use the charts that come with most execution platforms and make a serious run at trading forex. Execution platforms are for execution. And remember that you can get eSignal forex charts, which I endearingly call eSignal "lite," when you trade with TradeDirectFX. If I sound like I am pretty excited about this, I am. I'm not trying to sell you on anything, but when you can get full-featured charts and reliable data from the most trusted provider around—and for free* when you open a $1,000 account with one of the most established forex brokers in the business—it's a no-brainer.

MY CHARTING TOOLS

Before some critic writes this book off as some sort of pitch for my software (and believe me, I had enough of those pop out of the woodwork after my first book was released), let me repeat what I have always said about my automated software: It's a luxury and not a necessity. Heck, I didn't even automate my own charts until the fall of 2004! So I had been trading for more than 10 years with manual drawing tools. Is it more work doing it manually? Of course it is. But it's best to start out knowing how to do these things without the mental crutch of automation.

You'll see that my trend lines, support and resistance level, the Wave, pivot points, and a few other tools were done using my automated tools. (Sorry, currently the software works only on eSignal.) I also have eSignal's forex charting running on my laptop and draw lines and Fibonacci levels manually, too.

My automated software doesn't tell me when to buy or sell, and it doesn't automatically execute anything. What it does do is automate the manual tasks of drawing trend lines, drawing support and resistance, calculating pivot points, finding candlestick patterns, drawing Fibonacci levels, plotting the Wave, and a couple of other tools.

By the way, the name of my software, "EZ2Trade," was born out of sarcasm and satire—both of which I was born with two heaping spoonfuls of. Trading is not, nor will it ever be, "EZ." I found it absolutely comical how many trading software companies out there made it sound as if a piece of software would allow traders and investors to decode the secrets of the market in little time, with little experience and little work. Does such a tool exist? Let me be the first to burst that bubble for anyone who still believes in the tooth fairy, Santa Claus, and unicorns—it doesn't exist! However, it was my goal to make the process as simple as possible using a three-step methodology with three tools that almost anyone can learn, my "Three Classic Tools to a Three-Step Setup."

*Please see details at TradeDirectFX.com.

I can't tell you how many people have asked me where I trade and what charts I use. So here, I've told you. It's all out in the open now. If you have used some of these tools and like them, great! If you've had some trying or bad experiences, I'm sorry to hear that, but nothing and no one is perfect. Beyond that, these are just the tools I use and, by the way, pay for, too! I don't get executions for free. I don't get eSignal for free. And once upon a time I had to pay a programmer for my automated tools. My hard-earned money was spent on all these opinions I have. I wouldn't have it any other way.

If you want to see the EZ2 Trade Charting Collection in action, head on over to www.ez2tradesoftware.com and you can watch multimedia videos on how this software works and read some articles about the "Three Classic Tools to a Three-Step Setup."

FOUR KEYS TO TRADE EXECUTION

Ideas strike in the strangest of places. I have sticky note pads all over my home for when an idea comes to mind. *Write it down immediately or lose it forever.* So when an idea hit me in the shower I had one of two choices: run out soaking wet or yell for my husband to come and write it down for me. *I started yelling.* Funny enough, I had never narrowed my trading rules down to a handful of simple guidelines that would keep traders from wandering off the path. So here are four simple keys to following the trading approach outlined in this book, thanks to my husband Herbie.

1. *The decision to enter and exit must be based on price,* not *emotion or fundamentals.* We have already discussed hot zones at length, so I hope you understand that fundamentals do not set up a trade. They do give you a way to time potential volatility. They cannot offer a specific price at which to enter a trade nor manage the trade with stop price and profit target. There are, at minimum, three prices that complete a trading plan. You must know the price at which you will enter, the price at which you will place your stop-loss, and the price(s) at which you will place your profit target(s). None of these levels can be determined by news or fundamentals, and all must be determined before you enter the trade by your charts and specifically by price.

2. *You must identify whether the market is trending or chopping before you enter.* The most important tool I have is the Wave. Be sure that the three 34-period EMAs on the high, low, and close are on every one of your charts. The first step of analysis is to take a clock angle reading. The Wave offers the easiest and most reliable way to determine whether the market is trending, and it will give you the quickest and best way to see transitions in market cycles. The clock angle will also and most importantly determine the way you will enter the market. It will determine

whether you will be looking for a breakout or breakdown in a sideways market or a pullback or bounce in a trending market.

3. ***You must determine your risk-to-reward ratio before you enter the trade.*** Identifying a potential trade is only half of the equation. Once you do find a momentum or swing trade, the next step is to do the chart work and find your risk-to-reward ratio. Notice I mention "chart work." Finding your risk-to-reward ratio is about locating support and resistance on the chart. It's not, nor should it ever be, about using a fixed risk goal and a fixed reward goal. When I sit down with traders to discuss their trading plans, too often I see trading plans that are based on some fixed profit target and a fixed pip or percentage stop-loss. The fact that a trader only wants to risk X and make Y doesn't have a bearing on the price action or the lines and levels on the charts. When you are deciding on a stop-loss level, your first question should be "Where is this trade no longer valid?" Once you enter long in any market, your stop should start the thought "Where is this buy no longer valid?" and then you should look for support below your entry. If you enter short in any market, you're looking for resistance above your entry with the same idea in mind: "Where is this short sell no longer valid?" You will pick from one of these levels. You do want to keep some things in mind as you are choosing from the levels you could place your stop-loss at. There are multiple choices. Some price levels will give your entry some wiggle room, which is what we traders call the amount of price fluctuation you will tolerate. Wiggle room typically refers to the space between your entry and your stop-loss, but it can and will eventually be applied to current price and your profit target. The difference between your entry price and stop-loss price is of course your risk.

When you begin considering profit targets, you are not looking for one price level. Profit targets are multiple levels along the path of the trade as it goes in your favor at which it can be exited. *Think of it like a sprinter running down the track with hurdles to jump over.* These levels should not factor in some sort of dollar amount but rather focus on the potential price "hurdles" that are on the "track." In an uptrend you should be focusing on resistance levels, and in a downtrend you should be focusing on support. These levels can be decided on by using major and minor psychological levels, Fibonacci levels, trend lines, or horizontal support and resistance. You can also alternatively use pivot points. Remember that these levels all have one thing in common regardless of what they are or how they are calculated: They are all simply different types of support and resistance. We will use these levels to help identify not only our stop-loss, but also our profit targets. There will be multiple profit levels at which a trade can be exited. This brings us to the last of the four keys.

4. ***Enter the market with a single trade with your full complement of lots and exit scaling out at your predetermined profit target(s).*** Exiting a trade is one of the most difficult orders to execute. The challenge is more widely acknowledged as true concerning stop-losses—most traders are aware of that. However, most peo-

ple do not associate this difficulty with the profitable side of the trade, and if you ask me, it's the profit target that is psychologically more difficult to follow through on because most people think the profitable side of the trade is easier. This observation comes from watching literally dozens and dozens of traders. I think we all have a certain preconceived notion of what we would like to make in terms of money. It's only human. I do it to a certain degree, too. *Gee, we're only human and we do this not only for professional satisfaction but also to make a profit.* So I understand the urge. I've been there. But I have to tell you, I have seen more positive trades turn to mud because a trader wanted to make $400 on a trade and $392 just wouldn't do. These are traders who placed their stops and knew where their profit targets were! But as the money added up on the open position, greediness took over. Profit targets are placed irrespective of any kind of dollar gain. Resistance is resistance and support is support, and a dollar consideration is just not part of that equation. This goes obviously for stop-loss placement, but it often seems to be forgotten in profit target order execution. So what's the culprit of this behavior, and, more importantly, what's the fix?

It's actually pretty simple. One reason we do this is what we just spoke of: fixating upon a certain dollar profit. The other reason is because we don't want to get off the ride too soon. We all have this fear. At first we're just hoping that the trade goes our way, and then that hope gives way to the "pig" and it's the pig that wants every last pip of the trade. We can satisfy the pig, though; we trick it with discipline. So how to we do this? Easy. We utilize multiple profit targets. This allows us to do two things. First, we can pocket profits by peeling out of our position as the market moves in our favor. *We can exit the market when we can, not when we have to.* This method of exiting the position a little at a time can be done only if you enter with multiple lots or contracts. This brings up a very common question I get, which concerns position sizing. I don't use fancy calculations for position sizing. I do have criteria, though, and these are easy enough for anyone to follow.

Again, and just so I know I have made this point abundantly clear: We are entering the position in a single trade. We place our stop-loss based on the thought: Where is this trade no longer valid? And while that level may not be the actual price point we use for our stop order, it's the initial point we work from. We then scale out at our predetermined profit targets. If a trade is entered with one contract, then the first profit target represents your exit point for the trade. With two contracts, you will exit one contract at the first profit target and the second contract at the second profit target. Get the picture? The point here is to lighten your position as the market moves in your favor. I see far too many traders add to winning positions, but what they are erroneously doing here is adding lower-percentage entries to their initial position. Any entry, long or short, must be a valid trade entry on its own merit. What happens when you enter with more than one contract and peel out of your position as the trade moves in your favor is that you get a chance to capture a greater amount of the move and you can also pocket profits along the way, reducing your risk.

There is an interesting thing I have noticed because I have been able to speak at length with many floor traders and many off-the-floor traders in both stocks and commodity futures. And these two groups enter trades in often drastically different ways. Being on the floor affords a trader not only better execution but also a much more acute feel for the ebb and flow of price action. That's why so many of them can scalp—make a series of small trades that go with the current trend until there is a reversal. That's also why you will hear me say that if you are trying to scalp off the floor, it's very, very difficult.

But I digress. The conversations that I have continually found eye-opening are with traders who were once floor traders and have successfully made the transition off the floor. One of the main differences I see in this transition is the way trades are managed. Off-the-floor traders will adapt their trade management so that they scale out of positions. Not only does it reduce the volatility of their trading basket, but I can tell you that it also reduces stress.

I know I said this already, but these are two of the most important points that you can come away with from everything I will tell you over the next 30 days: Always remember, a stop-loss represents the point at which the trade is no longer valid, and scale out of your position as you reach your profit targets.

There is only one exception to this advice, and that is my 60-second stop. Sixty-second stops are used during entries that accompany hot zones, and we'll certainly discuss that process throughout the next 30 days.

Want to get more about the Four Keys to Trade Execution? Head over to www.trade directfx.com and you can watch a multimedia video series of examples of each one of these four keys.

MULTIPLE TIME FRAMES

If you read *Forex Trading for Maximum Profit*, you already know that I watch multiple time frames when trading the forex market. I watch the 30-, 60-, 180-, and 240-minute charts and the daily or end-of-day chart for a total of five time frames. However, I do not use multiple time frame confirmation. In other words, I do not confirm trades on, for example, the 60-minute chart with the 180- or 240-minute chart. Multiple time frame confirmation usually means that you will confirm a trade on a shorter time frame with the trend on a longer time frame. Again, I do *not* do this. In fact, each time frame stands alone in its relevance, and each setup is confirmed on its own chart and time frame. Using a longer-term time frame to confirm a shorter one makes little sense when you consider that any kind of price change on a longer time frame will begin at the shortest time frame. You will see a reversal on the 30-minute chart before it shows up on the daily. However, there is an important concept that I do want to elaborate on concerning watching multiple time frames.

Since I am watching five time frames I have to weight each chart with a certain amount of strength or relevance. As a rule, longer time frames will be more relevant. What do I mean by relevant? Relevance has to do with the attention each chart garners. A longer time frame, specifically the daily, will be more relevant than the 30-minute. A triangle that sets up on the daily is more relevant that one on the 30-minute. This makes perfect sense when you think about the price action and time it takes to create a triangle (or any pattern, for that matter!) on a daily chart versus a shorter-term intraday chart. Now let me say before we go any further that I don't want you to just trade off the daily thinking that watching it alone is best. What I do want you to do is start making some distinction between setups. I think that there is slightly more relevance in the 60-minute chart than the 30-minute chart. The same can be said about the 180 and the 240; the 240-minute chart is slightly more relevant than the 180-minute.

Since I have been encouraging you to use the setups described in this and all my books on not only all time frames but all markets, let me share with you some specifics with the stock and futures markets. First, I trade the stock and futures markets only off the daily chart. The only exception to this is when I decide to trade E-mini futures, like the S&P 500, NASDAQ-100, Russell 2000, and mini-Dow contract. I trade these only on their respective electronic (that's what the "E" stands for) mini contracts. On these intraday futures charts I typically trade off the three- or five-minute chart and have some confirmation tools that are specific to trading a futures contract that is based on a basket of stocks. But the chart patterns, chart tools, and confirmation indicators are the same! In fact, my use of the MACD histogram as a confirming tool was reinforced by my intraday trading. So it all has roots in my foundation of the "Three Classic Tools to a Three-Step Setup."

Another point to consider when discussing the choice of time frames that I'm presenting in the book is that with this flexibility you can find a time frame that will suit your schedule. For example, finding and managing a trade based on the 30- or 60-minute chart may not be suitable for your schedule or on a particular trading day. However, the 240 or the daily might be perfect when you are not able to spend the time and attention often needed to trade short-term intraday charts. So use this flexibility to your advantage. The five time frames present choices, so don't get trapped into the mind-set that one time frame is superior to another. I call each time frame a universe unto itself and therefore independent in its own chart setups. What we can do when viewing multiple time frames of the same market is find, among the choices that will be presented, the best setup to use.

A discussion of multiple time frames is also a great time to discuss an inevitability of trading forex: missing trades.

It's part of the whole 24-hour market. Right here and right now you must accept

Even though I will talk about my five time frames, the setups work on any time frame. Some traders tell me they use the "Three Classic Tools to a Three-Step Setup" on 10- and 15-minute charts or on 120-minute charts, even weekly charts. And that's great! The tools are equally robust on any time frame, so if there is a particular time frame that you trade from don't think you must use the five I do. There's a lot of room here for adapting these concepts to other markets and, of course, time frames.

that you are going to miss some setups that confirm, whether it's because you were having dinner as a trade was confirming during the Tokyo session or you were sleeping during the London open. It's all going to depend on where you live and the hours you work, play, and sleep. The two scenarios I just mentioned are my typical "missed the trade" times. Here's where having five time frames to choose from can help, though. I will never advocate chasing a trade. That's just plain stupid and shows a lack a discipline. But think about it: If you see a trade setup and confirmation that you missed and the first profit target and the stop-loss for the setup were not reached, go ahead and enter if your entry price is still available. This does not happen very often. We call it a second-chance entry. In addition, using our multiple time frames, everything starts on the shortest time frame chart, which for us is the 30-minute. If you miss a trade on the 30-minute chart you can look to the 60, the 180, or the 240. The 30 and 60 will have much in common in terms of lines and levels, while the same is true for the 180 and 240. But there is no reason that you cannot look to these other charts to see if the price action that triggered a trade on one chart might not also be setting up a trade on another. That setup may not have existed earlier or maybe it wasn't your first choice . . . but you've got it now and maybe it's a trade that will suit you and offer a new opportunity.

In high school I wrote down this quote from Theodore Roosevelt and taped it above my desk, and throughout college and my trading career, really my whole life, I have lived by it: "Do what you can, with what you have, where you are."

MY DAILY TRADING SCHEDULE

Many of my students have wanted to know when I trade and why. I hesitate to put this in the book, because *I don't want you thinking that just because I choose not to trade during certain hours that you shouldn't.* Forex is a 24-hour market so you can trade almost anytime you want, but there are times that are better suited for trades according to when different financial centers are open or closed. The main consideration before trading is "who's awake." Here is a list that I keep handy to remind me when to trade and when not to trade. The more financial centers that are open—creating market overlap—the better.

There are basically five trading time blocks that you should know. Since I live in Florida all times here and throughout the book are in eastern standard time (EST).

Starting at 2:00 A.M. EST the European and Asian financial centers are active. This is the first overlap of the trading day. It lasts until 4:00 A.M. to 5:00 A.M. when Tokyo closes, followed by Hong Kong/Singapore. These sessions don't just stop on a dime. They fade over the course of about an hour.

The European session, of which the U.K. market is the most important, goes from 2:00 A.M. EST until about 11:00 A.M. to noon EST.

Starting at about 7:00 A.M. EST we have the U.K./U.S. overlap. This overlap lasts until 11:00 A.M. to noon EST. After this overlap is done, I highly recommend hanging it up for the day. This is because after noon EST the only financial center open is the U.S. market, and this creates a lull in activity. The only exception to this would be on the Federal Reserve's Federal Open Market Committee (FOMC) policy statement days, when you are going to see volatility after the decision at 2:15 P.M. EST.

At between 6:00 P.M. and 7:00 P.M. EST the Tokyo and Hong Kong/Singapore markets are just opening. (Hong Kong/Singapore is one hour behind Tokyo.) Keep in mind that the Australian and New Zealand markets have been trading for about two hours by this time. So you have an overlap of Sydney, Tokyo, and Hong Kong/Singapore at this time.

Ideally, I would be up at 2:00 A.M. EST to trade the London open with the Tokyo and Hong Kong/Singapore overlap. That's in a perfect world. *Now for the real world.* I am usually up and in my trading office between 4:00 A.M. and 6:00 A.M. EST. I'm coming in after the Asian market closes but I am trading the heart of the London trading day. Between 7:00 A.M. and 8:00 A.M. EST we get the best overlap of the day, the U.S./U.K. overlap, and I will be active until noon EST. And just like I recommend, I hang it up for the day after that point except for managing an open position. I won't initiate any new positions until 6:00 P.M. to 7:00 P.M.

So now you know who's awake, when, and for how long. With this knowledge you can decide for yourself when you can make time to trade. Consider that with the understanding of how to place limit, stop, OCO, and if/then orders you can make your entries, and then with the assistance of these order types, which make less demand on your time, you can manage your open positions effectively.

The Thirty Days
of Trading

Tuesday, January 31st

Welcome to my trading room. It's day one and I'm excited to get this trading diary off the ground today. Each day is going to present different lessons and distinctions. What I want to do is point out and explain the reasons I make the decision to enter or exit. The setups we are going to discuss are not complicated. There really are only two types of entries: swing and momentum. Having these two entry styles at our disposal allows us to handle both sideways and trending markets. If you take the time to learn how to read the Wave and draw trend lines, support, and resistance, you are well on your way to recognizing entry opportunities. Add to those tools the price levels created by Fibonacci retracement and extension levels, psychological levels, and pivot points, and you have all the lines and levels you need to set your stop-loss and identify profit targets.

It's an interesting day because after 18 years, Alan Greenspan has retired as Federal Reserve chairman. Like him or not, you must respect the man's insight over the past two decades. I see and hear a lot of Monday morning quarterbacking about Mr. Greenspan's decisions, but regardless of your opinion, today is the end of the Greenspan era and the first day of the Bernanke era. It's history in the making. And although Benjamin Bernanke's first testimony and congressional grilling won't take place for another two weeks, there will be plenty of speculation between now and February 15th.

On a personal note, one drawback I am dealing with—and this is life—is that I am getting over the flu and still am oversleeping it seems every morning. I'm not 100 percent but am feeling well enough to do my homework and stay on top of some light trading. Light trading can be done one of two ways. If you have a set amount of time (preferably at least two hours) you can scan the longer-term charts for setups or you can watch and trade any intraday setups. A scan through the time frames is going to tell you which is more viable. Your other choice if you have only an hour or less is simply to focus on the longer-term time frames, and if there is nothing setting up tomorrow will be here before you know it. With that in mind, I'm going to look at the longer time frames this morning. I'll scan all five time frames with particular attention on the 240-minute and the daily. By the way, I am flat going into this, our first day; I'm not managing any existing trades. I'll be starting a fresh scan of the markets to see what's on my radar this morning.

Speaking of my radar: I will scan through the euro/U.S. dollar pair (EUR/USD), as well the Australian dollar (AUD/USD) and the British pound (GBP/USD), and re-member these three typically move opposite the U.S. dollar, especially the EUR/USD. I will continue with the Swiss franc (USD/CHF), the Canadian dollar (USD/CAD), and the Japanese yen (USD/JPY). The Swiss franc moves almost tick for tick with the U.S. dollar. These six pairs make up more than 90 percent of daily trading activity. That means all over the globe as traders are waking up long before the sun's own alarm clock goes off, the only thing on their minds is: Where is the U.S. dollar going? Never forget that you are trading the U.S. dollar when you trade forex. Yes, these are pairs and that means two, but don't lose the pulse of the U.S. dollar because, like I said, 90 percent of every day's trading volume focuses on traders' varying opinions of the USD strength or weakness.

Let me add this: If you are looking at the EUR/USD long and the USD/CHF short, you are in essence entering two markets but with the same opinion. If I do put on a trade in each one of these pairs like this, then I will take into consideration that I am en-tering essentially the same trade in two markets.

I will also take a look at the New Zealand dollar/U.S. dollar pair (NZD/USD). There are cross rates to consider, too, but they don't comprise a great deal of my trading activi-ty. Think about this, though: Since the most active trading pair in forex is the EUR/USD, the cross rates based on the euro are certainly viable options. I watch some of the most watched and actively traded cross rates like the euro/Japanese yen (EUR/JPY) and euro/British pound (EUR/GBP). So on any given day I'll be watching the six majors and perhaps a few of the euro cross rates.

Figure 1.1 shows what's on my radar this morning. The daily chart of the Swiss franc (USD/CHF) has nearly leveled out to a three o'clock Wave so I'm thinking "mo-mentum trade." And while I'm not going to assume which way the break may happen, I see that the MACD histogram is above the zero line and *if* prices do break out through the horizontal resistance level then I will have a confirmed trade. I'm not wild about this view, though, simply because the Wave, the first thing I look at, is not at the flat three o'clock angle that I prefer to set up momentum trades with. The angle, however, is well within the two to four o'clock area that would qualify as a sideways market. I'll be keeping an eye on this chart going into tomorrow.

Anytime I see a setup on the Swissy I will automatically take a look at the euro. Since it is my goal to train your eyes to the nuances that I use to differentiate setups, let's spend a few moments looking at the chart of the EUR/USD (Figure 1.2). First notice that the Wave is in what I call *transition*. Transitional Waves are simply those Waves that are making the shift from one recognized clock angle to another. In this case we see that the Wave is trying to level out to a three o'clock angle from an uptrending twelve to

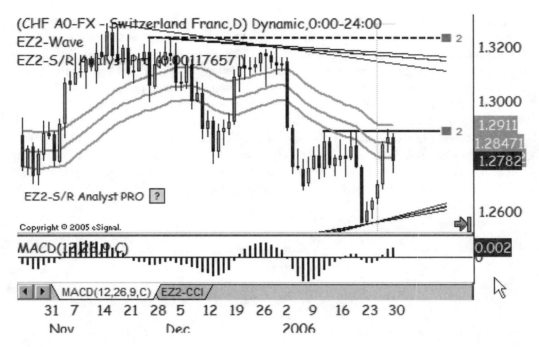

FIGURE 1.1

FIGURE 1.2

two o'clock Wave. The last three, maybe four, candles have leveled the Wave out to a flatter, more three o'clock direction, and on the 30th you can see that the candle pierced the uptrend line. The MACD histogram had a negative reading, which plotted it below the zero line, and thus it's a confirmed, albeit a little aggressive, short because the trade is setting up fresh from transition. The sideways Wave was not in place for very long.

For the sake of example, let's set this trade up so that we can walk through the three price levels that will start a trading plan.

Let's rewind back one day to January 30th. (See Figure 1.3.) The EUR/USD broke the uptrend line at 1.2075. The MACD histogram had already gone below the zero line the previous trading session so at the time of the break the confirmation was there and waiting. I have also added the most recent Fibonacci level.

Fibonacci levels using the last major move as well as minor highs and lows are covered in my book *Forex Trading for Maximum Profit*, so while I will explain the levels I am drawing the Fibonacci levels from, I will not go into great length to explain the basics of last major moves and Fibonacci retracements and extensions. However, I use the following Fibonacci retracement and extension levels: 0.250, 0.382, 0.500, 0.618, 0.786, 0.886, 1.272, 1.618, 1.886. Yes, you do need them *all*, and your charting platform should allow you to draw these levels if you are going to use Fibonacci retracements and extensions.

FIGURE 1.3

There is resistance at 0.786 and 0.618, near-term levels at which we could place a stop-loss. But first we have to ask, "Where is this trade no longer valid?" That level in its most basic definition would be if prices broke through the major psychological level of 1.2200. This is because if prices can be buoyed above that level, the higher prices will attract buyers and thus be support. Even though prices are trading very close to the major psychological level of 1.2100, it is only 25 pips above the short entry and just doesn't give this trade enough wiggle room. A daily chart, due to the fact that prices typically trade in a significant range through the entire trading day as compared to, say, the 60-minute chart, needs some room for price fluctuation. But this level is an important point to watch in case prices level off above this level in the coming days. The other level is the downtrend lines that represent the top of this triangle pattern. Do you see the triangle pattern—the convergence of the downtrend lines and the uptrend line? A pierce through the upside would certainly nullify the short trade. So there's the starting point. We have two levels that clearly represent where this short trade will no longer be valid: The downtrend lines and the 1.2200 major psychological level. Does that mean we must use these levels? No, of course not, but it's good to start with this knowledge. Then we can move to closer levels that would be relevant but we acknowledge are not ideal. This examination gives us reasons for placing our stop-loss. *And it starts with understanding where the trade is no longer valid!*

What are our other choices? There are other levels that I consider. The two most obvious are the breakdown candle's high as well as the previous candle's high. Since the breakdown candle (the third candle from the right) didn't make much of a high, I can look to the 1.2235 level of the previous trading session. But it's above the 1.2200 level that I am already gauging as a danger level for attracting support. So I will settle on the 1.2200 level. Here's the part where you have to make some judgment calls. This stop level represents a potentially significant loss if our stop is hit. Could you use the 0.786, 0.886, or even the 0.500 Fibonacci retracement levels? Sure, and that's where I can't tell you what to do. *Do you think these decisions are easy?* They are definitely not even in the vicinity of easy. But then again, these are decisions that separate the successful from the unsuccessful trader. There's a reason you hear the saying "Experience is the best teacher" so much. It's true! When I refer to "experience" I'm not talking about hours logged into a demo platform. That's platform training because all you're really doing is practicing how to enter orders on the platform. There's no reality of trading there. No emotion. No fear. No greed. So once you are familiar with finding the setups we're going to examine through the book, sure, go ahead and acquaint yourself with a good order entry platform. In fact, head over to TradeDirectFX.com. But after that, take the next step when you have about $1,000 of risk capital and open a minimum account. I don't want to help contribute another member to the national demo traders association.

Okay, back to the EUR/USD short entry. We've got the stop-loss discussion out of the way. Next is the profit target. Frankly, this consideration is easy because there will be more than one profit target. All we have to do is locate the support levels as prices trade lower. The easiest ones to identify are the "00" major psychological levels. You must exit as prices approach a double zero price level. That means I'm watching the

1.2000 level for potential support. Just like 1.2100 and 1.2200 are upside resistance, 1.2000 will be downside support. Next we'll use the Fibonacci levels; in this case we're below the 1.000 full retracement so we're looking at 1.272, 1.618, and 1.886 for support, which means they will all be good profit targets. This also means that I could potentially see 1.9000 and 1.8000. There is no way of knowing which one of these support levels could catch this fall and cause a reversal or bounce. That's precisely why we will be ready for any possibility and take our profits off the table as prices reach each one of these support levels. The rule of thumb as we approach "00" is to exit three to five pips before we reach "00," which means as we trade down to "00" we actually want our profit target order, specifically a limit order, to be placed at "05" to "03." This means that our limit order to buy back a portion of our short position would be at 1.1905 or 1.1903.

This entire process is what must be done before every trade, which may begin to explain why my shortest time frame is 30 minutes. With practice, finding all three levels of a trading plan (stop-loss, profit target, and entry) can be done relatively quickly—and I mean within a few minutes of recognizing the initial setup.

If the Swissy sets up in the coming days, then we will go through that process with it. But let me say that you don't have to wait until prices trigger an entry to start this process. You should be more proactive about it. You can set up multiple scenarios, and it's good practice to do so. So let's take a look at Figures 1.4 and 1.5 of the USD/CHF. One shows the long setup; the other shows the short setup.

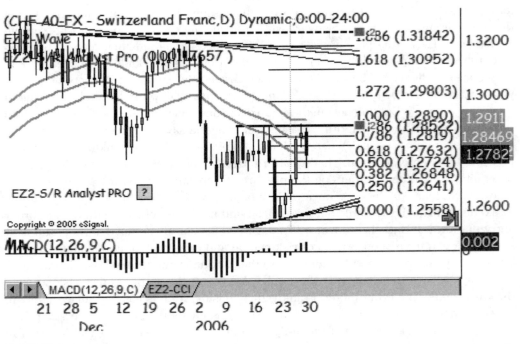

FIGURE 1.4

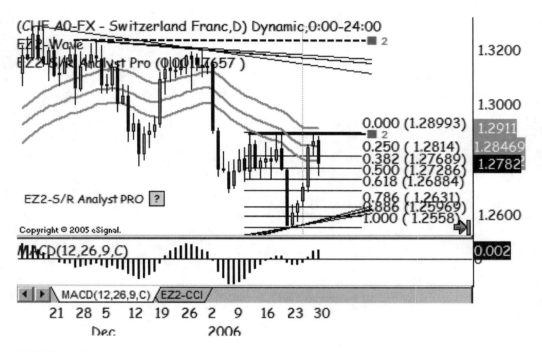

FIGURE 1.5

The only difference between the two charts is the last major move that is used to draw the Fibonacci level. Consider the first of the two charts: If prices break to the upside, we want to have a Fibonacci level that is drawn from the last major move down or sell-off. Fibonacci levels presuppose a reversal, so they project levels that prices will have to overcome as they reverse direction. So by drawing the Fibonacci level from the last major *down* move (Figure 1.4), we're getting the projected resistance levels. Conversely, if we use the last major move *up* (Figure 1.5) we will have the projected level at which we could expect to see support as prices reverse from that last major move up and trade lower.

Wednesday, February 1st

The *blessing* of a 24-hour market is also the *bain* of a 24-hour market. When you trade stocks or futures, because of the daily, defined trading time you know that you can track and set up trading opportunities right from the open. *But there is no daily open in the forex.* Whenever you see a setup on any chart you must ask yourself: What preceded it?

I liken it to watching a movie. When you come into a movie 30 minutes after it started you know you missed something because you weren't watching when the movie began. Did you miss a major plot point? Did you miss a major character development scene? There are a number of things you may have missed because the movie started 30 minutes before you began watching it. You lose a certain degree of understanding and framework because of this. Trading the forex works the same way. You're almost always coming into the market after it began playing.

If the movie is on your DVD player, the fix is simple: Rewind and play it back. Well, we can do something very similar on our charts. Most charting platforms allow you to "play back" a certain amount of price data. eSignal does, and I utilize the replay mode daily. In fact, all my charts are in permanent replay mode so I never forget to rewind the charts while I am setting up a potential trade. And folks, you can use whatever charting platform you like. It's just that I use eSignal, and that's why my chart images are from that platform. It would be like you and me having a discussion about buying a car and not mentioning large automakers like Ford or Honda. eSignal is the largest, so naturally it is going to be in a conversation about charting platforms.

A good rule of thumb when rewinding a chart is to rewind two to three hours on a 30-minute chart, 10 to 12 hours on a 60-minute chart, and two to three days on 180- and 240-minute charts. On a daily chart, a week is a good amount of time to rewind. But the best approach when rewinding is to jump back to the last point at which you observed price action or did your chart analysis.

We already know what's on my radar from yesterday, but let's see if there is anything that we can add to that as markets traded overnight. A habit that we must develop in order to be ready for "hot zones" is to check what economic reports are scheduled to be released. We'll start with that today. The 10:00 A.M. Construction Spending number as well as the Institute for Supply Management (ISM) will inject some volatility this morning, and the Crude Inventories number will be released at 10:30 A.M. We'll watch the Canadian dollar nearing 10:30 A.M. In fact, let's go ahead and glance at the 30- and 60-minute charts of the USD/CAD in Figures 2.1 and 2.2.

Both these charts show a consolidation setting up in front of the 10:30 A.M. release, and that's pretty typical of prerelease price action. I have no hesitation taking a confirmed setup before an economic release. I just want you to be aware of a couple of points. First, the release will create volatility, which brings up my second point. I have to be ready to use a 60-second stop, which is used only if my entry is immediately before a report. I'm sure to have my profit targets in place using limit orders. However, I remove my stop-loss orders for 60 seconds right after the release to keep from getting stopped out just due to volatility, which as a rule needs about a minute to settle down. The basis behind this time-based stop is that reports will inject emotion but after the initial emotional reaction, most often prices resume their prior trend. After 60 seconds and if prices are at (or beyond) my stop-loss, I will execute the stop and get out. In this case I am taking a larger hit than the initial stop-loss price repre-

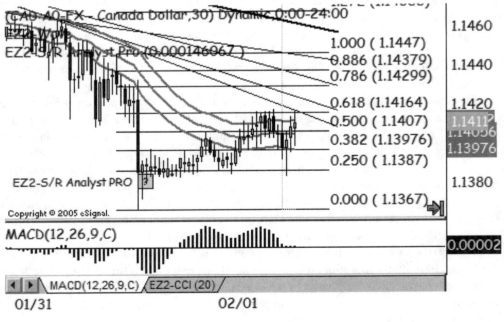

FIGURE 2.1

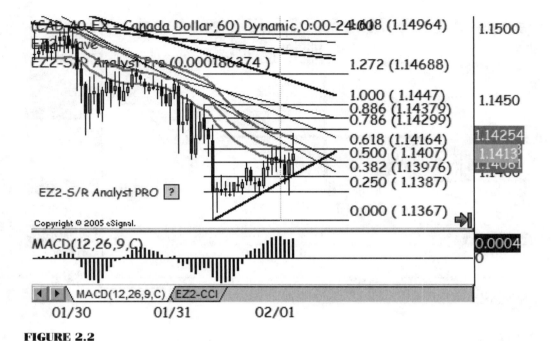

FIGURE 2.2

sented. *Trade during hot zones only if you are able to accept the volatility of the release time.*

With the host of economics hitting the airwaves today I will focus on the 30- and 60-minute charts for setups. It's just good common sense to do this but only if you already have some experience watching price action around these reports. If not, watch a few releases, note the price action, and then you can begin to understand how these hot zones work.

I wanted to share two views of the 30- and 60-minute chart on the EUR/USD on which I have drawn pivot points (Figures 2.3 and 2.4). Pivots are a great alternative for those of you who (1) are learning to use Fibonacci levels or (2) just don't like to use them. Whereas I think Fibonacci levels are the most accurate way to find support and resistance from recent price action, I won't say that if you don't use Fibonacci levels all is lost. In fact, here's a great alternative. Use pivot points, a simple calculation that is valid for one trading session. The math is pretty simple. You add together the high, low, and close from the previous session and divide the total by 3 to generate the pivot point (PP):

$$PP = \frac{H + L + C}{3}$$

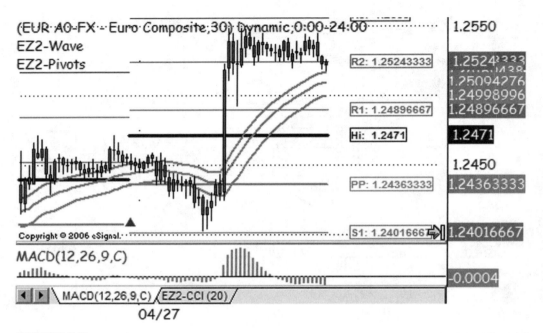

FIGURE 2.3

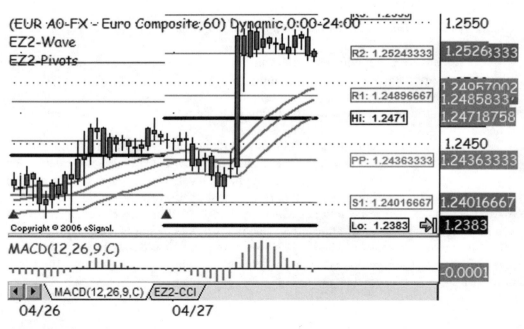

FIGURE 2.4

The Support 1 (S), Support 2 (S2), Resistance 1 (R1), and Resistance 2 (R2) are calculated like this:

$$R2 = P + (H - L) = P + (R1 - S1)$$
$$R1 = (P \times 2) - L$$
$$S1 = (P \times 2) - H$$
$$S2 = P - (H - L) = P - (R1 - S1)$$

Add the prior session high and low as well as psychological levels to this and you have an alternative to using Fibonacci levels. *But I'd still rather see you use Fibonacci levels.*

By the way, pivot points are great when there is no "last major move" from which to draw a Fibonacci series.

Thursday, February 2nd

We'll begin the day by seeing what hot zones we're going to have to contend with today. You can head over to TradeDirectFX.com and see the economic releases that I want to be aware of. If you're thinking that I trade economic news, please reread February 1st, and you'll see that the EUR/USD trade was triggered and was reaching profit objectives well before the release. I want you to remember this, because it's no fluke; and if you think by playing only hot zones you're positioning yourself for the best price action of the day, think again. It's not that I don't respect fundamentals; quite the contrary! It's just that time and time again I have found that focusing on them and using their volatility doesn't increase my success. As a chartist, though, it still serves me to know when these hot zones will occur. Does that make sense?

Today will have the Initial Claims number coming out at 8:30 A.M. EST. That's a huge number. So let's see what's on my radar.

The 30-minute EUR/USD is setting up nicely and has triggered a long at the 7:30 A.M. candle. I'm going to show you two views of this chart: one with pivots (Figure 3.1) and the other with Fibonacci (Figure 3.2). But before you start thinking that I don't trade anything but the EUR/USD, keep in mind that it is the most actively traded pair. Of our six majors it accounts for the most volume.

Both of these views show the upside resistance if prices continue trading higher. The stop-loss on either setup could initially be placed at the bottom line of the Wave. But remember that if we are still long going into the Initial Claims release (and this applies to any release) we will make sure our profit target orders are in place using limit orders. We will remove the stop-loss for 60 seconds after the release time and let prices absorb the news.

As it turns out, the 8:30 A.M. release doesn't create much volatility and prices only range between a high of 1.2073 and a low of 1.2057. It's 10 to 15 minutes later that we're stopped out as prices break down through the bottom line of the Wave and the 1.2050

49

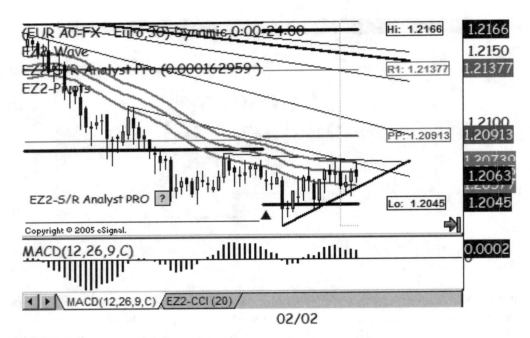

FIGURE 3.1

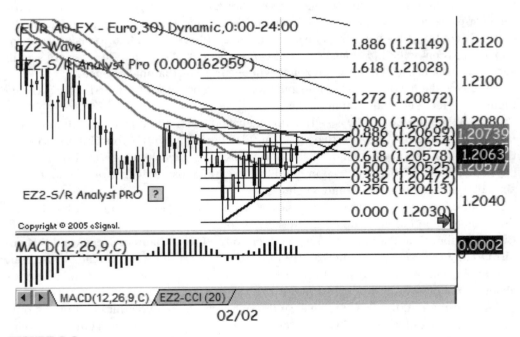

FIGURE 3.2

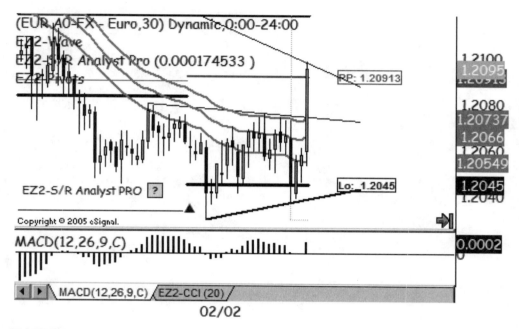

FIGURE 3.3

psychological price level. The Wave is continuing sideways, and that means that I will still watch the triangle pattern for a breakout or breakdown. This brings up an important lesson: Don't give up on a pattern just because it stopped you out earlier. It's tough, but it's a part of *recognize, react, repeat.* (See Day 20 and Day 24 for discussions of the three Rs concept.) With that in mind, let's look at the view of the same setup and a new break at 10:00 A.M. in Figure 3.3.

The breakout trigger price is 1.2075 and the MACD histogram confirms it. The 1.2100 price level will be significant resistance and certainly a profit target. The pivot point (PP) and the 1.272 Fibonacci level (Figure 3.2) will be support depending on which chart you are managing your trade with. Remember that as prices trade higher, we must scale out of the trade.

Friday, February 3rd

Today's action will be focused on the Non-Farm Payroll (NFP) number. This is one of the most significant reports in terms of fundamental reaction. I can only think of the FOMC decision as having more impact, so I have fastened my seat belt and am ready for the day.

Let's take a look at the U.S. dollar to start the morning. I want to focus on the shortest-term time frame, which for us is the 30-minute, and the longest time frame, the daily chart. We should do this if for no other reason than that trading forex, the majors specifically, is all about our judgment on the strength or weakness of the U.S. dollar. I use the U.S. Dollar Index Cash to do this. It's almost 6 A.M. EST and I'm just getting through my first cup of Earl Grey. The 30-minute Dollar Index Cash is moving at between two and four o'clock with a slight angle upwards, as shown in Figure 4.1. Anytime prices have established themselves above the Wave, I call this the strong side. A close above the Wave is enough to prove this to me, and continued trading and closes above the Wave strengthen this belief. So while we never carry a bias, prices are on the strong side of the Wave in the 30-minute chart.

The daily view in Figure 4.2 is neutral, with a three o'clock Wave that has successfully made a transition from a downtrending Wave to the past four trading days during which the range-bound USD has leveled out just below the 89.50 psychological number. There is a horizontal resistance level just above that has been pierced, and the MACD histogram is above the zero line. So while prices are not on the strong side of this Wave like they are on the 30-minute chart, the daily has shown its first signs of strength with the piercing of the resistance level. Whereas this may be absolutely nothing after the Non-Farm Payroll number comes out, I will trust the price action as any chartist would do and say that the U.S. dollar is strong as we are approaching the NFP release.

The function of this type of analysis is not just academic. The U.S. dollar can and will function as secondary confirmation for the majors and most directly can assist us in

FIGURE 4.1

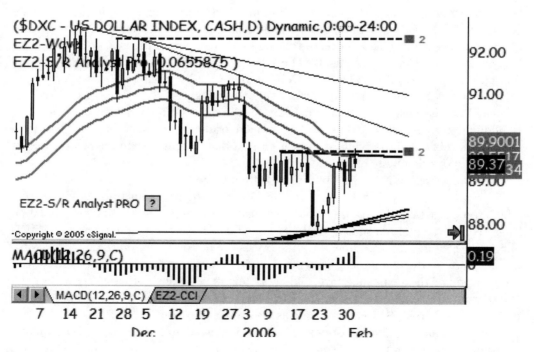

FIGURE 4.2

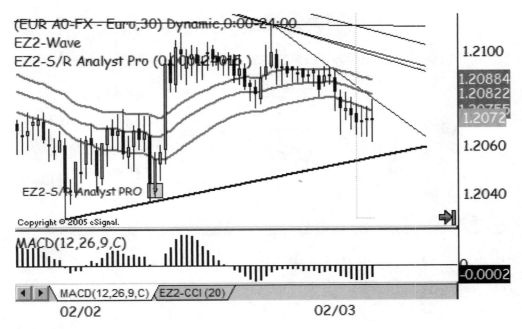

FIGURE 4.3

determining support and resistance in the EUR/USD and USD/CHF. These two currency pairs will be perfect for today's action. The view of the 30-minute EUR/USD in Figure 4.3 shows that prices are on the weak side of the Wave, which should be no surprise when you look at the 30-minute U.S. Dollar Index Cash chart. The EUR/USD is trading below the 1.2100 level, which is resistance. The Wave is not at an ideal, flat three o'clock angle, but it's well within the two to four o'clock area and it's still early.

The daily chart of the EUR/USD in Figure 4.4 is neutral in much the same way that the daily chart of the U.S. dollar is neutral. There is a larger triangle pattern that has formed as the Wave leveled out to a three o'clock angle. The MACD histogram is negative, but until we get a price trigger it really doesn't mean much. **Price comes first, then the indicator.**

The EUR/USD and the U.S. dollar move in opposite directions almost tick for tick. If the U.S. dollar ticks up, the EUR/USD ticks down. The negative correlation is tight. The USD/CHF and the U.S. dollar move together almost tick for tick. The 30-minute view of the USD/CHF in Figure 4.5 shows that prices are bouncing from some earlier weakness and level off at the bottom lines of the Wave.

The daily chart of the USD/CHF shown in Figure 4.6 is almost identical to the U.S. Dollar Index Cash daily chart. The Swissy has broken up through some significant resistance. There is horizontal resistance that has already been broken, but what's most important to me is the fact that 1.2900 has been pierced. The MACD histogram has been

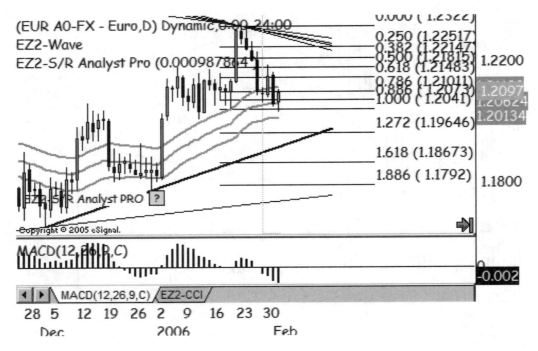

FIGURE 4.4

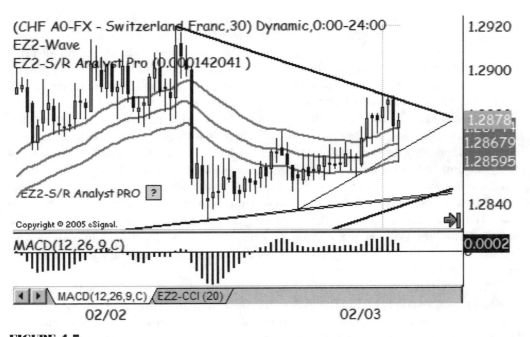

FIGURE 4.5

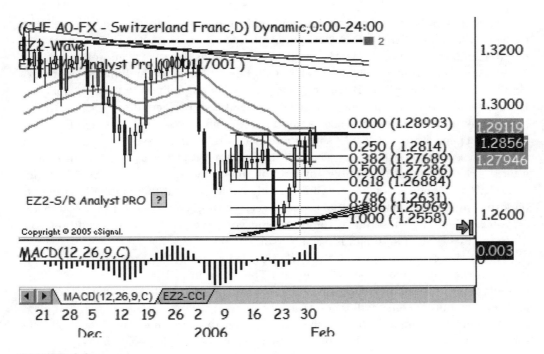

FIGURE 4.6

above the zero line for several days, so even though the Wave is flat, price action has shown that there is new strength and buyers are coming into the market. Psychological levels have a way of attracting order flow. Above the 1.2900 level there will not only be buy orders waiting but as prices stay above the 1.2900 level more buyers will come. This works the other way around, too. The resistance that waits at and just below 1.2900 is significant as well. Prices will resist going higher until there are no longer any more sellers at 1.2900. If sellers stay at the 1.2900 level, then prices will continue to find resistance there. It's not a line in the sand, either. There can and will be price fluctuation of typically three to five pips above and below the psychological level of "00."

The reason we are spending so much time examining these prereport charts is because I want to get across any setups that only chartists can act on. Many traders erroneously believe that the report itself will yield not only the overriding opinion of the market but also the trade trigger. *That's just not the reality for chartists.*

We're ready for the report. As 6:30 A.M. nears the Swissy breaks up through a downtrend line at 1.2885 with MACD histogram confirmation and we're off! Prices are showing strength and we'll go with it. The euro is conversely getting weak and breaking down through uptrend support at 1.2055. We're still two hours from the report but prices are triggering entries. This is not an uncommon scenario at all as we approach any report, not just the NFP. So do not think of this as an exception, and moreover, get used to recognizing it and reacting to it. Here's the payoff, literally and figuratively. Figures 4.7 and 4.8 are views of the EUR/USD and CHF/USD at the report's release.

Here's the way this entry works: As the report comes out we are in profit mode. We knew where our profit targets are back at 6:30 this morning, so the limit orders to exit should already be in place. If we are in any trade as the economic news is being released, remember that each stop must be changed to a 60-second stop *before* the release. How soon before the release? A good rule of thumb is seven to ten minutes. Let's also take a peek at the GBP/USD, since there is a correlation there as the GBP/USD generally moves with the EUR/USD. The GBP/USD did not register any kind of entry until after the release and did not allow any kind of preemptive entry like the EUR/USD and USD/CHF did. When this happens you certainly could utilize if/then and OCO orders to park the entry, stops, and the initial profit target, but this is not what I do very often and as you are learning these entries and training your eyes to the setups, putting your trades on this level of autopilot is not advisable.

As the day comes to an end, the AUD/USD is breaking down through a major uptrend on the daily chart. (See Figure 4.9.) The Wave is well within the two to four o'clock angle but not perfectly flat at three. Here's another lesson that experience and some common sense will teach you:

If I were to compare momentum setups on our two extreme time frames, the 30-minute and the daily chart, I would say that the Wave should be absolutely flat and

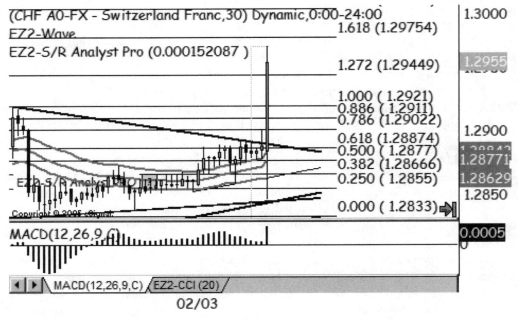

FIGURE 4.7

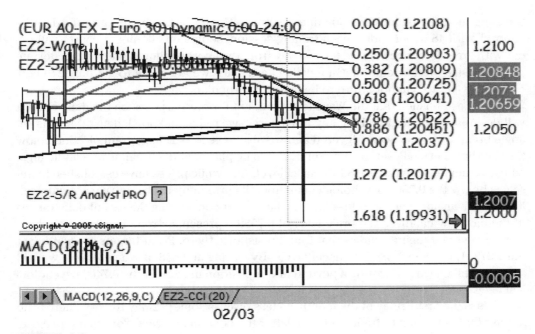

FIGURE 4.8

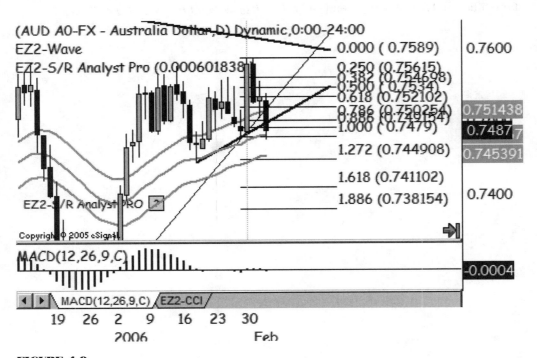

FIGURE 4.9

traveling at three o'clock for 30-minute setups. This is because we can afford to be choosy! With 48 new candles each trading session, setups on 30-minute charts will occur with great frequency. As we move away from the shortest time frame we can deviate from this strict interpretation. On a daily chart, since we are going to get only 240 new candles a year, we cannot afford to be quite as particular.

We've established that the Wave is not flat, but for our purposes on the daily chart it will do. And we're not breaking any rules here—we're just acknowledging that this triangle breakdown has been triggered and we also have MACD histogram plotting below the zero line. Let's talk setup. Our stop-loss can be placed at the breakdown candle high, which coincides with the 0.618 Fibonacci level. And while prices have established themselves below the 0.7500 psychological number, its proximity to the entry price won't allow it to be an adequate stop-loss for this daily chart considering the recent daily ranges of the past few candles. The price level of 0.7589 represents strong resistance as there were two large-ranging candles that found resistance there. Profit targets are waiting at the 1.272, 1.618, and 1.886 Fibonacci levels. By exiting at 1.618, if we get there, we will have also taken care of exiting a portion of our position in front of the 0.7400 psychological level.

This is the first Friday of the month, so let's discuss some "Friday Rules." There is no market that is waiting to trade on Friday after the London and New York markets close. After noon the only market open is the U.S. market. There will be no Sydney open, nor Tokyo, Hong Kong, or Singapore, so after noon on Friday I recommend that you head out of the office and start the weekend early. *Think of it as a forex trader perk!*

Monday, February 6th

It's a brand-new week and our first Monday of the month. Since we haven't discussed the open, which is on Sunday afternoon, let's do that now. I don't make it a habit to do anything on Sundays related to trading other than look at the open itself as Sydney and then, more importantly, Tokyo start their trading day. The Hong Kong open is also becoming more and more relevant. These are the first trades and opinions of the week, and if for no other reason than the market has opened after being closed Saturday, it's a significant time. I won't enter trades until London has opened, and the only time I watch any price action at all on Sunday is if I am still holding a position after Friday's close.

By the way, just so you know, I already checked: There are no significant U.S. market reports today. And since my waking and thus trading hours are on most days no earlier than 5:00 A.M. EST, the reports of other countries are not hot zones I usually have to contend with. However, if I am up much earlier I will certainly make sure that I am aware of hot zones in other countries. My trading platform lists them all. (See Figure 5.1.)

The lack of reports is no reason not to trade, but if you were going to try to schedule errands and days off, these days are certainly the better choices. That's certainly not to say that you won't see setups occur; you most certainly can and will. But the absence of volatility that surrounds economic reports will make for typically a quieter trading day. Let's see what's on my radar for this morning.

The AUD/USD is still weak on the daily chart and my OCO order is taking care of my stop order and my limit profit target order. Let's imagine that we're not in the daily chart trade and look at another setup of the same pair on the 30-minute chart. Before we get to that chart, though, let me address a common question. It's not an uncommon scenario that you may want to enter a trade on the daily and also on one of the intraday time frames. Sometimes these are setups and trades in the same direction and sometimes

FOREX.com

| Position | Economic Calendar | Charting |

	Time	Country	Name	Period ▲	Previous	Forecast
...	1330	US	Continuing claims	w/e 3/4	2.506 mio	n/a
...	2200	US	ABC weekly consumer ...	w/e 3/13	-9	n/a
...	1330	US	Initial jobless claims	w/e 3/11	303K	300K
...	1200	US	MBA mortgage applicati...	w/e 3/10	0.7%	n/a
...	1445	US	Univ Michigan consume...	Mar-prelim	86.7	88.0
...	1000	Germany	ZEW econ. sentyiment ...	Mar	69.8	71.0
...	1000	EC	ZEW econ. sentiment s...	Mar	66.0	n/a
...	1800	US	NAHB housing market in...	Mar	57	56
...	1330	US	Empire (NY Fed) manuf...	Mar	20.3	18.9
...	2330	Australia	Westpac consumer con...	Mar	n/a	n/a
...	1700	US	Phila. Fed index	Mar	15.4	13.4
...	1000	Germany	ZEW current situation s...	Mar	-19.5	-15.0
...	0500	Japan	Coincident index	Jan-final	100.0	n/a
...	0430	Japan	Industrial production MoM	Jan-final	0.3%	0.3%
...	0430	Japan	Industrial production YoY	Jan-final	2.1%	2.1%
...	0500	Japan	Leading economic index	Jan-final	85.0	n/a
...	0430	Japan	Capacity utilization	Jan-final	106.5%	n/a
...	1330	Canada	Manufacturing shipment...	Jan	1.4%	0.4%
...	1400	US	Net foreign security pur...	Jan	56.6 bio	n/a
...	0930	UK	ODPM house prices YoY	Jan	2.9%	3.2%
...	0930	UK	Avg earnings ex-bonus...	Jan	3.8%	3.8%
...	1330	Canada	New vehicle sales MoM	Jan	-0.4%	1.0%
...	2350	Japan	Current account total	Jan	JPY 1748 bio	JPY 659 bio
...	1000	EC	Eurozone industrial pro...	Jan	0.1%	0.4%
...	2145	NZ	Retail sales MoM	Jan	0.0%	0.5%
...	2350	Japan	Adjusted current accou...	Jan	JPY 2024 bio	JPY 1581 bio
...	1530	UK	Coincident indicator ind...	Jan	0.2%	n/a

FIGURE 5.1
Source: Forex.com.

these trades are in opposing directions. They won't necessarily happen at the same time, but you could be already in a trade off the daily chart when an intraday setup confirms. The only way to do this is to have two accounts. These can be with the same broker. This is not a big deal at all. If you have a question about this or even setting up an account in general, e-mail info@tradedirectfx.com.

Back to the 30-minute AUD/USD. This setup is the first swing trade we'll examine together. The majority of my trading involves momentum entries, the three o'clock Wave, and the MACD histogram. In Figure 5.2 we're looking at something completely different.

The first thing you want to notice is the angle of the Wave. This is the swing trading

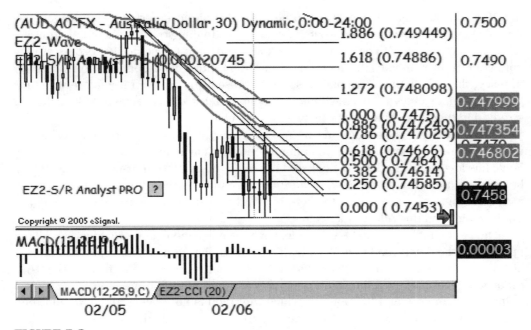

FIGURE 5.2

telltale. This is the most important element of the trade! The Wave must be traveling downward at between four and six o'clock to register a swing trade. Then we wait. Shortly after 1:00 A.M. EST prices bounced into the Wave, registering a short (but I'm not going to tell you I was up at 1:30 A.M.). The trade we are examining was triggered first at 5:00 A.M. and then again at 5:30 A.M. I don't know where on the planet you may be, and that's the point. I can't expect you to trade at times that are not realistic for you to be awake and at your desk! Five o'clock in the morning is realistic for me. You need to figure out what is reasonable to you. Maybe 1:00 A.M. to 1:30 A.M. EST is a realistic time for you to be awake and in that case, take the entry! Sydney, Tokyo, Hong Kong, and Singapore are open, and London will be active in less than an hour. Certainly this trade rates high in terms of "who's awake" and multiple financial centers being active.

The first opportunity to enter short in this four to six o'clock Wave is at the lowest line, which is plotting at 0.7468, so that's the price you're looking for. For order execution, you can use a limit order here. Placing a limit order will allow you to park a short entry that will wait until prices trade up to the 0.7468 level. This is the best way to position yourself for swing trades. This is not the case for momentum entries.

Although we have already covered order types, I believe repetition is the mother of skill. While the limit order positions us well for entries that are based on corrections, limit orders are not suited for momentum entries. You must use stops or market orders. Do not make the error of thinking that stops are merely a risk management order type. Although that is what they are certainly synonymous with, their function is much more multifaceted than that! If you want to be proactive about entering swing trades, use limit orders. If you want to be proactive about positioning yourself for momentum entries, use stop orders. If you're at your desk and you want to use market orders or execute your order manually, that's certainly an option. But if your confirmation is already in place, then being proactive makes sense because at times, even if you are watching your charts like a hawk, prices will move fast and trades will be triggered like lightning strikes and that proactive order will be your only chance.

As the morning progresses and we near the U.S. market open, the Canada also has my attention this morning, the 180-minute chart in particular. (See Figure 5.3.) The Wave has leveled off to three o'clock and has been this way for more than a day. Prices had broken up through the downtrend line one candle earlier, but take a look at the MACD histogram: It was below the zero line and thus did not confirm the trade. If you think I ever bend this rule, think again.

The next candle, the 9:00 A.M. candle, gave me a second-chance entry with a pierce up through the downtrend line. The MACD histogram has gone positive and has plotted above the zero line. *All systems are go!* This breakout is further confirmed by the 0.618 Fibonacci level that is at the same point as the downtrend line breakout. One logical point for a stop-loss and the point at which the trade is no longer valid is the uptrend line, which is the other side of the triangle pattern we have here. A pierce of this line would register a breakdown. Using that level as a starting point, where are the other support levels that might afford a more closely positioned stop for this entry? Keep in

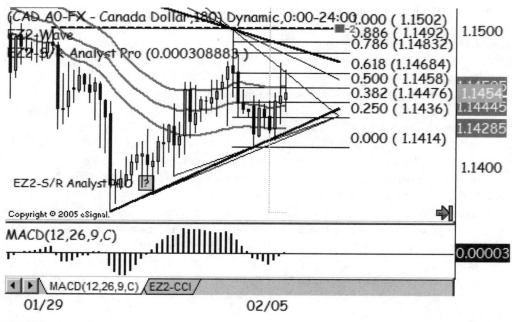

FIGURE 5.3

mind that this is a 180-minute chart and the stop must be able to handle the ebb and flow of three hours of trading per candle. The breakout candle has a low that is at the middle line of the Wave, which is also plotting just below the psychological level of 1.1450. The 0.382 Fibonacci level helps further reinforce this support area.

The profit targets for this trade are as follows—and of course each profit target is a price point at which we must scale out of our position. *How much of the position you choose to scale out of is up to you and your risk tolerance, but you must scale out at the predetermined profit targets.* (The only exception is if profit targets are within 10 to 12 pips of one another.) Keep an eye on the 0.786 and 0.886. The 0.886 Fibonacci at the 1.1492 price level will also allow you to scale out in front of the 1.1500 psychological number so you won't have to set another exit at 1.1495/1.1497. *Got it?*

Tuesday, February 7th

Another day sans economic reports. Actually, that's not entirely the case but the Consumer Credit number won't be released today until 3:00 P.M. EST and, as I have said before, after lunch I'm gone. By noon EST I am in need of either lunch or a nap. If it's an FOMC decision day, I'll hang around, but other than that there's no reason to. So like I said, the 3:00 P.M. release won't affect me. The daily chart of the AUD/USD in Figure 6.1 is a pretty, pretty sight. It's a great way to start the morning.

But you can't let a winner go to your head! Act like you've been here before; act like a winning trade isn't a reason to celebrate but rather, it's just your job. Because frankly, that's all that it is. The more you celebrate your winning trades, the more you will be depressed for your losing trades. The pendulum swings both ways, so either way, act like you've been there before, winner or loser. My goal each day is as simple as this: When my husband walks in the door after his day at work, he shouldn't know whether I had a good or bad day. I'm a fighter and my ring is the market. I give my all in the ring and then I walk away from the ring.

I want to share this example of a setup in the Japanese yen (USD/JPY) with you this morning because the chart image in Figure 6.2 is a great setup that I want you to begin recognizing. *Recognize, react, repeat.* There are some great pieces that are in place as well as small distinctions we want to make as traders. Oh, let me mention there was one piece that was not in place here: *me.* The trade set up at one o'clock this morning. I was asleep but for those of you who could find yourselves actively trading during the Tokyo session, I don't want to neglect the action that can be very productive there.

The Wave is just four candles into the three o'clock angle but has certainly completed the transition from the uptrending Wave just four hours earlier. There are some price levels to watch on this chart. First, make sure you get in the habit of picking up on major "00" psychological levels as soon as you set your gaze to any chart. Here prices have established themselves below the 119.00 level, which is now resistance. This level

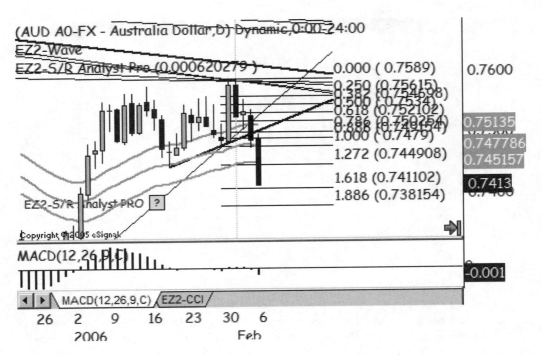

FIGURE 6.1

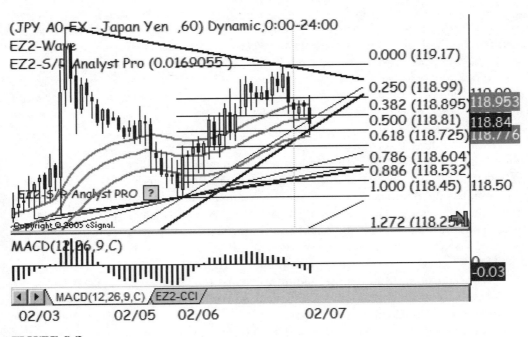

FIGURE 6.2

is further confirmed by the 0.250 Fibonacci level. The MACD histogram is negative and this confirms this pierce of the uptrend line.

Let me point out a distinction that makes this setup just a little less than perfect. Anytime you have a triangle pattern, which is what we have here, you must take note of where prices are trading. You can visualize that the triangle is divided into middle, top, and bottom. The middle slices right through the center of the triangle (heavy line in Figure 6.3).

What I am trying to show you is that prices do not always travel in the center of a triangle pattern. This fact alone will not render a triangle pattern useless; I'm just trying to make a point. Triangle patterns are the most common to momentum trading setups. Momentum trading triggers are best when there is a breakout or breakdown with some conviction behind it. This is not always the case with triangle breakouts. Because triangle patterns put a squeeze on prices, at some point there will simply be nowhere else for prices to go except through the downtrend line or through the uptrend line. Even if prices just go sideways, eventually they will break from the confines of the triangle pattern. All I want you to be aware of is this distinction. Breakouts or breakdowns with conviction are often not going to give you much time to react. The prices will come fast and change faster. This is where parking stop orders can allow you to proactively trade the triangle. You know there's a reason I am mentioning all this.

The follow-through on the USD/JPY chart brings us to 6:00 A.M. EST. (See Figure 6.4.) The breakdown was fast and furious. If your order was not already placed using a

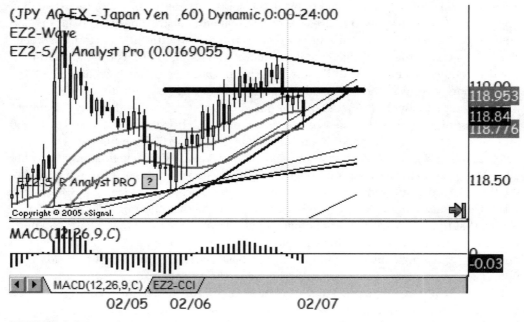

FIGURE 6.3

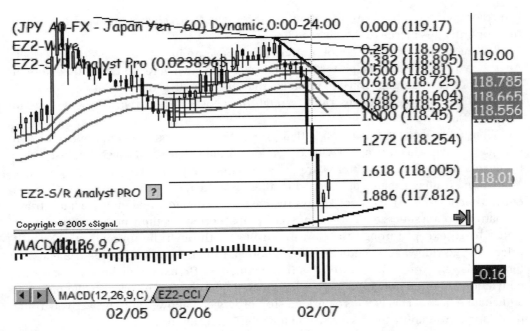

FIGURE 6.4

stop-loss, you probably did not get to place the short entry at the break of the trend line. This chart also allows me to address another frequently asked question: What do I do when my Fibonacci levels come in close succession with little price gap in between? This is especially true of 30- and 60-minute charts. Here's a good rule of thumb, and we'll use this follow-through chart of the yen to explain. Once the breakdown happened, the first support level was the 0.786 Fibonacci. Remember the cushion that we use if the first price target is within 10 to 12 pips of our entry. Well, this same thinking can be utilized for profit targets that come in close succession. The breakdown occurred at 118.80 and means the 0.786 Fibonacci is our first objective at 118.60. The next support level down is the 0.886, which is only seven pips away at 118.53. Because this level is within 10 to 12 pips, you have the option to ignore it. If you do ignore it because of its proximity, then the 1.000 full retracement must be your next scale-out price at 118.45. Below this level the scale-out levels are obvious: The 1.272 and then the 1.618 Fibonacci levels. Notice that the 1.618 is at the psychological number of 118.00, and that means you must exit three to five pips above 118.00 so as not to get lost in the mass of orders that will flood this psychologically relevant price. Even past the 118.00, this is not the end of the fall. *There is no single level that can be depended on to reverse prices in any move!* That's why we are ready to react at a number of levels. Any one of them could have been where this drop in the yen reversed. It just happens to be that the 1.886 finally caught and reversed the fall. This is the level that not only buyers felt comfortable stepping in but where sellers weren't pushing hard. It's supply and demand, and at 117.81 (another reason we should watch the minor psychological levels of the "20" and "80" pips!) prices finally held: more demand than supply. Again no one knows at which support level a sell-off will reverse. For that matter, no one knows where a rally will find resistance and reverse. So don't guess; just be ready at each decision level. The decision levels are already marked on your chart by psychological numbers, by Fibonacci levels, or by pivot points. That's why trying to pick tops and bottoms is such a low-percentage entry.

Wednesday, February 8th

Y ou'll hear me mention this from time to time: taking it easy. I don't charge into every trading day with guns blazing. There are days when I will, for one reason or another, either take the day off or take it easy. With that said, I am taking it easy today. Why this day in particular? Well, years and years ago, one of the few things I could get my hands on about trading was *Technical Analysis of Stocks & Commodities* magazine. This was pre-Internet so there was a certain isolation a budding trader lived in. *TASC* was my monthly party, a celebration of the fact that I wasn't alone in my pursuit of trading. I am not unlike many of the traders and students I meet online and in person every day, so when I was asked to do an interview for *TASC*'s forex special, you had to peel me off the ceiling. It was surreal. It feels like only yesterday that I was going to the trading expos as an attendee and now I present on stage. I don't say all this to brag. I just want you to understand that I wasn't born knowing how to do all this. I didn't study this in college; I was an English major who studied Dante, not derivatives. Trading is something you *can* learn to do—and learn to do well.

At 7:30 A.M. EST I short the pierce of the uptrend line on the daily chart of the EUR/USD. (See Figure 7.1.) Prices have broken through the psychological level of 1.1950, which is where I wanted to see prices go so that I could get short.

I am going to watch the 1.1900 psychological level for support! Make sure you always give respect to the "00" pip levels; they are the most important and strongest levels of the four major and minor levels we watch ("00," "20," "50," and "80"). Notice that I also used the major psychological level of 1.1950 as my trigger since it coincided with the uptrend line support I was waiting to see break. I'm placing my protective stop at the middle line of the Wave, which is at 1.2045. I like this level because it gives my daily chart the wiggle room a daily chart setup needs. (Remember that you have to take into

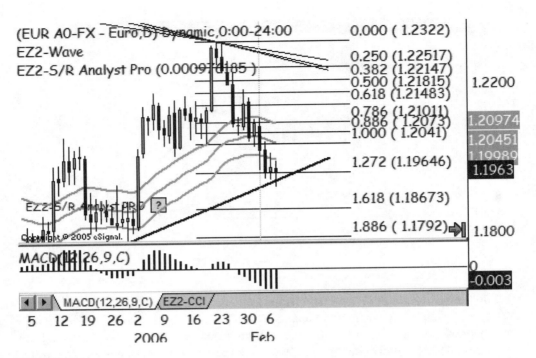

FIGURE 7.1

account that you are now managing your stop based on the range within which prices could trade over the course of 24 hours!) The 1.2045 level is also buffered by the fact that *both* the middle line of the Wave and the 1.000 full retracement level are there. Now there are two reasons that this level should hold as resistance. Because I am shorting, I will also refer to the high of the preceding candle and the breakdown candle for shorter-term resistance so guidance. My first profit target is 1.1900 and then 1.1867, which is the 1.618 Fibonacci extension level.

The Crude Inventories report is out today and will be released at 10:30 A.M. It's usually a U.S. dollar mover so let's take a look at two charts that are most directly affected by the U.S. dollar: the USD/CHF and the EUR/USD. (See Figures 7.2 and 7.3.) I'll scan the time frames that are usually best for pre–hot zone setups: the 30-minute and the 60-minute.

The Swissy is not near an entry trigger . . . yet. You can see where the resistance and support are waiting. Also notice that while it will not generate an entry on its own, the MACD histogram is already above the zero line. This could change, of course, but as long as it is above the zero line, parking an entry at the resistance breakout above the 1.3000 level is okay. Remember that the resistance here is a downtrend line and it will

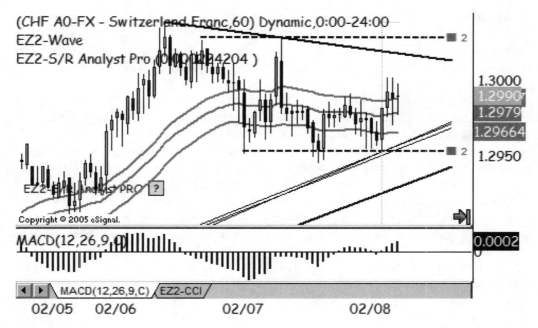

FIGURE 7.2

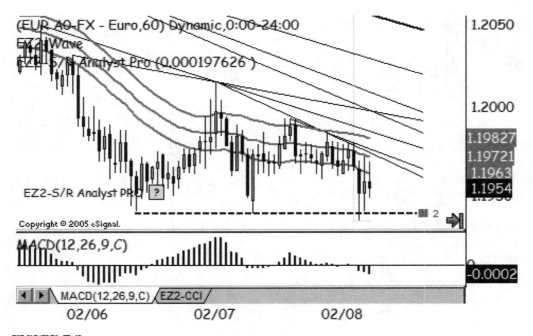

FIGURE 7.3

continue lower as time goes on. Regardless of where it is plotting, we cannot go long below 1.3000. We must wait until price breaks through 1.3003 or 1.3005. By they way, three to five pips is not a random number. It's meant to represent the typical spread between the bid and the ask in most currency pairs with the exception of the EUR/USD, which is three pips.

The daily chart has already set up a short trade in the euro (that price also triggered a short on the 60-minute earlier this morning but has bounced slightly since then). The MACD histogram confirmed the short entry and the Wave is still heading sideways. We didn't move past the horizontal support level enough to reach any profit targets, so we have a second-chance entry here. Keep an eye on the middle line of the Wave for resistance and, of course, the downtrend lines just above it. If prices go up through the downtrend lines, then this short is no longer valid. You can choose to take both entries if you'd like to do so, but they will be managed on the respective charts. You can also choose between them. It's really all up to you. Having multiple time frames gives us this flexibility!

Figures 7.4 and 7.5 show where prices are at 11:00 A.M. on the two 60-minute charts. My interview (see back of book) is in one hour so I am going to go relax. My limit orders are in the market so my positions are managed.

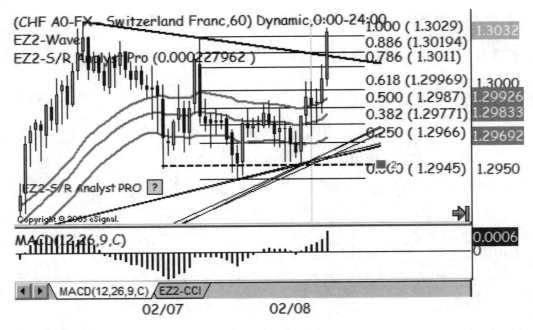

FIGURE 7.4

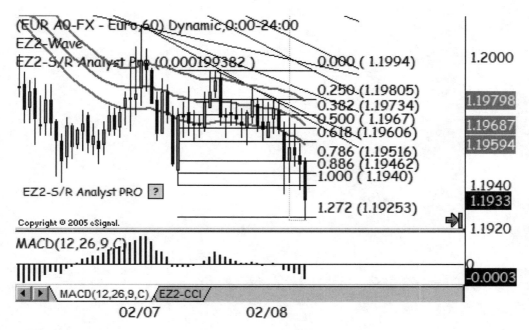

FIGURE 7.5

I took both setups on the euro because both charts were compelling and offered me excellent setups. It wasn't a stretch in this case at all to short the 60-minute intraday weakness as well as the daily chart's breakdown. These are two distinct setups that don't diminish each other. Realize that a move on the 30- or 60-minute chart can be just a small percentage within the entire range on a daily candle.

Thursday, February 9th

I check my overnight trade on the daily chart of the EUR/USD. It's holding on, trading s-l-o-w-l-y lower. Because I used the middle line of the Wave as my protective stop, I have to recheck the price of the middle line of the Wave to make any adjustments. It's lower by about two or three pips so I'm not going to worry about updating the price on my stop. Let's see what else is blipping on my radar. I'll take a little extra time on my scans and rewind today since I wasn't watching the market closely yesterday. We'll be dealing with a big report today and that means hot zones. The Initial Claims number will be released at 8:30 A.M. EST. I set an alarm clock to get me up a little early so that I would have time to catch up on price action well before the release. I don't typically use an alarm clock. I am lucky to be one of those people who can just wake up when I need to. But just in case I want to be ready. Initial Claims will be a market mover and I trust my charts to put me where I need to be. *When you can say that and believe it, you are a chartist.* I'm going to go pour a cup of tea and then see what's on my radar. It's 4:00 A.M. and I can use all the help I can get.

I'm scanning through the pairs on my screen (they're listed alphabetically). The AUD/USD didn't show any potential on any of my time frames but the short on the daily is still in play from the 3rd. I am going to continue to trail my stop down by using my prior profit targets, which were support on the way down but are now resistance as prices break down from the 1.272 (remember to place the stop-loss order three to five pips above the Fibonacci price level!) to the 1.618, and because prices have taken out the 1.886 level we can use that level as the trailing stop. (See Figure 8.1.) Here's where your own risk tolerance comes in. Both the 1.618 and the 1.886 are resistance levels. If you'd rather give this daily chart of the Aussie more wiggle room, use the 1.618. If you want to protect your profits tightly, use the 1.886. We have also broken down below the psychological level of 0.7400, so that could be a resistance level you could use, too. *It's your choice.* There are no "right" answers here, just choices based on your preference.

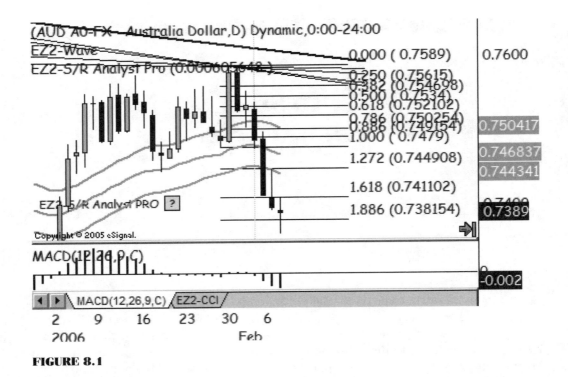

FIGURE 8.1

I want to point out a chart (Figure 8.2) that has a confirmed breakout that I am *not* going to take. The 30-minute USD/CAD is taking out not only the downtrend line but also the middle line of the Wave (resistance) and it's being confirmed by an MACD histogram that has been above the zero line for better than six hours.

So why am I not going to take the breakout of the 30-minute USD/CAD this morning? Question: At what price is the Canada breaking? Answer: 1.1500. This places any entry long right at psychological resistance. The high of this candle was 1.1501 and not the three to five pips above this level we would need to see to trigger an entry. I also want to call your attention to the horizontal resistance that is waiting at 1.1507. If our ideal entry is 1.1503 or 1.1505 and we have a resistance level by way of a horizontal resistance line overhead just two to four pips north of our entry, *is this a good place to enter?* Keep in mind that flat, horizontal resistance (and support) levels are not common. And since we're going to have to have enough momentum to take out 1.1500 and then 1.1507 (the horizontal resistance), *wouldn't it be better to just wait for both levels to be broken?* It's not as if we are giving eight to ten pips up; we're taking only about two to four pips and those few pips could give us a much stronger indication of a breakout. *Do you see how to weight these factors together?* Waiting gives us a chance to enter after two significant levels are broken! At this moment, this succession of questions probably is not going to come naturally, but eventually it will. I will be sure to revisit that chart in

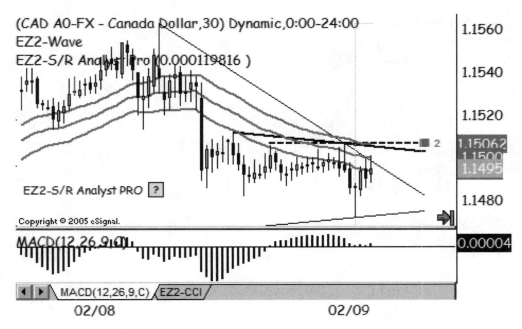

(CAD A0-FX – Canada Dollar,30) Dynamic,0:00–24:00
EZ2-Wave
EZ2-S/R Analyst Pro (0.0001 19816)

EZ2-S/R Analyst PRO [?]

Copyright © 2005 eSignal.

MACD(12,26,9,C)

MACD(12,26,9,C) / EZ2-CCI /

02/08   02/09

1.1560
1.1540
1.1520
■ 2   1.15062
         1.1500
         1.1495
1.1480

0.00004

FIGURE 8.2

a couple or hours to see if the resistance level held or if we can look for a breakout entry if 1.1507 is taken out.

The Swissy has already triggered an entry this morning. (See Figure 8.3.) The breakout is confirmed and far enough below the 1.3000 level that the trade has some room to move up in our favor before hitting that psychological resistance.

The resistance at 1.2991 is within 10 to 12 pips of the 1.2981 entry, so I will use 1.2995 as the initial profit target and place a limit order there. Near-term support for a potential stop-loss is at the breakout candle low of 1.2973 but the trade will no longer be valid if prices break down through the uptrend line, which at the moment is at the 0.250 Fibonacci level. Mind you, this will change with each new candle that plots.

It's 4:30 A.M. I've been awake for only half an hour and we've already entered a trade. The Swissy has broken to the upside and traded through my 1.2995 level, so I want to trail my stop, the Wave, and the 0.500 Fibonacci level. The high of the breakout candle is only 1.2998, which means that the 1.3000 is still resistance.

The EUR/USD has broken down on the 30-minute chart (Figure 8.4). The Wave is not as flat as it is in the USD/CHF but is well within the two to four o'clock angle. That alone could make you decide on the USD/CHF setup. Frankly, the breakdown happened fast enough that while I was busy with the USD/CHF, the entry price on the EUR/USD already traded by. But I can rest assured that the long in the Swissy has positioned me to take advantage of the strength in the U.S. dollar. A short in the EUR/USD and a long in

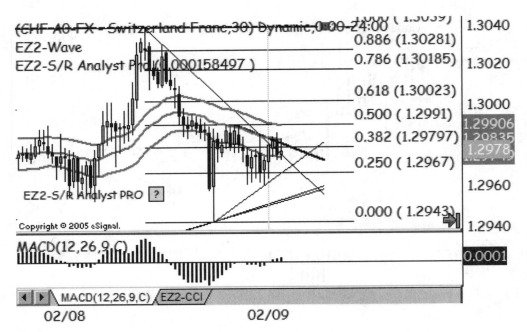

FIGURE 8.3

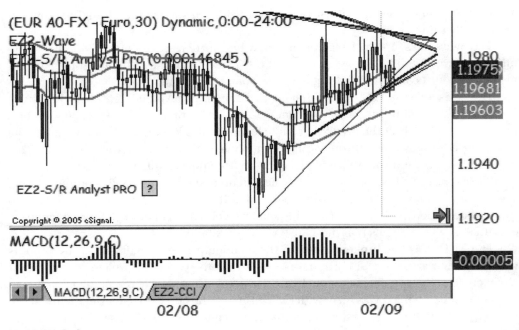

FIGURE 8.4

the CHF/USD are essentially the same position. Don't forget that we're already short on the daily euro from Wednesday.

As I take a look at the GBP/USD I see it has tanked, and tanked hard. The setup most obviously formed earlier. It does me no good now, so I am moving on to the USD/JPY.

The yen is presenting an interesting dilemma for me—that is, if you consider having two different setups on the same pair a dilemma. As I scan through the charts I see that the 60-minute chart is registering and confirming a breakdown while the 180-minute chart is breaking to the upside. (See Figures 8.5 and 8.6.)

This is not a difficult decision. If presented with this type of conflicting entry setups, as a rule take the longer-term setup. The 180-minute chart of the yen also has a few other distinctions that would make it a better setup besides the fact that it is the longer of the two time frames. First, the triangle pattern itself is a more balanced pattern as compared to the 60-minute chart. The 180-minute chart also has a better MACD histogram reading. The 60-minute histogram, while fitting the prerequisite of being below the zero line, has been bobbing along the zero line instead of being firmly established on one side or the other. By the way, there are two types of MACD histogram neutral readings: bobbing and treading water. I will refer to both. Bobbing typifies a histogram that is going back and forth between a positive and negative reading whereas a histogram that is treading water is just barely registering a positive reading. (Figure 8.5 is bobbing.)

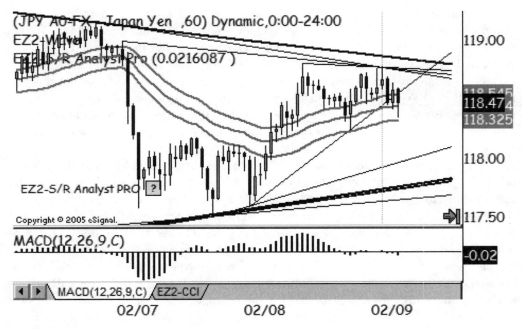

FIGURE 8.5

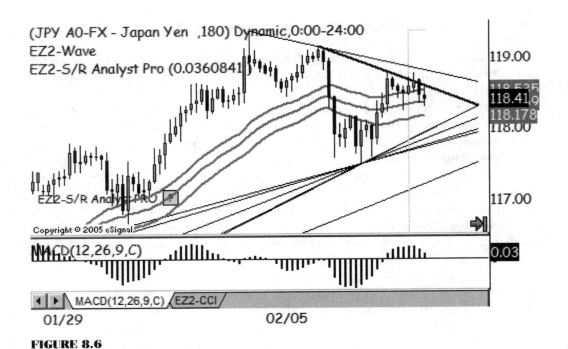

FIGURE 8.6

Look at the more definite histogram reading on the 180-minute chart. The Wave is also flatter and traveling at a truer three o'clock angle on the 180-minute chart. *All that considered—case closed.* The 180-minute yen chart also shows that there already was a confirmed breakout at midnight EST. Prices did not climb much higher subsequently and then actually dropped, giving us a nice second-chance entry. Let's set up this momentum trade. We need a decent last major move to the downside to draw our Fibonacci levels and I am not happy with any other last major moves on this chart. Either they have already been retraced or they are not major enough. That's why we have backups. I will use psychological levels and pivot points. (See Figure 8.7.)

The breakout candle low is at the pivot point (PP) and the middle line of the Wave, at 118.33. There is certainly some short-term support there. The point at which this trade will no longer be valid is if we break the uptrend line, which is the other side of this triangle. But I am not willing to give this trade that much wiggle room, so I will look to see what support levels are closer to my entry. We all have to make this decision on our own, and how close we put our stop should be based on our own risk tolerance. But let me warn you, **if you begin placing stops in accordance with a low risk tolerance and ignore the point at which the trade is no longer valid, you will not be setting your stops correctly.** Look for logical support (or resistance) levels that the trade is likely not to break beyond. Here I think that the Wave and pivot point can do the job, and I will place my stop three to five pips below that level (the spread). This puts

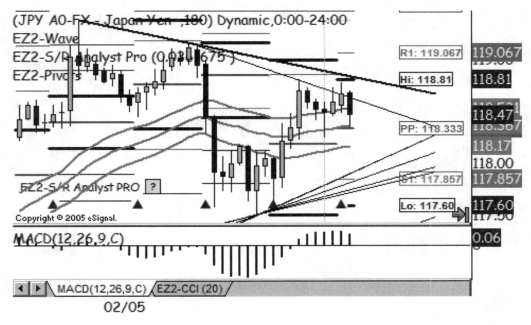

FIGURE 8.7

me at 118.28, and if I want to give myself a little extra room I can use the 20-pip minor psychological level.

Meanwhile, the USD/CHF 30-minute chart has reversed, stopping me out after a quick profit. Prices topped out at 1.3000 during the 5:00 A.M. candle when sellers had complete and utter dominance. (See Figure 8.8.)

If you are wondering whatever happened to the USD/CAD trade where we were waiting to see if prices could break 1.1507, take a look at Figure 8.9 as USD/CAD trades at 6:00 A.M.

As 7:00 A.M. rolls around the Swiss franc—which had already stopped out the long entry earlier this morning—is still trading sideways with a three o'clock Wave. (See Figure 8.10.) We're still an hour an a half from the Initial Claims number. *I don't hold a grudge.*

The break to the upside has my attention, but I can't execute here for the same reason that I placed my profit target in the earlier trade this morning and got stopped out later: the 1.3000 level. Prices topped at 1.3002, and with the MACD histogram still poised above the zero line I am ready to get long as soon as I see 1.3005 trade. I know there will be volatility with the Initial Claims so I will be sure to use my 60-second stop when the time comes. For now I will place an if/then order to get me long 1.3005 and place my first profit target order at 1.3018, which is the 0.786 Fibonacci level.

Initial Claims were pretty muted on the USD/CHF and my order to buy was never even touched so I am still flat. Figure 8.11 shows a view of the U.S. dollar at the 8:30 A.M. candle.

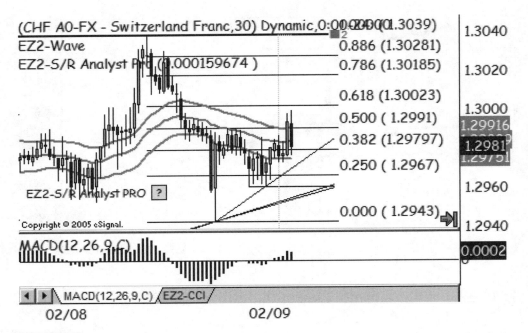

FIGURE 8.8

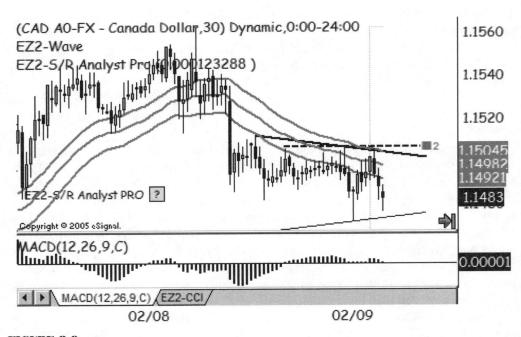

FIGURE 8.9

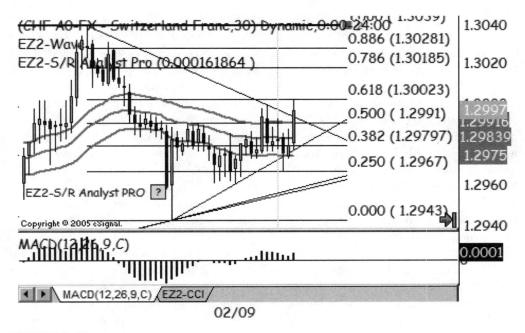

FIGURE 8.10

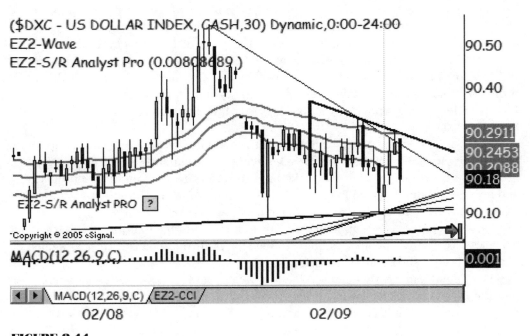

FIGURE 8.11

Let me address another frequently asked question: How long will I stay in a trade? The answer is until it either hits my stop-loss or hits my profit target(s). I don't exit a trade because it is not going anywhere. I am focused on the two decision levels that will force me to follow through on my trading plan. Somewhere along the line, traders were told by someone (who needs their butt kicked!) that you should exit the trade after a certain amount of time has passed. I frankly have never run across this advice, but enough traders ask me about this that somewhere out there, someone is extolling this useless drivel. I don't want to sound too mean-spirited, but that advice is just plain wrong. Conceivably if a trade has been monopolizing your margin (your buying power) for an extended amount of time, I could see why you may be tempted to exit a trade going nowhere. But this is not the fault of the trade itself. It is the fault of the trader for not setting aside enough margin for when another trading opportunity comes along. You always need to keep reserves, not just from a risk management standpoint but from a trading opportunity standpoint as well.

I bring this point up because the Swissy is still moving within a range that was set earlier this morning. This neither bothers nor worries me. The low established during the 6:30 A.M. candle at the 0.250 Fibonacci level and the high set during the 7:30 A.M. candle at the 0.618 Fibonacci level have defined the support and resistance so far. I am comfortable with the fact that prices seem to be bouncing back and forth between these levels because it confirms that if and when prices finally break, I should see some follow-through! It's 9:30 A.M. when the resistance at the 0.618 gives and my entry price at 1.3005 is triggered. This price was the first part of my if/then order and this has also triggered my limit order to sell at 1.3018. Since I am now long I will go ahead and place my stop-loss for protection. During the past couple of hours I have seen that the 1.2979, which is a minor psychological level, as well as the 0.382 Fibonacci level, have been holding. The bottom line of the Wave is at 1.2976 and my stop will go there for now, until it is (hopefully) time to trail it up! Prices continue upwards and take out the initial profit target so it's time to make sure I place my second profit target at 1.3028, the 0.886 Fibonacci level. I can update my stop-loss, too, which I will place just above the 1.3000 level at 1.3003.

At 10 A.M., prices hit 1.3028 and my trailing stop must now be moved way up to the prior profit target, which was resistance but will now be support. It's the 0.786. (See Figure 8.12.) Unfortunately, it doesn't take long for prices to weaken after hitting 1.3028 and my trailing stop is hit at 1.3018. So the remainder of my position that was left after reaching 1.3028 is now exited at 1.3018. I'm flat.

I also wanted to follow up with the yen chart. I've returned to my desk and it's about 3:00 P.M. EST. The yen finally (trailing) stopped my trade out. The OCO orders kicked in, and what I see is shown in Figure 8.13.

The pound had slowly been leveling out all day and its range tightened enough so that the four to six o'clock Wave it had been traveling at slowed into transition and by 6:00 P.M. this evening it is actually triggering a breakout, even though the Wave is not completely flat, and by 9:00 P.M. the Wave has moved enough to complete transition and is now flat. Sydney, Tokyo, Singapore, and Hong Kong are all active and I know the

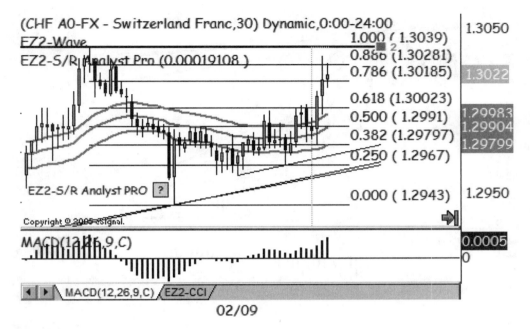

FIGURE 8.12

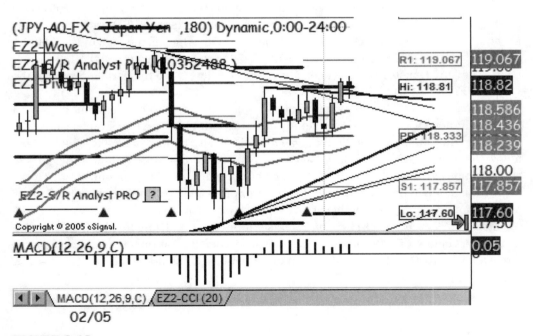

FIGURE 8.13

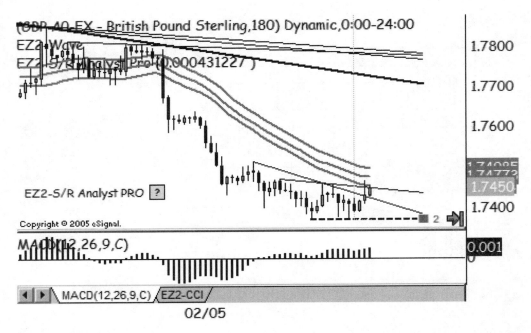

FIGURE 8.14

pound has enough trading activity in these financial centers that an entry wouldn't be too high-risk. The pound is breaking up through resistance as the USD trades lower this evening, which is to be expected. I enter long at 1.7455, which is the high of the 9:00 P.M. candle and above the psychological level of 1.7450 based on the setup on the 180-minute chart. The MACD histogram has been above the zero line since the early morning of the 7th. (See Figure 8.14.)

I'll be putting this trade on autopilot as I will be heading to bed in about an hour. I place an if/then OCO order to bracket my entry. My stop-loss is a buy stop based on the low of the first breakout candle that traded at 6:00 P.M. The low is 1.7409, which is just above the psychological level of 1.7400. I place my first profit target, a limit order to sell, at the minor psychological level of 1.7480 where I will unload half my position. Then I think for a moment that maybe I would be better off using the 1.7400 support level in my favor and place a stop below this at 1.7395. *That would make better sense . . . so I edit my stop with just a few clicks of my mouse.* If prices stay strong I will unload another quarter just below 1.7500, and this way I will have a small position left just in case prices move above 1.7500. With my conditional order in place, I call it a night.

Friday, February 10th

The Trade Balance number will be released at 8:30 A.M. EST and this is a significant hot zone, so I'll be sure to use 60-second stops on open positions. I have been watching the market since just before 7:30 A.M., and here's what's on my radar.

I'm still managing the EUR/USD short from Wednesday. So I want to check the reading of the middle line of the Wave to see if I have to update my protective stop. It's just above 1.2040 and only five pips from where my initial order was placed, so I will leave it where it is. (See Figure 9.1.)

As the Trade Balance number steps into the ring at 8:30 A.M., the U.S. Dollar Index takes a hard shot on the chin, moving from just above 90 to 89.75. So now I am seeing some strength in the EUR/USD. This doesn't exactly make me happy because I am short the EUR/USD based on the breakdown that occurred on the 8th, but my long position in the pound is flying. My first profit target was easily hit on a spike early this morning before I was even awake and my OCO unloaded half my position, and I see that prices are already just above 1.7550 so I immediately place an order to unload the remainder of my position. Spikes or sudden moves certainly don't make a trend, so it's time to just relax and trust my charts and exit the GBP/USD at logical resistance levels. *It's so far above where I would have exited that it's all gravy at this point.* I'm flat the pound within minutes.

I have a habit of going through my charts alphabetically, and usually from the 30-minute to the daily. So if you're wondering why I look at certain charts when I do, it's just the way they are listed on my quote screen: alphabetically.

The Aussie broke to the upside earlier this morning around 4:00 A.M. on the 30- and 60-minute charts, but it looks like there is a setup on the 180 that appears to be poised for a breakout. (See Figure 9.2.) The MACD histogram is established above the zero line and therefore a proactive entry to buy can be placed at the breakout level of 0.7440.

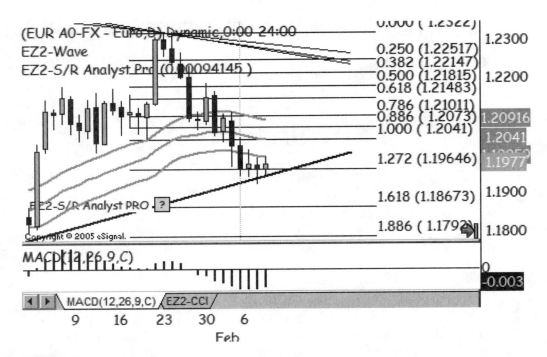

FIGURE 9.1

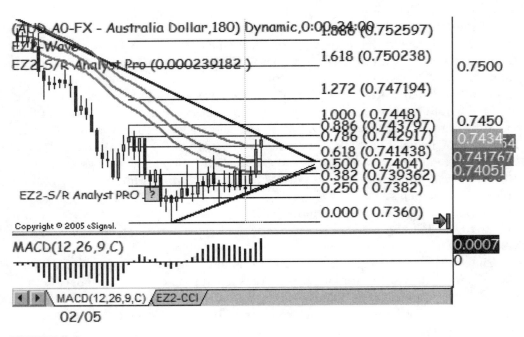

FIGURE 9.2

Notice that the breakout level and the 0.886 Fibonacci level are at the same level, giving this resistance level more relevance. It's always good to see that there are multiple reasons for a price level to be in play. Think of it this way: If you watch support and resistance levels and trend lines you would consider this level important. Traders who use Fibonacci levels would also consider this level important. So now you have two groups of traders watching this price level. Everything looks good, right? All we need is price to trigger our entry. Remember this is a two-sided pattern and support currently waits at the 0.382 Fibonacci level just below the psychological level of 0.7400. During the next candle we see our break. (See Figure 9.3.)

This is a great example of how and why to expect the *unexpected*. There was *no way* we could park a proactive entry order due to the fact that the MACD histogram was not confirming the break*down*. There was no way the trade triggered long, either, as prices never broke 0.7440; in fact, the high was 0.7338.

As I mentioned earlier, the U.S. dollar traded down sharply right at the Trade Balance release at the 8:30 A.M. candle. (See Figure 9.4.) Let's take an in-depth look at what happened on some of the short-term intraday charts that we often examine for setups when we have mornings that will be ruled by economic data.

With the breakdown of the U.S. dollar there was certainly weakness in the Swissy and strength in the euro. The USD/CHF sold off sharply through support, while the EUR/USD rallied up through resistance. (See Figures 9.5 and 9.6.)

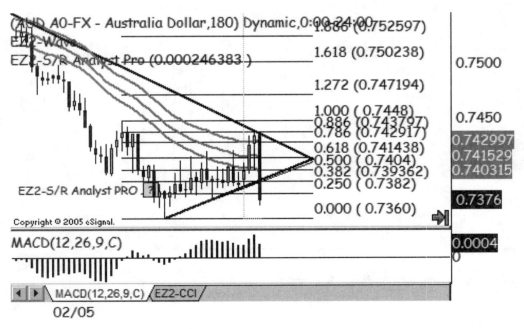

FIGURE 9.3

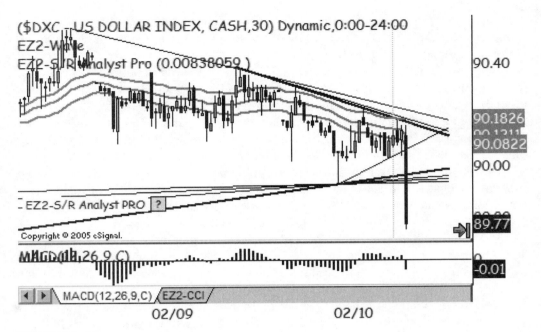

FIGURE 9.4

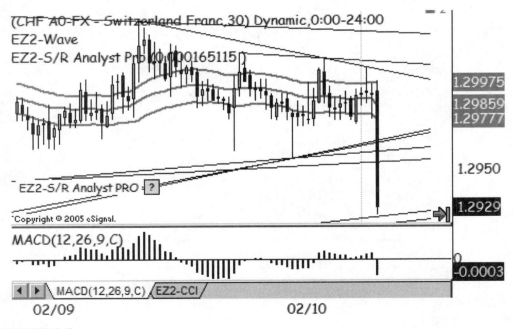

FIGURE 9.5

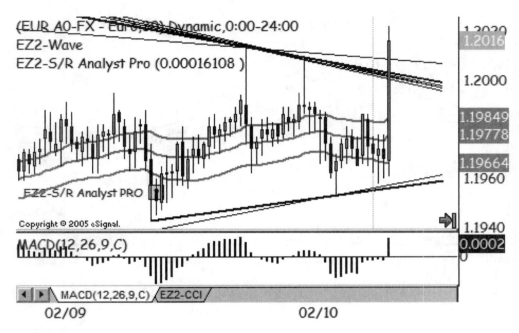

FIGURE 9.6

Figure 9.7 is a view of the U.S. dollar during the 10:00 A.M. candle. Within 90 minutes the U.S. dollar rallied and the moves in the Swissy and euro both reversed their prior direction. (See Figures 9.8 and 9.9.)

Mind you, none of this was tradable by my setups and confirmation because none of the setups could have been triggered by proactive entry orders due to lack of MACD histogram confirmation and the all-out velocity of the moves. All this has completely skewed prices to such a degree that it's best to walk away.

I have also decided to exit the EUR/USD trade on the daily chart (Figure 9.10). I'm out at 1.1905 in front of the 1.1900 psychological level and go into the weekend flat.

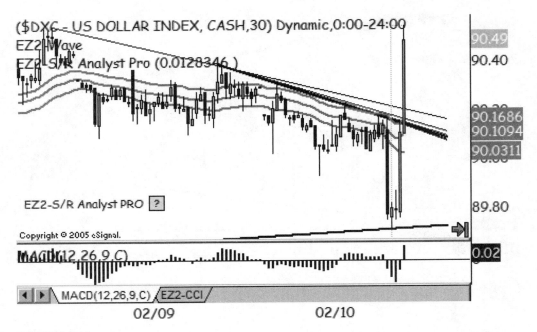

FIGURE 9.7

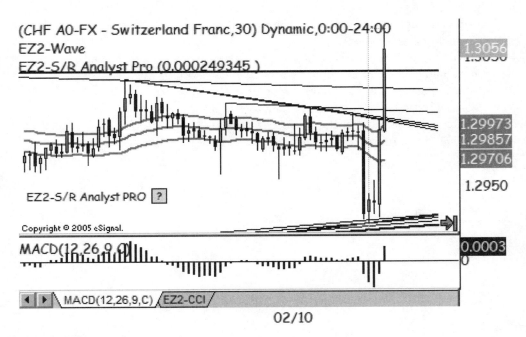

FIGURE 9.8

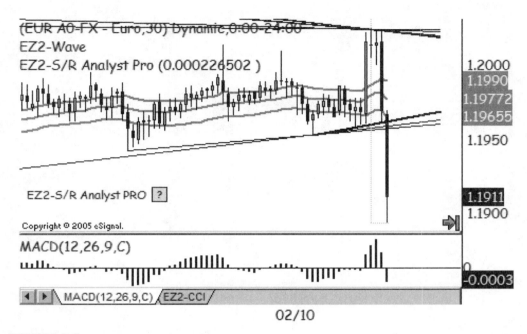

FIGURE 9.9

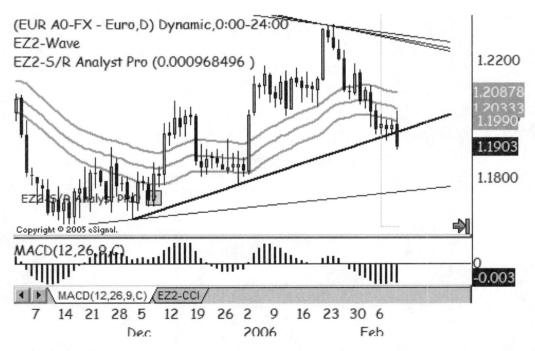

FIGURE 9.10

Sunday, February 12th

I feel really good today. Maybe that's because it's a Sunday and I have spent some time out on the water in my boat. The ocean air is amazing and seems to heal anything that ails me. This is probably the best I have felt since I got sick in January. It's about time! Knowing I am in such a good mood, my husband asks me why I am grumbling over at my desk. It's about 4:00 P.M. and, as you know, I exited Friday's entry short on the daily chart of the EUR/USD. The 1.1900 psychological level was support and it was Friday and the market was acting crazy so I played it safe just in case the 1.1900 level acted as a launchpad come Sunday evening. Now I see that 1.1900 has not held and prices are currently trading just below 1.1900. I know better than to be unhappy about my decision. I know that Sunday night's price action doesn't necessarily mean anything, to tell you the truth. We'll know what the real status is in about six or seven hours when London rises and shines because it's 7:30 P.M. Sunday night EST and 1:30 A.M. Monday morning in London. But right now I see that prices are breaking 1.1890, and as long as prices are trading below 1.1900 that level will now be resistance. Even though I am flat now, I'm certain that if prices want to make another move south, I can find an entry on the 30- or 60-minute chart if prices consolidate around the psychological 1.1900 level.

Monday,
February 13th

Fundamentally things are going to be fairly quiet today, so that means that I won't be playing within any hot zones. Here's what's blipping on the radar, though.

The AUD/USD confirmed, and although the break wasn't showing a great deal of upward momentum—I am happier when I do see upward momentum—it was a break nonetheless, so I will take a small position of two contracts. (See Figure 11.1.) A certain

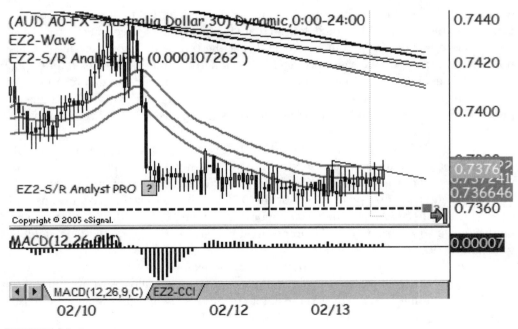

FIGURE 11.1

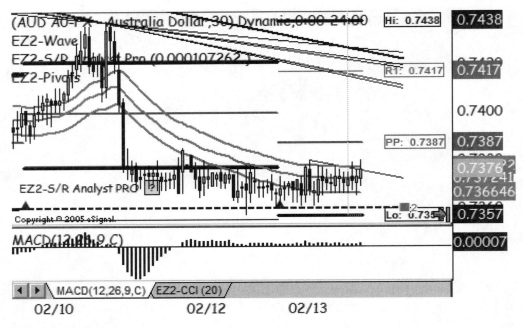

02/10   02/12   02/13

FIGURE 11.2

part of position size is just feel, and when I see a break like this I am not going to ignore the entry but I won't take a huge position, either. I'll look at the first two to three profit targets and then enter with enough lots so that I can peel out as prices meet each target.

In this case you can see in Figure 11.2 that the 0.7400 psychological level is just north of our entry. I have therefore decided to take the trade no further than 0.7395, where I can peel out of a minimum one contract, or both contracts. I am not happy with any of the recent major moves to draw a Fibonacci retracement from so I will use my pivots. The pivot point at 0.7387 is within the 10-to-12-pip cushion, so we can forgo exiting there and focus on the 0.7395 level.

The USD/JPY confirmed and I short 117.91. (See Figure 11.3.) There are two profit targets I'll be watching, and since I am going to be at my desk, I will execute my stop and second profit target manually. But I will go ahead and place a limit order to buy at 117.76, which is the first profit target at the 0.886 Fibonacci level. That's because the 0.618 is within 10 to 12 pips. The next support level is the 117.70 at the full retracement, but it's only six pips from the 0.886 profit target exit so we can ignore that one and look to the 1.272 Fibonacci extension.

I want to make sure that I continue to include examples of trades that have confirmed but, because of other charting and price cues, I have chosen to not enter. The New Zealand dollar/U.S. dollar is an example of that today. It's 10 A.M. and the 0.6800 level is resistance in the NZD/USD. (See Figure 11.4.) For the breakout level to be of any use to me I have to see that 0.6800 is support instead of the resistance it now represents.

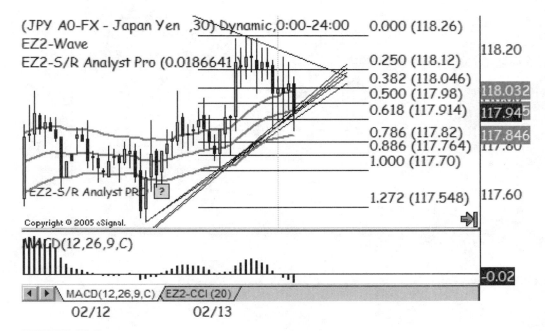

FIGURE 11.3

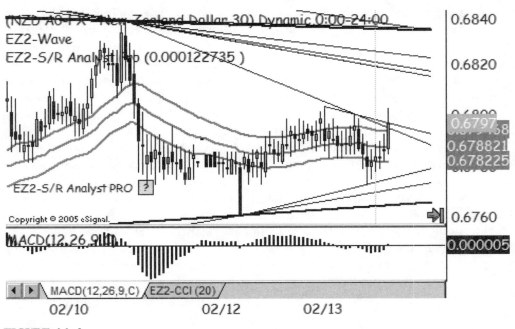

FIGURE 11.4

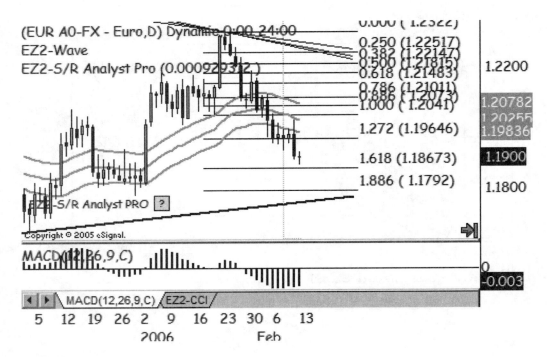

FIGURE 11.5

I like to wrap up my trading around 11 A.M. EST, noon at the latest. This trade has a sizable obstacle to scale in the 0.6800 level and despite a few pierces through 0.6800 it doesn't feel or look determined to stay above 0.6800 so I have decided to leave this one alone. Game over.

By the way, despite my Sunday evening grumblings, Monday morning proved to be more telling as the EUR/USD has formed a doji, a candle that signals a stall or potential reversal as the open and close are at or very near the same price. (See Figure 11.5.) A doji is a candle that I will keep an eye on within the context of a trend. If prices are meeting support or resistance and form a doji, it's an alert because a doji is most commonly perceived as a reversal candle. That certainly doesn't mean that prices are going to rally from here but it does mean that the selling pressure at least for the short term is easing up. A doji is a candle that represents balance. Imbalances are what make up a trend but balance is a trend killer. Nevertheless, my trailing stop is at the prior support level and onetime profit target of 1.1873. My next profit target is the 1.618 Fibonacci level. If prices can establish themselves with a close below the 1.618, I can consider trailing the stop down to that level, but for now I'm just waiting for that level to trade so I can exit more of my position.

Tuesday, February 14th

Early to bed, early to rise. I'm at my desk just before 6:00 A.M. so I'm definitely getting closer to being ready at least near the tail end of my ideal start time. Small successes and consistency equal confidence. It would be easy to get down on myself after being sick, getting to my office later than I'd like, but confidence is really the best asset I have. If I lose that, no matter how great my methodology and tools, I will be lost. So I am trying to string together a few well-prepared trading sessions so that I can get back in the groove.

In Figure 12.1 I see the EUR/USD breaking down below the uptrend line support with MACD histogram confirmation, and I take it. It feels a little "aggro," which is what my husband named my aggressive trader alter ego. That's because even though during most of my nontrading waking hours I am a high-energy, pitbullish multitasker, when I trade I am calm and focused, almost disconnected. So it's not in character when I take this EUR/USD short early. I know it's been trading tightly near this 1.1900 level, never straying too far above or below the level. Today is probably going to change all that. By the way, I am also still in the daily chart of the EUR/USD with my trailing stop and next profit target in place with an OCO.

There is a whole host of economic reports today and with the hot zones we are looking at today, *something's gonna give.*

Speaking of "something's gonna give," the USD/CAD has been range-bound since yesterday. (See Figure 12.2.) The Wave is at a nice, flat three o'clock angle. The market let loose around 3:30 this morning but as of right now, 7:00 A.M. EST, prices have begun to consolidate tightly once again. Also noteworthy is the fact that the MACD histogram has just become positive after many hours below the zero line.

If you were to be aggressive with setting up your trades this morning and park some stop orders to ready yourself for sudden breaks and entries, that's fine. Of course, these

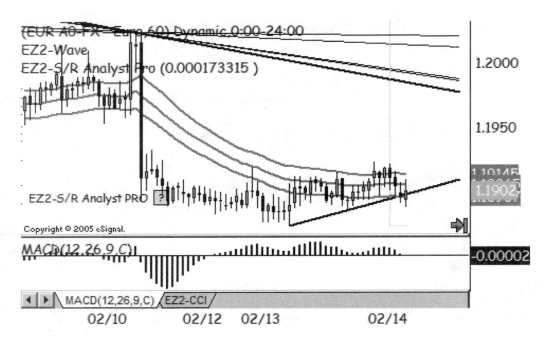

FIGURE 12.1

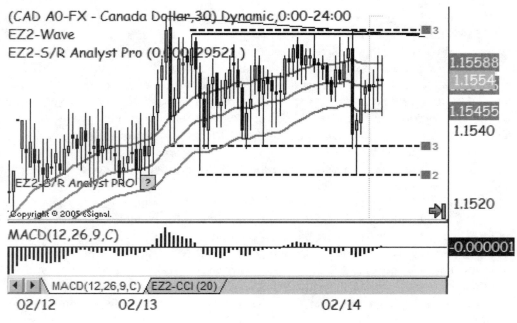

FIGURE 12.2

> This entire book, every one of our 30 days together, is about noticing the small nuances of the market. The breakouts and breakdowns, the pullbacks and bounces—those are the easy part. It's the small details that make the difference.

parked orders must already have MACD histogram confirmation in the case of momentum trading examples like this one.

In the case of swing trades, the same thing is true. Once you have a Wave traveling at either twelve to two or four to six o'clock, you can check the price of the Wave correction line and place an order. By that I mean for a downtrend, check the price of the bottom line of the Wave and for an uptrend, check the top line of the Wave, because these will be the first available opportunities for an entry (short or long). Also consider that if you are setting up a 180-minute chart, for example, you have to be aware that the Wave will have to be updated as the new candle and thus new Wave reading plots. The same is true for a 30-minute chart or whatever time frame you are setting up.

Right now, since the MACD histogram is above the zero line, if you wanted to park an entry (a proactive order), then the only way you could do it would be to park the buy stop. If the MACD histogram was below the zero line, then your only option would be to park the sell stop. Does that make sense? The reason I am spending so much time on how to be proactive about placing your entry orders is because you will find that far too often not doing so leaves you with no entry opportunity at all.

> If the forex market was a sport, at times I think it would have the most in common with drag racing.

In Figure 12.3 you can see the fast break up through the resistance. *It was like the light went green and from that moment on it was full throttle.* And as we already know, the confirmation of the MACD was already in place as the histogram went above the zero line during the prior 30-minute candle.

Today is Valentine's Day and I want to be sure to wrap up my day a little earlier, which means I won't spend any time tonight going over the charts to look for any setups that may confirm early tomorrow. I'll make a point of getting up earlier tomorrow, but I'll be wrapping things up for today so I can enjoy a nice evening out with my husband, Herbie. But I want to leave you today with this important point: *You must exit at your predetermined profit targets.*

Let's walk through the details of the trade management of the 30-minute chart of the Canadian dollar in Figure 12.4.

Prices are still climbing, and if you were scaling out of your position with the rally you must have already been stopped out as prices pulled back to the 1.272 Fibonacci

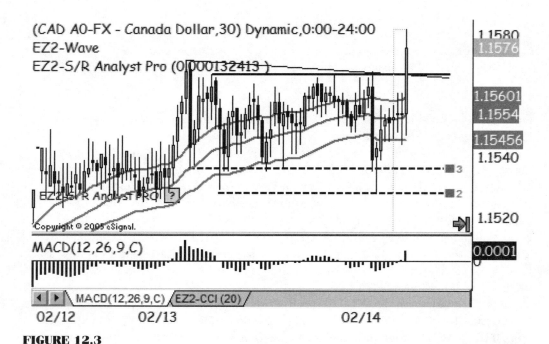

FIGURE 12.3

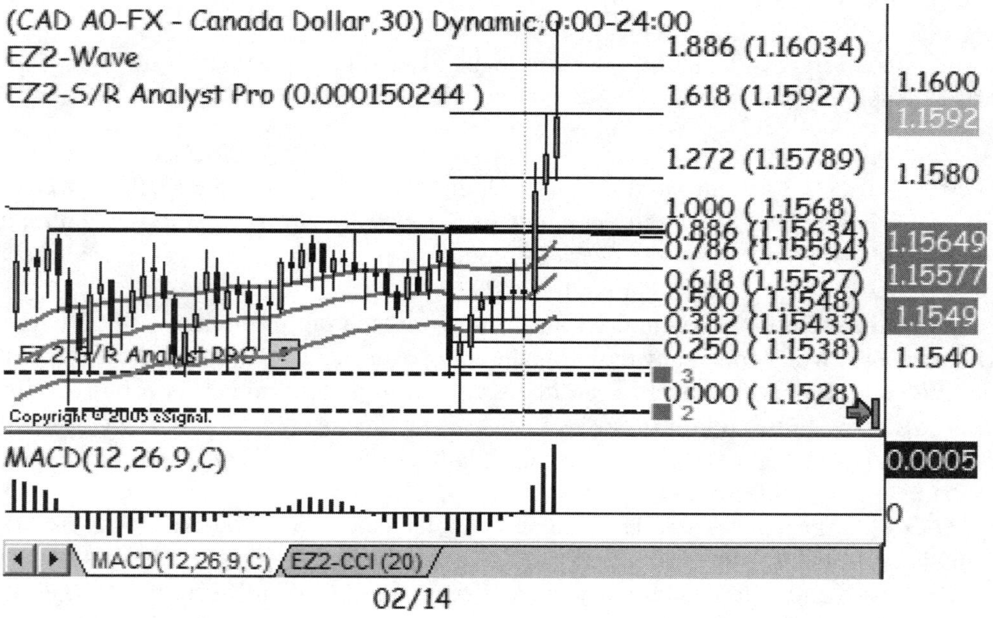

FIGURE 12.4

level at the 8:30 A.M. EST candle. On the chart, the 8:30 A.M. candle is the most recent candle and the one that continued upwards through the 1.886 Fibonacci level. As far as the mechanics of trailing a stop go, there are a few things to think about. Of course, the order type is a stop order. But beyond that, I am commonly asked when I decide to move my trailing stop. I've already discussed how I decide on the levels. Fibonacci takes care of that for me as long as I have a viable last major move. In those cases when I do not, I can utilize pivots. And I will always use psychological levels and, without exception, the "00" pip levels. But I can understand that there probably are questions as to when all this should happen. Frankly, it's just a little common sense. Because I use support and resistance to enter and manage my trades, deciding on when to trail a stop is a matter of defining when a support level becomes a resistance level and when a resistance level becomes support. Setting the initial stop is a *risk* management decision. Setting a trailing stop is a *trade* management decision. These are two distinct mind-sets.

> A stop-loss is about preserving capital and focuses on where an entry is no longer valid.

Setting a stop-loss is based on first answering the question: *Where is this trade no longer valid?* Answering this question is the first step in preventing you from hanging on to a trade long after you should have been stopped out. When traders place a stop based on a dollar loss, it is easy to tell yourself you are willing to change the stop and take more heat because you still feel the trade is valid and are willing to accept more risk. You have simply rationalized taking a larger unrealized loss.

Setting a stop based on where the trade is no longer valid helps prevent the rationalization that happens from dollar-based stops when the trader is concerned with the profit or loss of the trade in an account. When you have already defined where the trade is no longer valid it is a chart-based decision. This does not mean a trader will not rationalize this, too, but it's more difficult to argue with a chart-based stop because the stop-loss placement has nothing to do with you or your risk tolerance. It's the first step to removing emotion from the trading process.

> Trailing stops are about profit preservation and trade optimization.

I want to take the trade as far as it will go as long as it is valid. We identify the pullbacks or bounces that we are likely to see in a trend so that when they occur we can still have a basis for deciding on whether the trade is reversing or just correcting. A correction is not necessarily a reason to exit a trade, but we want to be able to scale out of a position at correction points. The reason we actively want to scale out at these levels is because any one of the correction levels could be where a reversal begins. We just don't know where that will be. *Not* managing trades in this manner reduces our trade management to

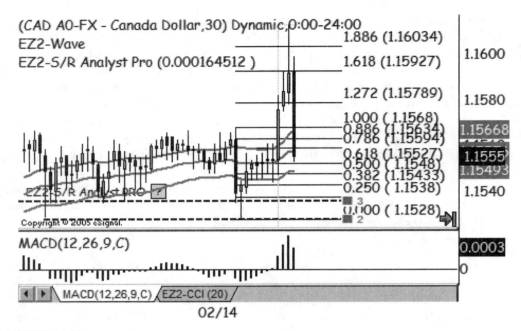

FIGURE 12.5

merely picking tops and bottoms. This is not only vanity, but also an unproductive and inaccurate approach to trade management.

The chart of the USD/CAD shows how quickly prices accelerated through multiple profit targets. As each profit target was traded through on the Canadian dollar, it became a support level. As the Canada traded higher, we did not want to tighten the trailing stop until a profit target, which was once resistance, became support. You could define this process by saying that the moment prices trade up through resistance, that level immediately becomes support. You could also define it by saying you would like to see a close above the level. Waiting for closes in longer time frames, like the 180-minute, 240-minute, or daily chart, can be ineffective because of the length of time before the candle closes. There is no clear-cut answer. Experience does help, but in the end it is really about you and how much price fluctuation you are comfortable taking. This entire process is about getting you started on asking the right questions.

Let's leave today with another chart of the Canada, one candle after the height of the run-up. (See Figure 12.5.)

> Successful trading has little to do with certain strategies, indicators, or software. Successful trading is about asking and answering the questions that help you manage both the risk and reward of a trade. Good traders know to ask the questions. Great traders know what the answers are for them.

Wednesday, February 15th

New Federal Reserve Chairman Benjamin Bernanke's first testimony is today and the markets overall seem to be holding their collective breath waiting to see what is going to be said during this, Bernanke's first appearance before members of Congress. Today is also the 35th anniversary of the NASDAQ. I used to joke during my active stock trading years—when most of my teaching was focused on stocks—that two things were born in 1971: me and the NASDAQ.

Except for the GBP/USD move earlier this morning coinciding with London's open, the markets are giving me plenty of consolidation patterns that are just looking for a reason to break. There are a few hot zones that I will have to contend with today, not to mention a headache that feels like a vice tightening on my temples.

Okay, back to the hot zones. We're looking at two hot zones this morning. The hotter of the two is the Treasury International Capital (TIC) data (the net foreign purchases number) that will be released at 9:00 A.M. EST. The Industrial Production and the Capacity Utilization numbers will be released at 9:15 A.M. EST. Fed Chairman Bernanke's testimony begins at 10:00 A.M. EST and the U.S. dollar will begin gyrating on his every sentence.

I focus mainly on the six majors, as I have said before, but there are other pairs I watch as well. Two are the NZD/USD, which is the seventh major and the largest cross rate pair, and the EUR/JPY. It's the cross rate that has my attention this morning. I'm going to go about trading this morning gingerly as I just don't feel that well. Do not dismiss the importance of your well-being on any given day—if you are not up for trading, if your mind and body are not ready for the kinesthetic and emotional effects of trading— take it easy as I am going to do today or walk away.

The EUR/JPY is trading within a narrower channel compared to any of my other pairs this morning. Typically when I am looking at the EUR/JPY, I will also look at the USD/JPY as well as the EUR/USD. But again, taking it easy today, I will focus solely on the EUR/JPY, which has a great Wave setup as well as a tight congestion pattern on the 60-minute chart. (See Figures 13.1 and 13.2.)

Let me try to explain why these two charts caught my eye. First, the breakdown is visually apparent and confirmed. Before you start relegating your trading to your gut or intuition, you must have the price action and pattern to even begin thinking about a setup. I also like the fact that the setup is below the psychological number of 140.00 on both the 30- and 60-minute charts. All double zero pip levels get my attention, and this one is a decade number (140.00) as well. The MACD is not flat or bobbing between going positive and negative at the zero line on either chart. Both histograms have been established below the signal for some time. *Remember that if the MACD is bobbing at the zero line the reading has less credibility.* The only difference between these two charts is that the 30-minute chart has a one-sided pattern while the 60-minute chart has a complete symmetrical triangle. I'll go with the 60-minute chart because of this.

The 60-minute chart in Figure 13.3 shows where I enter short (139.93), my stop-loss (140.12 until before the release, when I will use a 60-second stop), and my first two profit targets (139.73 and 139.55). By the way, I try to always start with two profit targets, in terms of completing my trading plan. If you're just starting out developing the habit of scaling out of your positions, two profit targets allow you to take 50 percent of your position off the table at the first target and then take the other 50 percent at the second profit target. Since I am most likely still going to be in the trade when the TIC data comes out, I will play my stops mentally, which is to say that I won't leave a live stop-loss order in at

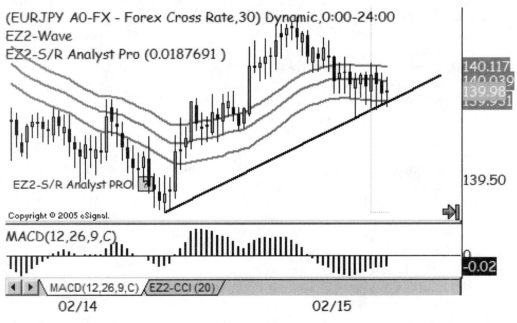

FIGURE 13.1

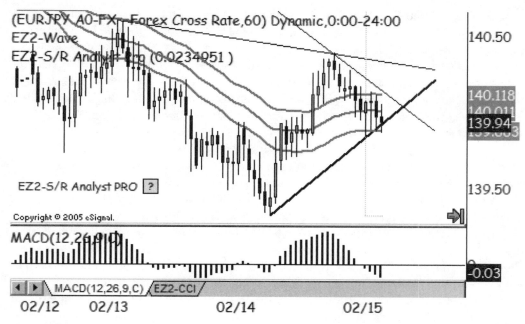

FIGURE 13.2

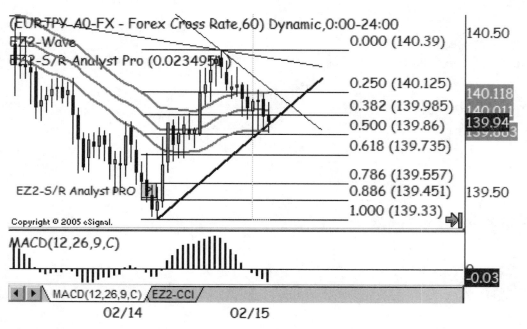

FIGURE 13.3

140.12. This technique is only for advanced and experienced traders who can stand the heat. I will employ my 60-second stop at the time of the release. If you needed a refresher, this is the strategy of waiting 60 seconds to let the market simmer down after the initial excitement of an economic data release. Getting stopped out during the volatility of a hot zone, after entering a confirmed trade, is usually not the most effective risk management approach. Now, let me also say that if you are *not* prepared to take this kind of heat, either don't take a trade before hot zones or do get flat before the report comes out. The heat can be fast and wide, and if your account and your brain aren't braced for it, get out.

The EUR/JPY sell-off follows through the first profit target with relative ease. (See Figure 13.4.) Now our trade management must kick in. Remember, just as we discussed at length yesterday, the profit targets provide excellent trailing stops!

You can see in Figure 13.5 that soon after trading through the 0.786 Fibonacci level (the second profit target!) prices are bouncing fast. There is resistance at the 0.786 since we traded below it, almost reaching the 0.886 Fibonacci level; we can use this level as the trailing stop. If that's too close because the low of the candle was 139.48, then feel free to use the 0.618 Fibonacci level. The fine line we seek here is giving the market enough room to move but not so much room that we give back too much profit. Let me give you a little insight here, though, because it's easy enough to recognize that you can put it to use next time you see a fast breakdown like the one here on the EUR/JPY. When prices break down fast, think of these moves like rubber bands, because they often snap back hard. (See Figure 13.6.)

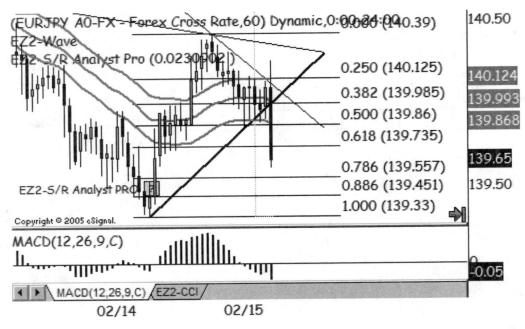

FIGURE 13.4

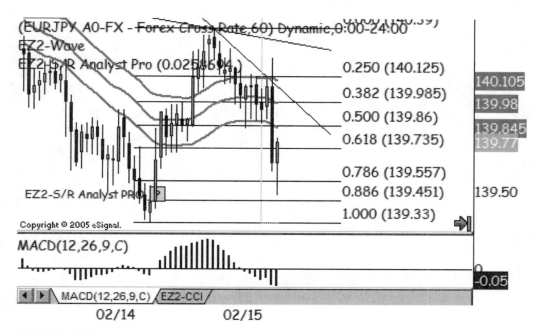

FIGURE 13.5

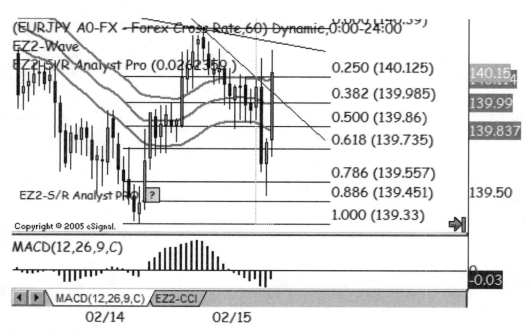

FIGURE 13.6

Thursday,
February 16th

This morning yielded Waves that are typically the result of some prior breakouts/ breakdowns in earlier sessions. I scan the markets looking for some three o'clock Waves and find only three markets that might yield some momentum setups this morning: the AUD/USD, the USD/JPY, and the EUR/JPY cross rate. I will look for swing setups as well, but they must have the twelve to two o'clock or four to six o'clock Waves that signal a trending market. Then and only then will I begin looking for corrections.

The AUD/USD in Figure 14.1 is trading in a slightly downward-angling Wave but well within the wiggle of three o'clock nonetheless. The MACD histogram has been below the zero line for almost an entire day so the confirmation of a breakdown is not an issue—it's already there and waiting for prices to trigger a trade, which is exactly what happens when prices pierce the 0.7372 level. This trade will be bearish as long as we stay below 0.7383 to 0.7387. The first profit target will be the 0.7353 level.

As the time approaches 10:00 A.M. EST, Fed Chairman Bernanke is gearing up for his second day of testimony on the economy. Even though the fundamental data that was released this week was way above expectations, especially today's housing starts, the U.S. dollar's response was fairly muted—*and that's exactly why we don't set up trades with fundamentals!* The running joke right now is that Bernanke's style is so clear and easy to interpret that the Greenspan Fed interpreters will be out of a job. Either way I am prepared for a second day of sentence-by-sentence U.S. dollar gyrations. So far I still see strength in the 30-minute chart as prices are trading above the Wave (strong side) and I will look to the Wave to support a continued move up. (See Figure 14.2.)

Notice that my positions today hinge on a continued upward move in the U.S. dollar. I am mindful of when I may be taking positions that hedge—that is, to be short the USD/CHF and the EUR/USD at the same time on the same time frame. By the way, this does preclude me from entering, for the sake of example, the daily chart of the EUR/USD and buying the USD/CHF on, say, a 30- or 60-minute chart.

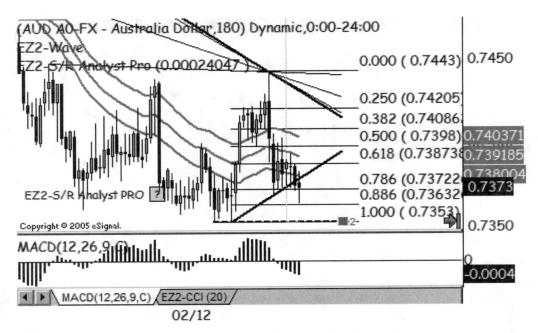

FIGURE 14.1

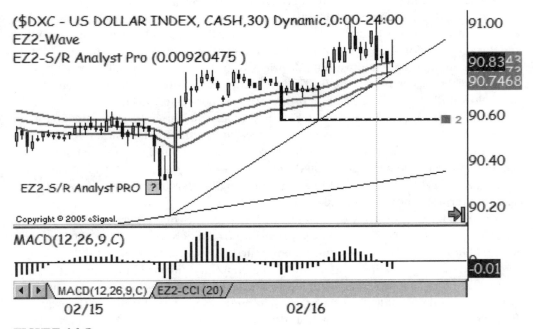

FIGURE 14.2

The 180-minute USD/JPY is trading just above the 118.00 psychological level and I enter long at 118.05. (Remember you want to be sure prices can establish themselves above a "00" level like this by at least three to five pips.) (See Figure 14.3.) I'd like to see this trade stay above 118.00 first and foremost; more specifically, I will keep an eye on the 6:00 A.M. breakout candle's low of 177.87 and the 0.618 Fibonacci support at 117.70. The first and most logical places to look when considering stop placement are the near-term lows preceding the breakout and at the breakout candle itself. My first profit target is the 0.382 Fibonacci resistance at 118.34 and then I will have to keep an eye on the major downtrend that will be resistance if the market continues past the 118.34 level.

I passed on the EUR/JPY trade, and this leaves me with two positions on the morning. The AUD/USD is being a little more temperamental but hangs around my entry price within a few pips in either direction. Finally, 0.7387 gets hit in the AUD/USD and I'm out with a 15-pip loss.

My OCO is still hard at work in the yen bracketing my stop and profit target, until I see that midafternoon my stop-loss was hit when prices fell below the 117.70 level. So I am now flat with a 35-pip loss. Not the best day in the books, but now that the action has completed and I am looking back on the minefield I was running through, I can see how price action just didn't go my way today. That happens, and since I followed my trading plan and adhered to my stops, I still walk away with confidence. This day, and any day when you follow your trading plan, is a success.

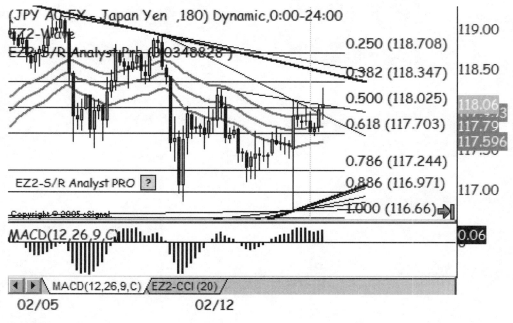

FIGURE 14.3

The real proof will be tomorrow and how I bounce back. *Recognize, react, repeat.* I've been at this long enough so that year after year I have seen the setups work in forex, futures, and stocks. *But you haven't.* So when I talk about bouncing back, I really have *you* in mind. I won't kid you; just because I say this works for me doesn't automatically mean that your brain is going to put 100 percent confidence into this. You, too, will have to put in the time, reinforcing you brain, training your eyes, and developing trust in what you see and confidence that you can manage no matter where prices can go.

Friday, February 17th

I stop trading at noon on Fridays, pretty much without exception. Today I will most likely wrap things up even earlier because I have a chiropractic appointment. I can let OCOs handle any position I may be in come 10:45 A.M. when I have to leave for the appointment. I will also be heading up to Orlando just after lunch for an Internet marketing seminar. It's a three-hour drive from where I live in South Florida, and I really enjoy road trips. Pop in an audiobook and I'm gone. The seminar I am attending this weekend is all about the innovations and methodology of marketing anything on the Internet. I love the Internet and I find marketing fascinating, so this will be a great way to relax and clear my mind of the markets for a couple of days. This may sound pretty geeky, my relaxing at an Internet marketing seminar, but I am a geek and quite proud of it. I enjoy this kind of active relaxing. You have to find hobbies, even distractions, from the market. The market can become consuming. I speak from experience.

I've never been a "kick my feet up and watch TV" kind of person. So I'll no sooner get back home from Orlando late Sunday night and I will be off again Monday morning at 4:30 for New York City. The International Traders Expo is there this weekend and I will be catching the tail end of it Monday and Tuesday. I won't miss any U.S. trading on Monday since it's a holiday and I will be able to trade from my hotel Tuesday morning if I feel like it. While in New York I'll be meeting with my friend the trader extraordinaire Todd Gordon of Gain Capital, as well as some friends over at the eSignal booth. I look forward to picking all their brains. Realistically, after today I probably won't be trading until I'm back at home on Wednesday.

Here's what's on my radar this morning. First, the direction of the U.S. dollar is always of primary consideration. I never want to lose the pulse of the U.S. dollar market and I keep the pulse with the U.S. Dollar Index Cash. The one thing that has my attention, especially after watching the dollar tank from 91.01 during yesterday's trading session, is the way sellers came in near the year's high at 91.02. It should be no surprise to you now, after two weeks analyzing the markets and trading with me, that the 91.00 is a psychological number. Don't underestimate this. Until prices get above it, 91.00 is resistance in the U.S. Dollar Index Cash. This means that in a secondary way, the EUR/USD, GBP/USD, and AUD/USD will be supported in part by the resistance in the U.S. dollar. I will scan these three markets for potential setups. Again, I'm not going to enter a trade based solely on where I think the U.S. dollar might find support or resistance, but it is an undercurrent that I must be aware of. It's about 7:00 A.M. and the USD is heading back up toward 91.00 this morning after some consolidation earlier under the 90.90 price level. (See Figure 15.1.)

> I've been watching the U.S. dollar in one form or another since I learned to trade commodity futures. Back then I tracked the DX contract. In fact, it was a very natural transition from futures to forex. I think many futures traders are looking to the forex market. Futures traders are already accustomed to leverage and the risk involved with having 50 to 1 and higher buying power.

I see the GBP/USD on the 30-minute chart has formed a nice triangle pattern with a three o'clock Wave (Figure 15.2). I also see the same on the 60-minute chart of the GBP/USD (Figure 15.3). Looking at these two charts, here's a great example of

FIGURE 15.1

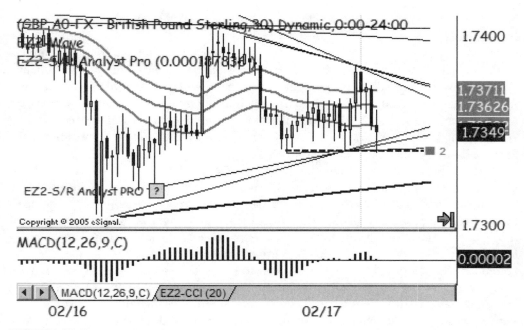

FIGURE 15.2

FIGURE 15.3

what I have referred to as a triangle that is breaking out versus one that has just run out of space.

It's easy to see that while both have triangle/three o'clock setups, the 30-minute triangle is clearly a better, more balanced pattern. Notice that the 60-minute chart is just coming down off a breakout through the downtrend line. The MACD histogram did confirm the breakout at 5:00 A.M. as prices traded up through the downtrend line (third candle from the right in Figure 15.3), and if you took the buy this morning, you're getting stopped out just about now. A quick rewind back on the 30-minute chart shows the same breakout at 5:00 A.M. (See Figure 15.4.)

There will be two hot zones this morning: one at 8:30 A.M. as the Core Producer Price Index (PPI) numbers are coming out, followed 20 minutes later by the Michigan Sentiment report. The PPI will move the market, and I expect that either we're going to bounce off the resistance of the 91.00 high of the U.S. dollar or we're going to blast through. And I have to tell you, here's where experience and some common sense come in. This is not gut or intuition; this is years of watching price action, my friends, and common sense. So you certainly don't need to put in the years; just apply some mass psychology. The U.S. dollar had been heading up since late last night. It rallied from a low of 90.54 to 91.01 in front of the 8:30 A.M. release. *How much higher can it go? How many people are still willing to bid it up from here?* And more to the point: *Have traders already discounted a good PPI number for this morning and run the dollar up in expectation?* We get what I think is the answer at 7:30 A.M. (See Figure 15.5.) The

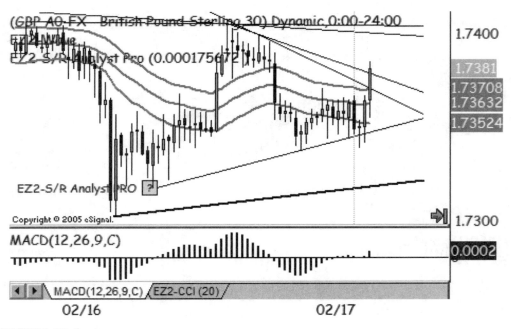

FIGURE 15.4

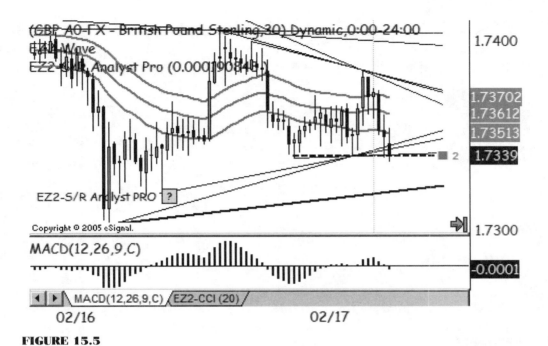

FIGURE 15.5

pound has broken down through the horizontal support level at 1.7339, with confirmation, on the 30-minute chart. And if you're curious, the 60-minute chart did not trigger a breakdown at all. *That's certainly an easy way to decide which chart to trade.*

The setup is confirming just above the 1.7339 price, which is the full retracement (1.000) and horizontal support level. The MACD histogram is confirming this weakness and the short entry. The breakdown candle has a high at 1.7354, and this will allow me to take advantage of the major psychological level at 1.7350. I know the trade will no longer be valid if it trades up through the lowest downtrend line resistance, but this is a 30-minute chart and with the first support level (our profit target!) at 1.7326 this trade is only yielding a support level that is within the 10-to-12-pip cushion where we'll be forgoing taking some of our position off the table at this initial level. This is an "aggro" setup, especially since it is poised just before a pretty impactful, dare I say massive, number. But then again, trading is all about assuming risk and *you* need to decide how much risk you are willing to accept on any given day.

As Figure 15.6 shows, this is one of those times where we miss our exit by a pip because the low of the 8:00 A.M. candle was 1.7327 and hovered just above our limit order to buy. As prices sharply trade higher, the stop is hit at 1.7354 for a loss of 15 pips.

Just for the sake of clarity, let's also examine a trade that was setting up and confirming at the same time the pound was in play. The EUR/USD, which I mentioned earlier as being a market to watch today (along with the Aussie), set up a short the same

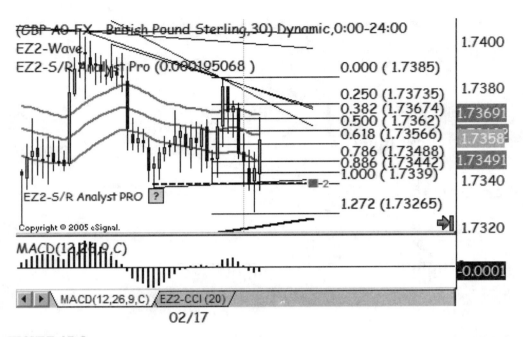

FIGURE 15.6

time the pound did. (See Figure 15.7.) The Wave in the euro was not as perfectly flat as in the pound, but it was well within the two to four o'clock angle and very close to three o'clock. The triangle pattern showed a breakdown level at 1.1864 and the MACD histogram was already below the zero line. With the setup entry established, the stop-loss placement will be very similar to my thinking in the pound setup. While I know the downtrend line is resistance and the point at which the short trade is no longer valid, the risk does not merit the reward, and I will enter knowing that I am using a near-term resistance level instead. I will use the breakdown candle high. The first profit target is 1.1854 (only 10 pips) and this is within our 10-to-12-pip cushion.

The drop once again missed my support by one pip, and after simultaneously seeing two bounces just short of the Fibonacci support *I'm almost starting to take this personally* . . . although in this case, I'm not reeling because this level really wasn't my profit target and I'm stopped out at 1.1578 for a loss of 14 pips. Both these bounces got me thinking about the triangle pattern I was looking at. The Wave in the EUR/USD was still traveling sideways at 9:00 A.M. and I wanted to follow up on my feeling that these bounces were telling me that the U.S. dollar was weak. Remember the 91.00 level we were watching early this morning? Like I said earlier, I don't assume anything; 91.00 could have been a rallying point or a reversal. Charts told the story . . . *and you know how I feel about the charts.* (See Figure 15.8.)

The weakness at the 91.00 resistance tells me that I should be looking for some buying opportunities on the EUR/USD, AUD/USD, and GBP/USD. The euro has the

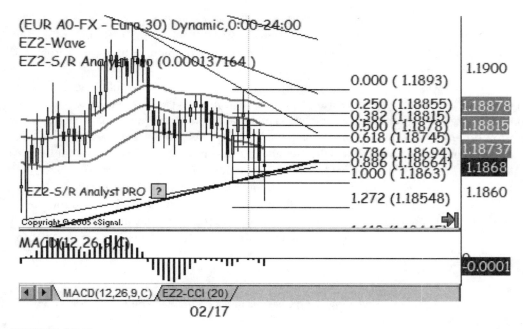

FIGURE 15.7

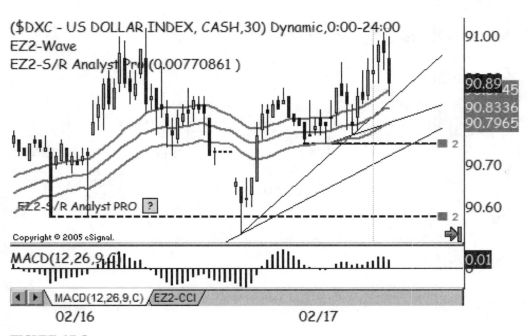

FIGURE 15.8

strongest (negative) correlation to the U.S. dollar so that's the best place to start. The euro finally took off about 60 minutes after the 91.00 level on the U.S. dollar was hit. (See Figure 15.9.) Remember that no matter what our opinion or analysis is, the U.S. dollar alone does not set up or confirm a trade.

The euro was still looking like a momentum setup, and while I would love to say that I entered long on the following setup, *that didn't happen.* The MACD histogram did not go above the zero line until the break occurred and that meant that I could not proactively set a stop order to get long. The break happened fast, too fast for an entry, and I won't even consider chasing an entry, especially considering the short time frame. On a daily chart? *Maybe.* I get the price my plan set forth or I don't enter. That may sound rigid and I wanted to show you that *I miss trades, too!* I stick to my rules, so this isn't a set of rules I am outlining to you that I don't follow; quite the contrary! The only reason I can outline these rules with confidence and consistency is because I do this every day and on every trade.

It's time to head out to the chiropractor's office and then to pack. I want to leave for Orlando before 1:00 P.M.

By the way, I conduct a Friday Morning Chat for Raghee.com each and every Friday and I discussed the day in detail. You can watch and listen to that webinar on the CD-ROM in the back of the book. In fact, there will be a number of lessons included on that CD-ROM and I'll be sure to tell you when to refer to it.

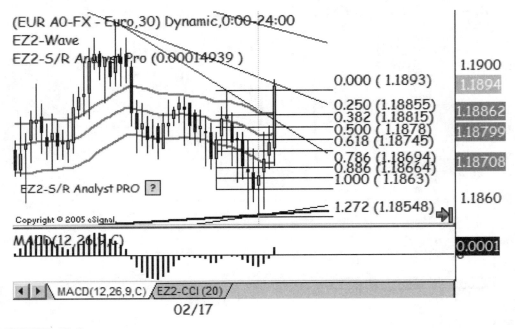

FIGURE 15.9

Monday, February 20th

As I look down on Times Square from my hotel room window I see that even the city slept in this morning. The usual herd of taxis is sparse and there is little foot traffic below on the streets. The U.S. markets are not open today while the rest of the world is trading. As a rule I do not trade the majors when the U.S. markets are closed and I'm sitting in my hotel room at my laptop, getting ready to go see some friends at the International Traders Expo. I'm not going to trade actively today but I do have time to scan the daily charts. On busy days *anyone* can scan six daily charts for potential opportunities. Because the U.S. markets are closed, this will exclude a scan of a few commodity futures and stock charts. The USD/CHF looks interesting. (See Figure 16.1.)

The Wave is traveling at between twelve and two o'clock and a pullback today to the top line of the Wave would allow for a long entry just above the 1.3000 psychological level. While it's not likely today, I will keep in place a proactive order (in this case an if/then) just in case. My order is to buy on a limit at 1.3005 and my stop-loss is at the middle line of the Wave, which is currently at 1.2952. I'll have to update this order each day, which is easily done by the edit feature on my order execution platform. This will be as easy as looking at where the top and middle line of the Wave are plotting and updating the if/then price orders, which is exactly what I will continue to do just as long as the Wave keeps a twelve to two o'clock reading.

On a personal note, with some time on my hands, I decided to start a weblog or blog today. I have been reading a couple of blogs on the Internet and have enjoyed the commentary. I decided to start sharing market commentary and articles at www.ragheehorner.com. It's interactive and I look forward to seeing your comments there.

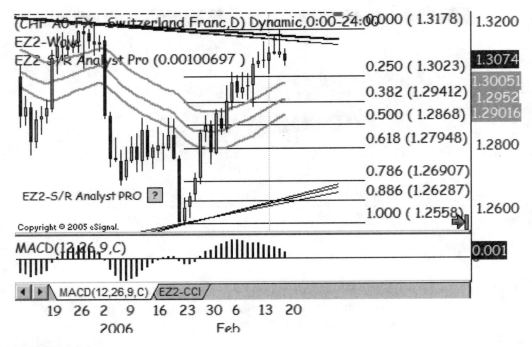

FIGURE 16.1

Tuesday, February 21st

Ah, back home to 80-degree weather and warm sunshine. I have really become a Floridian, much as I may have fought it for the past 23 years. I flew into Ft. Lauderdale at 4:00 P.M., and between the expo, meetings, and my flight I missed an entire day of trading. I am exhausted and want to review the notes from not only some presentations I watched but the meetings I had while at the expo. I also think I have brought home a souvenir cold because I feel lousy. I'll save my scanning for early tomorrow morning.

Wednesday, February 22nd

It's 4:30 A.M. and I'm scanning through my charts for the first time this morning. I want to check the U.S. dollar and I see that on the 30-minute chart prices seem to be trying to head back up to 91.00. The 3:30 A.M. candle in particular has my attention because it broke up through the resistance of the downtrend line. (See Figure 18.1.)

I've been away from the markets since the 17th and it already feels like déjà vu since this will be potentially the fourth test of this level since the 16th. This level has

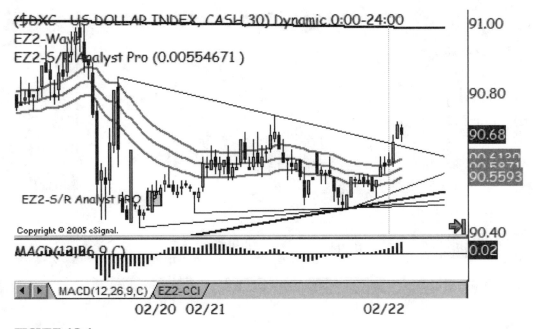

FIGURE 18.1

been formidable, and since the U.S. dollar seems to sell off with some vigor each time it approaches this level, I would think it will be no different this time. But again I will let my charts dictate my actions, regardless of my opinion. There is certainly enough space between where the U.S. dollar is currently trading and the 91.00 that prices in the majors can register trades to both the upside and the downside. We're looking at the consumer price index (CPI) number release today, so the hot zone we'll be watching is at 8:30 A.M. EST.

The Aussie already tanked early this morning around three o'clock—no good to me now. It was a beautiful setup, too. (See Figure 18.2.) I wasn't awake for the trade, but the chart is a great example of what we're looking for during active trading hours. Notice the way prices are bouncing at the horizontal support level that was already in place. This, regardless of other levels, would be one of our profit targets if we were short.

The 60-minute Canadian dollar triggered a break during the 3:00 A.M. candle . . . another miss. But unlike the Aussie, the breakdown is on the shorter time frame and if this strength persists, eventually we'll get a setup on one of the longer-term charts, so I will keep an eye on the 180- and 240-minute charts of the USD/CAD.

At 2:00 A.M. buyers lit a fire under the Swissy, which by 4:30 A.M. is retracing into a Wave but triggered and confirmed a long entry at 2:00 A.M. and a short entry on the euro. (See Figures 18.3 and 18.4.) So far this morning has been a busy London session.

The 180- and 240-minute charts on both the euro and the Swissy also triggered trades. The 240-minute chart of the EUR/USD had a flat three o'clock Wave in place for

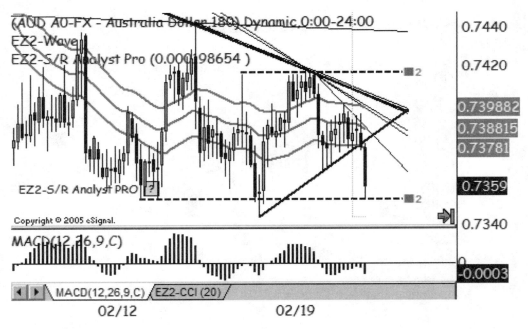

FIGURE 18.2

FIGURE 18.3

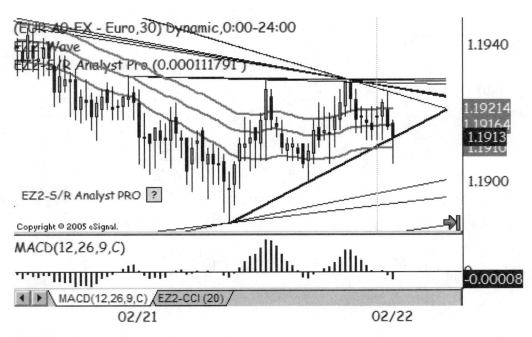

FIGURE 18.4

days and a symmetrical triangle breakdown. The MACD histogram also was negative for eight bars. Again, too bad I wasn't awake, but study Figure 18.5—the setup is textbook down to the fact that the euro broke down below the 1.1900 psychological level.

There's a reason I am outlining all these setups and confirmed trades: Most of the pairs triggered trades before, *well before*, the CPI numbers; when the numbers were actually released there were no setups! In fact, the release simply became part of the trade management and triggered one profit target after another. I also thought this was a great day that further reinforced one of the overarching lessons of the 30 days. *Trust the charts.*

As I got to the pound I saw that the 30- and 60-minute chart sell-offs were already in play, *but* the longer-term charts, the 180 and 240, were *not* triggering trades. So I put the pound on my list next to the Canadian dollar as a chart to keep an eye on. Let me mention something about these laggards. These charts did not all trigger trades on the longer-term charts for various reasons, but the bottom line is that price action on these longer-term charts just wasn't in a position to set up and trigger entries. That just means that later there may be some other reason for prices to move, but it won't relate to the hot zone. These setups will probably come later, since they are laggards to the pre–hot zone action, and I will keep in mind that as the day progresses and as we look to Initial Claims and Crude Inventories tomorrow, these two pairs, the Canadian dollar and the pound, could very well yield some entries later. If enough time passes between the report and another setup later in the day, then I can also look to the short-term intraday

FIGURE 18.5

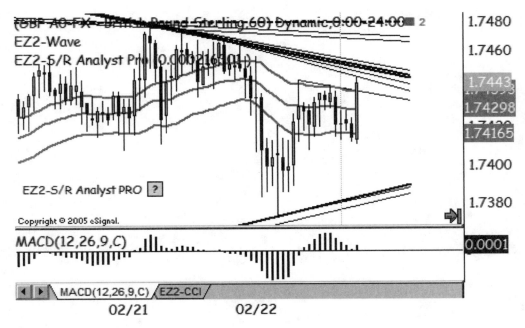

FIGURE 18.6

charts. The bottom line is that if you keep an eye on the charts and prices settle down enough from earlier volatility, you can find setups. I call this "resetting" because very often after volatile moves, prices have moved so far so fast they need to simmer before we can see a correction to enter on a three o'clock Wave that signals that prices have come off the markup or markdown and are back in accumulation or consolidation. *You do remember our discussion about market cycles in the Introduction, right?*

The pound became active just before midnight EST on the 22nd. The 60-minute chart, which had been setting up a triangle pattern since lunchtime today, finally broke above the first of multiple downtrend lines. (See Figure 18.6.) Earlier in the session, prices traded down as if they wanted to test the 1.7400 psychological level, with a low of 1.7411. Prices rallied from there and finally broke up through 1.7440.

There will be days like this when it feels like everything happened when you were not at your desk. It's a by-product of a 24-hour market. When I look back at the amount of trading this month, this is but one day and I will look to tomorrow for more opportunities. *And that, my friend, is what is so great about the markets!*

Thursday, February 23rd

With Initial Claims and Crude Inventories hot zones this morning we should have some active trading. Remember that on a morning when we have hot zones we're working against a deadline. We want to be ready as early as possible in front of the release. Here's what's on my radar this morning. I still have the USD/CAD on my mind from yesterday, so let's start there.

This chart in Figure 19.1 is showing a breakdown to the downside through uptrend

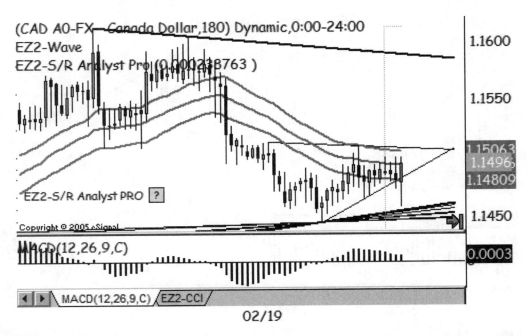

FIGURE 19.1

line support. But it's not confirmed, so I look to the 60-minute chart in Figure 19.2 to check whether there might be a confirmed setup there. That is, after all, why we have multiple time frames: so that we can *afford to be choosy* about our entries but also so that we can *widen our scope* of potential setups to a degree as well.

In the strictest sense, the 60-minute Canadian dollar is triggering a short but the chart is not an enticing one. Let me tell you why. Notice that the breakdown candle is confirmed by not only the pierce of the uptrend line support but also the MACD histogram—no problem there. The problem is the fact that just at the candle prior to the breakdown the triangle broke to the upside and even though it was not confirmed by the MACD histogram, this leads me to question whether the market is really breaking or just chopping. So I look to the 30-minute chart in Figure 19.3 to see if there is a *cleaner* setup. This is how I make decisions, this process of scanning through multiple time frames of a pair looking for a setup. In this case we have the 180-minute with a great-looking chart but no confirmed setup, the 60-minute chart with a confirmed setup but not a great-looking chart, and finally the 30-minute with both a confirmed setup and a great-looking chart—so that's where we enter.

The setup is under the 1.1500 psychological level, which is great, but I also see multiple uptrend lines that will act as support so I will no sooner get short at 1.1479 (both the uptrend line break and below minor psychological level!) and we will have to contend with the 1.272 Fibonacci extension level. At 1.1473, which of course due to my 10-

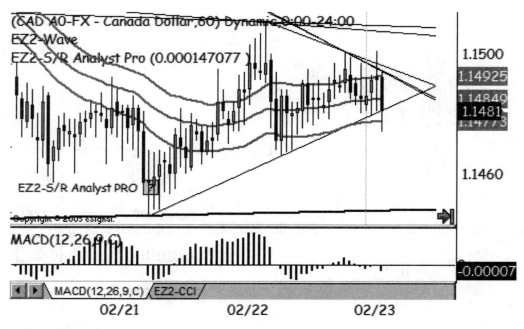

FIGURE 19.2

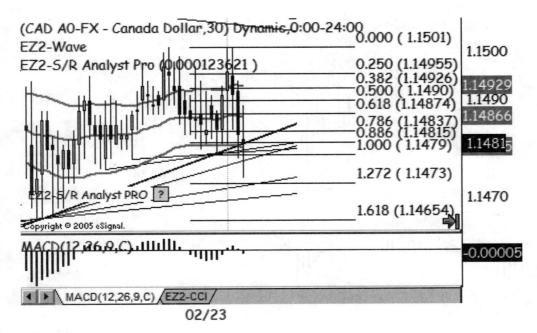

FIGURE 19.3

to-12-pip cushion I will not take profits at, I will park my limit order to buy at the 1.618 Fibonacci extension level at 1.1465 and then at the 1.886 Fibonacci extension level at 1.1459. My stop-loss on this 30-minute chart entry should be guided by the definition of "where this trade is no longer valid," but that level is pretty far north at the 1.1497 level; and so, although that is not too terrible in relation to my 1.1479 entry, I cheat my stop down to the top line of the Wave, which should also provide some resistance at 1.1491. By the 7:00 A.M. candle I am hitting the initial 1.1465 profit target and here I move my trailing stop down to the bottom line of the Wave. Looking at this chart I know that I could use the 1.272 Fibonacci level as resistance but these last couple of candles have been pretty "wicky"—that's my word for candles with a wide high to low range and a shorter body—so I think it's best to give the Canadian dollar a little room to move or wiggle. (See Figure 19.4.)

Well, it doesn't seem to have mattered because prices rallied up through the 1.272 Fibonacci level with ease and also to my trailing stop at the bottom line of the Wave, which also coincided with my entry price, so the remainder of my position, after exiting at the first profit target, is a wash. No worries, this was not a bad way to start the morning. If prices rally from here, I'm not short so that's not an issue and I still have the 180-minute chart that is waiting for the MACD histogram to confirm a trade in the triangle it's trading within. With the MACD histogram well established above the zero line and the bounce I am seeing on the 30-minute chart I was just stopped out from, perhaps it's

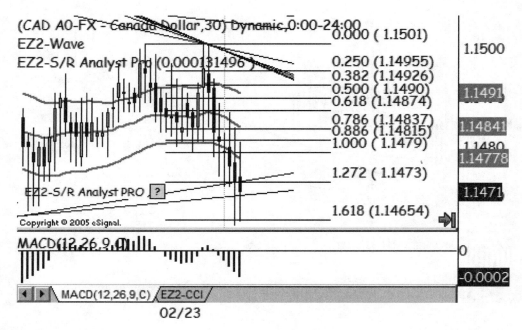

FIGURE 19.4

time to go park an order on the 180-minute chart setup. It's not quite 8:30 A.M. but it already feels like prices are beginning to move in anticipation of the Initial Claims release.

I place a proactive order for the 180-minute Canadian dollar. (See Figure 19.5.) I set a stop to buy at 1.1508, which allows me to enter long not only at the downtrend line breakout but also above the resistance of the 1.1500 major psychological level. I am not going to place a physical stop-loss order now because I will be dealing with the hot zone where I will want to use my 60-second stop. I am going to park a limit order to sell a part of my position at the 0.618 Fibonacci level at 1.1537. I am not using the resistance at the 0.500 Fibonacci level at 1.1520 because it's right at my 10-to-12-pip cushion. I've already considered where my stop should go, and just because the hot zone will make me use the 60-second stop, that's applicable for only 60 seconds! After that we still need a stop-loss price. And that will be at the low of the breakout candle, 1.1491, which allows me to use a few significant price levels: the middle line of the Wave, the psychological support at 1.1500, and of course the low of the breakout candle, which is near-term support. It's 8:30 A.M.! Hot zone! *Just as I thought—the hot zone triggers my entry and my first profit target.*

It's time to put in a trailing stop and the second profit target. I'm looking to the 0.786 Fibonacci level at 1.1562 for my next profit target. As much as I would love to put my trailing stop at the 0.618, prices did not yet trade above it enough to establish it as a sup-

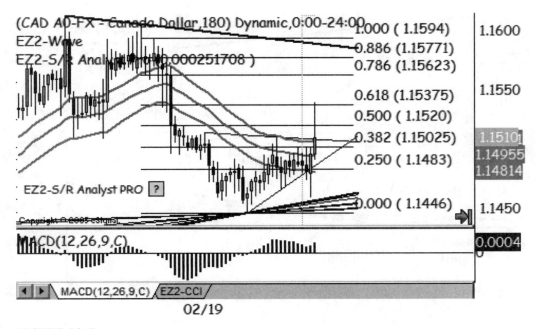

FIGURE 19.5

port level, so I am going to have to use the lower support level of 0.500 at 1.1520, which is also a minor psychological level. It's not ideal but this is the best decision because the only way to use a resistance level as support is when prices have traded beyond the price level far enough that attention can be put there and orders can congregate at the price and be of any use. So I have my OCO in place and now the trade is as any trade at this stage should be: on autopilot based on lines and levels on my chart.

As shown in Figure 19.6, the high of the breakout was the high, period. *Glad I parked a profit target there.* Prices slipped back down and my trailing stop was hit, so the remainder of the position is taken out at 1.1520.

It's time to call it a day. One thing I habitually do (and I realize I haven't mentioned it until now) is make sure that I glance over my order execution platform (also referred to as my trading platform) and take a look at what was executed today but more specifically to make sure that I don't have any single or contingent orders sitting out there that I may have forgotten. I only mention this because (1) *it happens* and (2) *I've done it.* So make sure you know what's on your platform. Don't be or get complacent about it. It takes literally just a glance to see what's waiting on my platform. I can check the order type and how many pips away a potential execution is very, very quickly, so there's no reason not to do it! It's a nice feature. As I am checking my own platform I see that the contingent order I placed back on the 20th has triggered. The Swissy is still traveling upwards at a shallow twelve to two o'clock angle, and I thought that maybe, as there was

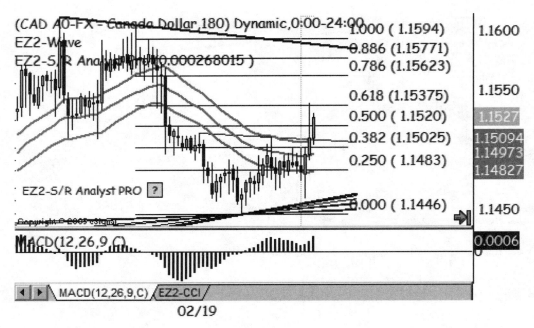

FIGURE 19.6

some weakness on the 20th in the USD/CHF, prices could touch the Wave high at 1.3005, which would also get me long just above the major psychological level. That didn't happen but I have been updating the order each day so that if we got a pullback, as the Wave was still traveling upwards, I could enter a long swing trade. I'm long now on this morning's sell-off. (See Figure 19.7.)

The pullback to the Wave is also confirmed by the 0.250 Fibonacci level, which certainly makes me happy. The trigger of the entry also has triggered my stop-loss order, which waits just in case prices sell off to 1.2974. I will place an OCO to handle my profit targets. I can place two limit orders to sell, one at 1.3178 and the other at 1.3195. By the way, the horizontal resistance level above 1.3200 is at 1.3220, which will be the next target I will look to if we can trade above 1.3200.

The daily chart of the USD/JPY also has my attention. (See Figure 19.8.) The chart is trading within a three o'clock angle and prices have traded down through the higher of two uptrend lines with MACD histogram confirmation.

It's a rather steep uptrend, which alone doesn't concern me too much. I also notice that prices are just selling off from a pierce of the downtrend line (without confirmation) but for some reason I am not comfortable about getting short right now. I am focusing on the lower of the two uptrend lines, which actually forms a better, more balanced triangle pattern. I can keep an eye on this chart. I am forgoing the short at 117.60 (the higher uptrend line) and will see if prices can take out the lower

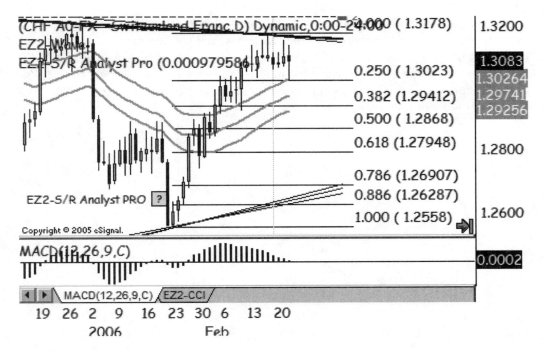

FIGURE 19.7

FIGURE 19.8

downtrend line between 116.60 and 116.75. Remember that this level is rising as we move forward with each new trading day. By the way, if you are wondering if I would have held off going short if I didn't have the second uptrend line, probably not. I'll keep an eye on it for the next few days and see if the weakness persists. In fact, I'm going to enter a proactive sell stop order to short at 116.65 since the MACD histogram is below the zero line.

Friday, February 24th

Fridays are like half days for me and it's really a nice way to start the weekend. Today we'll have the 8:30 A.M. EST release of the Durable Orders number so that's the only hot zone I'll have to deal with today. Remember that we wrap things up by noon and that means that I'll focus on setups that will confirm and hopefully allow me either to be in a position to take some profits out of the trade before noon or scale down the position, or to go into the weekend flat. I don't mind carrying trades into the weekend, but if I had the choice of going into the weekend with a position or going into the weekend flat, *I'd take flat. But I won't exit a position without a price reason, so the weekend is no reason alone to exit.*

I'm looking at the USD/JPY in Figure 20.1. Remember the proactive entry yesterday? It's easy to get caught up in what's going on during the day, especially on the intraday charts, and forget about the slower-moving daily. It's weaker this morning and I see that last night just after 7:00 P.M. EST, I got my fill as prices sold off. My stop-loss is just above the middle line of the Wave and psychological number at 117.55. My first profit target is 116.15, which will scale out some of my position north of 116.00. After that, I'll look for prices to trade down to 115.28.

I have the USD/CHF to manage as well, so I'll be sure to update my stop-loss as well as my profit targets. (See Figure 20.2.) *By the way, if one of my profit targets is hit, then I can update my stop-loss into a trailing stop.* This is the shift I make from *risk* management to *trade* management. This shift only happens after the initial profit target is hit. Until that point you must keep a stop-loss active, whether that be an actual stop order, a mental stop (only for advanced traders and only when you are at your desk!), or a 60-second stop. (Head over to thirtydaysoftrading.com for a stop-loss video.)

My end-of-day entry on the Swissy does not preclude my looking at some other trading opportunities in this pair. Don't think an entry on the daily chart keeps you from still

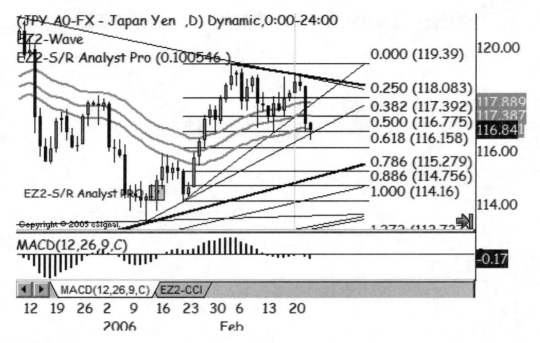

FIGURE 20.1

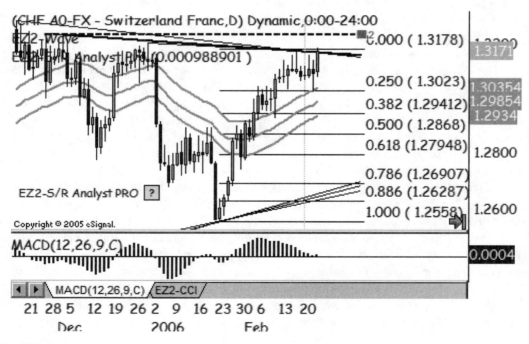

FIGURE 20.2

looking at the intraday charts. And this is equally applicable to when you are in an intra-day trade. Keep your eyes open. Different time frames will present different swing or momentum trading opportunities. Remember that you can't do both in the same ac-count, though. I keep an account for end-of-day trading and one for my more active in-traday trading. While scanning the time frames I see that the 240-minute chart on the USD/CHF has a great symmetrical triangle shaping up. (See Figure 20.3.) The Wave is sideways and the MACD is just now plotting above the zero line, which offers a chance for me to park a buy stop at 1.3140; this is where the downtrend line is coming down and also just above the 0.886 Fibonacci level.

The stop-loss I will park in my OCO is going to be just below the 1.3100 level, which will allow me to use the top line of the Wave and the psychological number. I ac-knowledge that this may be a little tight and that the better choice might very well be the middle line of the Wave and the 0.500 Fibonacci, but I am just not willing to give the trade that much wiggle room. My initial profit target will be the 1.3155 level, which I must recognize because it is the full retracement level (1.000) and 15 pips from my en-try. But what I'm really hoping to see is the 1.272 Fibonacci level at 1.3192. This level will get me out ahead of the 1.3200 psychological level and will represent a nice move to the upside.

The daily chart of the Canadian dollar is trading with a sideways Wave. (See Figure 20.4.) As of the last three, maybe four trading days the Wave has made a transition to a

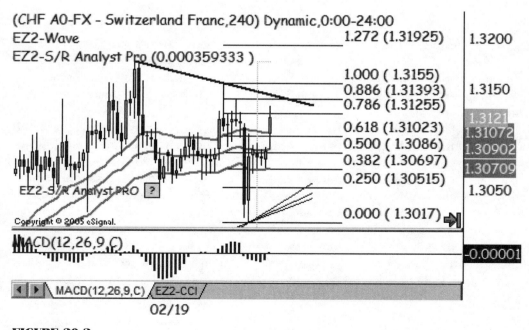

FIGURE 20.3

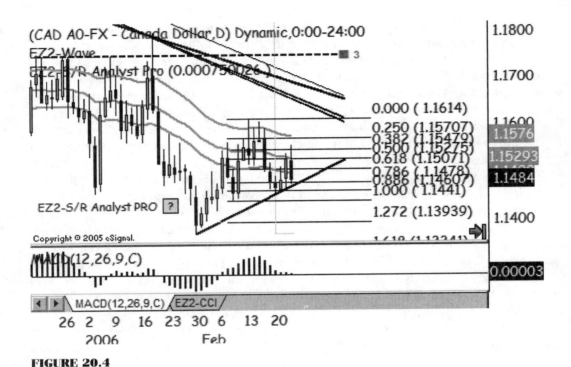

FIGURE 20.4

three o'clock angle. The pattern is not perfect as prices are favoring the bottom half of the pattern, but I'll keep an eye on this one. I can't park a stop order to sell but I can park one to buy, which seems not very likely since the downtrend line is so far north of current prices. It's on my radar, though, and I'm going to write up a sticky note so I remember to keep an eye on it.

It's right about 8:00 A.M. and 30 minutes until the hot zone when I see that the pound has been slowly leveling out over the past four to five hours to a flat three o'clock Wave. (See Figure 20.5.) The triangle pattern is favoring the bottom side of the pattern. But that's just an observation and you must still rely on price and MACD histogram confirmation; that observation means little to any eventual trade. What does mean more is the fact that the MACD histogram has been below the zero line since yesterday afternoon. The entry to go short will be the stop order part of my OCO, which I am placing at 1.7475. I will place an initial profit target at the 0.786 Fibonacci level of 1.7441 with a limit order to buy. Notice that I am not placing a stop-loss because with the proximity of the hot zone I will be using a 60-second stop. After 60 seconds I will put in the stop-loss order just above the psychological level, at 1.7505.

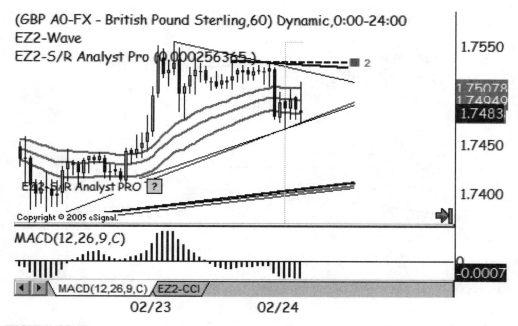

FIGURE 20.5

Without a proactive order this entry would probably not have been an executable trade. You'll notice in Figure 20.6 that not only was the entry triggered but also the profit target. I immediately am placing my second profit target as well as a trailing stop. Because prices haven't traded below the 0.786 Fibonacci level by much, it has not been

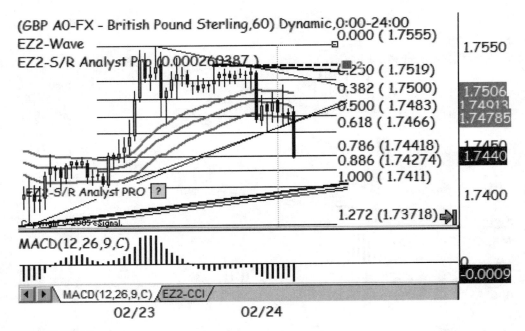

FIGURE 20.6

established as resistance yet, so I will use the 0.618 Fibonacci level at 1.7466 as resistance and my trailing stop. The next profit target is the 0.886 Fibonacci level at 1.7427. Shortly after hitting the 0.786 Fibonacci level I am watching prices trying to rally, but selling pressure is coming in well beneath the trailing stop at 1.7466. This pressure has now traded back through the 0.786 Fibonacci level and hit the 0.886. It's time to edit my trailing stop to 0.786 and place my next profit target at 1.7411. In Figure 20.7 prices have eased up on the sell-off and my trailing stop is hit as the Fibonacci support level of 0.886 has created a sizable bounce.

Did you forget about our play in the USD/CHF? (See Figure 20.8.) With the initial profit target hit, the 1.3155 level is not support and we'll be looking to the 1.3192 for the next profit target, where I place a limit order to sell. My trailing (sell) stop is 1.3155. Prices stall at just four pips above the minor psychological level of 1.3184 and pull back to the support (and my trailing stop!). (See Figure 20.9.) I'm out. Besides, if this strength persists, my entry based on the daily chart has me covered.

I'm taking the daily entry of the USD/CHF into the weekend. *And notice that you certainly can trade longer-term chart setups and shorter-term chart setups as I've done today!* The daily is looking strong and I know that I am taking some risk here as my stop-loss means nothing over the weekend because the market is closed and my broker cannot guarantee my stop-loss, and I remind myself that *trading is all about assuming and managing risk!*

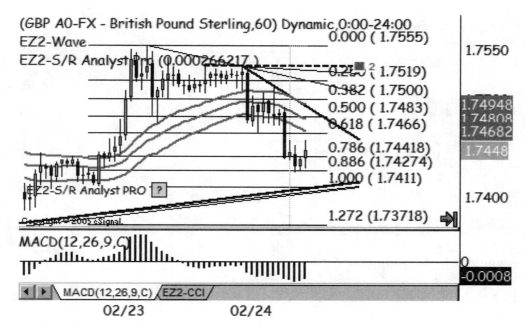

FIGURE 20.7

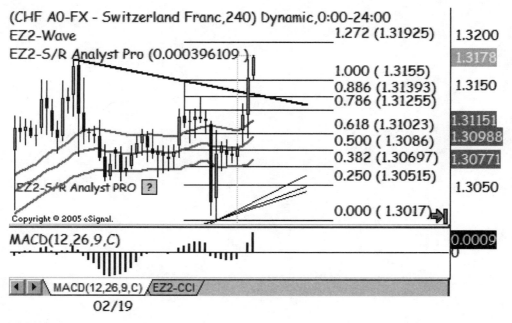

FIGURE 20.8

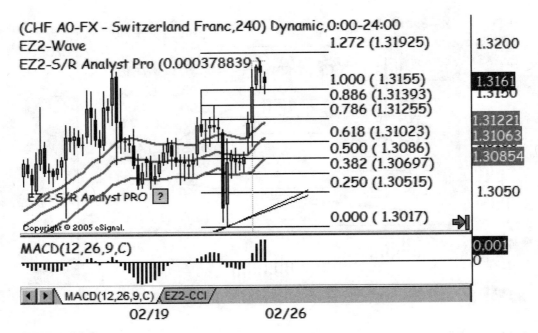

FIGURE 20.9

Monday,
February 27th

I'm a visual trader. That means I will trade what I see on my charts, not what I hear on the news or hunches I feel. I hope that now after more than three weeks and over 80 charts you see this and are beginning to believe.

We do have some big numbers coming out today and tomorrow. Today we have New Home Sales at 10:00 A.M. This is not necessarily a number you might associate with forex, but since we are experiencing a bubble or a rally in the real estate market, this number is one the U.S. markets are watching, and that will affect the U.S. dollar. Remember that the currency of any country will typically move in sympathy with the equities market of that country. They won't move tick for tick, but there's certainly a relationship there.

I am quick to check my swing long in the USD/CHF. This is not the first time I've looked at it. I also checked it yesterday (Sunday) just to see where it opened. It looks strong, so I am going to trust the orders I already have in the market to manage that position. Let's see what's on my radar this morning. It's late, later than I wanted to start my day. It's 8:30 A.M. and I have to see what—*if anything*—is setting up.

My USD/JPY short is following through to the down side, with my stop-loss and profit target in place. I'm going to continue scanning, as I have less than 90 minutes before the New Home Sales number.

Unfortunately, most of the charts are slowly trending or just choppy, with no clear setups. This is not completely shocking since we have a truckload of economic data coming out tomorrow. I don't think that if I had been at my desk at 4:30 A.M. or even 5:00 A.M. it would have made any difference. Here are a few examples of what I am finding so lackluster this morning. It's just as important when you recognize when *not* to do anything.

The view of the 180-minute pound in Figure 21.1 has a slightly downward-angling Wave; we're not close to a breakout or breakdown. Nor is the Wave steep enough to the downside to merit a swing consideration. And it's not just the longer-term intraday charts, either. Figure 21.2 is a shorter-term chart, and again, it's not that the Wave doesn't have po-

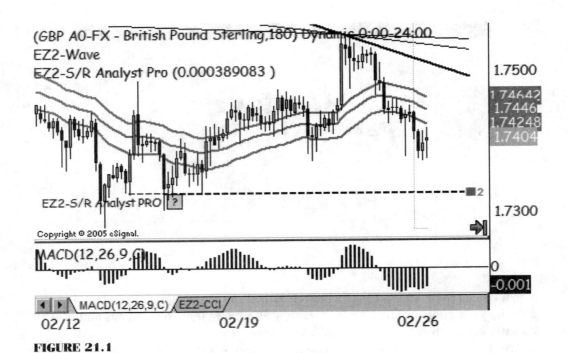

FIGURE 21.1

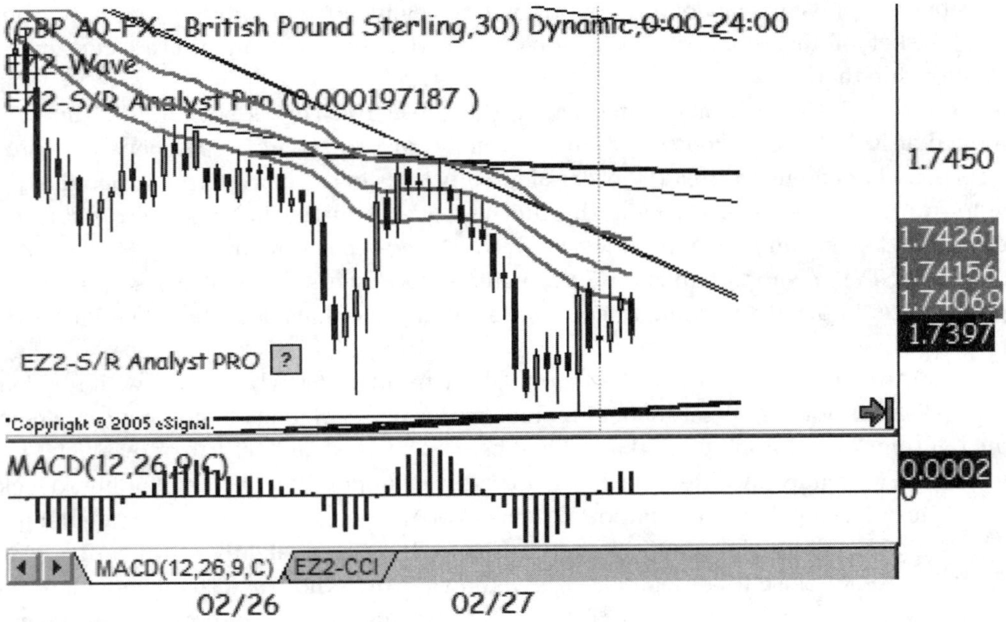

FIGURE 21.2

tential on the 30-minute chart. It's certainly trying to level out and it's within the two to four o'clock angle. However, I am going to be much more choosy about the Wave on 30-minute charts than I would be on the 180 or 240 or daily. Prices are not near any kind of break and it's almost 9:00 A.M. Everything just has a flat feel about it. Or maybe my head just isn't in it today. Let's take a look at a couple of other charts, starting with Figure 21.3.

The 60-minute chart of the Aussie actually did register a confirmed breakdown at 6:00 A.M.—almost three hours ago. Even if I had been able to enter that short at 0.7375, it's not going anywhere. Currently it is trading sideways with a slightly downward-angling Wave. It's well within the two to four o'clock angle, so I cannot consider a swing entry short.

Now, wait a minute. Just before I lose hope of any entry possibility, I see that the Canadian dollar is breaking down through 1.1475 with a MACD histogram that is plotting below the zero line. If you recall, I have been keeping an eye on this chart and have a bright green sticky note that has been staring at me since the 24th. The breakdown has already begun and seems to have weakened at 6:30 A.M. this morning but if you remember I am looking for a setup on the daily chart and am waiting for the MACD histogram to confirm the trade. I am seeing that now, and it looks like I can manually enter. I enter short at 1.1465 and place my stop-loss at 1.1527 (the middle line of the Wave as well as the 0.500 Fibonacci level) and my initial profit target at 1.1441 (the 1.000 full retracement level) and will hope to be able to see the next profit target of 1.1405. The entry is not the 1.1475 I wanted so I have about 10 pips of slippage between the entry I planned and the entry I finally executed at. This is not brokerage slippage! Slippage in the more commonly known

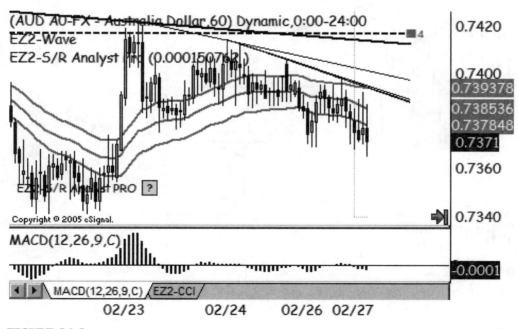

FIGURE 21.3

sense really doesn't exist in the forex market. What I am referring to is how much I was willing to give up to get my entry. If this was a 30-minute or 60-minute chart, I would never have given up 10 pips! It would even be borderline on the 180- or 240-minute, and the decision to do so on those charts would have more to do with where the initial profit targets were. Remember that this 10-pip slippage minimizes my profit target and increases my risk. I don't consider 10 pips a chase on the daily time frame. My entry has preceded the all-out tank by less than a half hour. And my initial support level of 1.1441 is hit almost immediately. I am moving my stop-loss up to this profit target (now resistance) as prices are slicing down through 1.1430. My next profit target is 1.1405 (just above the psychological number of 1.1400) and I place my limit order there.

Okay, not a bad morning at all . . . I'll take a peek again tonight and certainly early tomorrow. And I will be at my desk early. We have Gross Domestic Product (GDP), Purchasing Managers Index (PMI), Consumer Confidence, and Existing Home Sales. The hot zone starts at 8:30 A.M.

I think I'll go take my ma out to lunch today. When I return I will see where my entry on the Canadian dollar is.

Upon my return I see that the Canadian dollar did not disappoint. (See Figure 21.4.) Around 2:30 P.M. EST, while I was out to lunch, my second profit target was hit at 1.1405. I'm flat, as I had only two lots. So today I got to spend an afternoon with my ma after making some nice trades this morning. This is what a good day of trading is all about. This is the payoff. *Not a bad afternoon at all.*

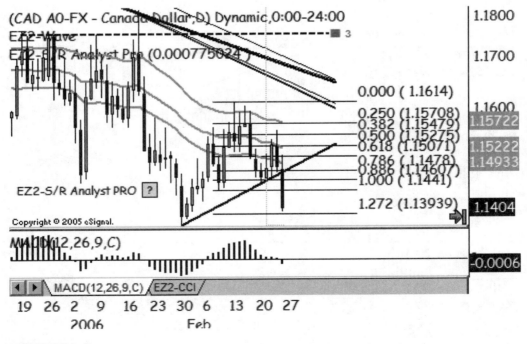

FIGURE 21.4

Tuesday, February 28th

It's early—too early for me, but I told myself I would get up early, so here I am. It's not quite 4:30 A.M. yet and there doesn't seem to be enough Earl Grey tea in Florida to get my synapses firing this morning.

I'm still keeping an eye on the USD/CHF daily chart and I see that the Canadian dollar is still falling. *Oh, well.* It doesn't mean that I can scan the intraday charts for another setup. Don't revenge trade. *I am telling this to myself as much as I am telling it to you.* After a couple of losses, after a missed trade, after exiting a trade and seeing it continue on without you, like the Canada this morning, *don't revenge trade.* So I will scan the 30, 60, 180, and 240 charts to see if there is an opportunity. The setup will have to stand on its own merit, and I'm not to be swayed in any way by the continued drop on the daily chart. *Got it?* The 240-minute chart seems to be setting just that opportunity. (See Figure 22.1.)

The Aussie is next on my list to scan. The 60-minute chart (Figure 22.2) is setting up a momentum trade—you know, sideways Wave, triangle pattern . . . *You don't really want to keep me spelling this out for you, do you? It's the last day of the month and you might be as sick of reading "sideways, three o'clock Wave" and "00 is a major psychological number" as I am of typing them. How about we agree that at this point we are now on the same page, you and I, and that I can refrain from assuming that you don't know what I am referring to? Cool?*

This chart of the Aussie is not one I am considering an entry in . . . yet. Let's review why. It's certainly not because the Wave is not flat or the triangle is not being broken to the upside, nor is it because the MACD histogram is after all confirming. There are enough reasons not to take the trade. These distinctions make the difference between taking a trade and not taking the trade. First notice the breakout's proximity to the 0.7400 level. The original breakout occurred between 2:00 A.M. and 3:00 A.M. EST. This is the second breakout level, which is not as desirable an entry as the first and lower of the

159

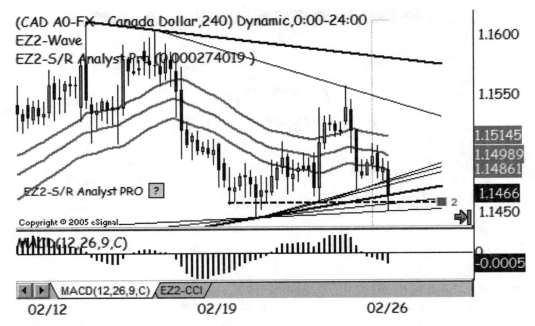

FIGURE 22.1

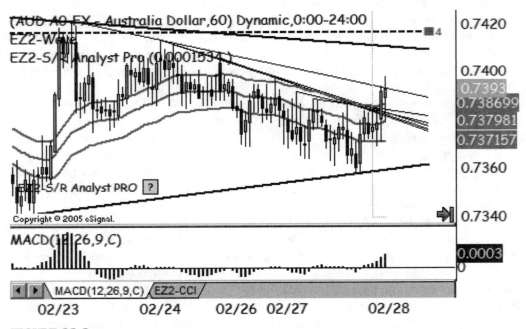

FIGURE 22.2

multiple downtrend lines on this chart. And even the original breakout is only 18 to 20 pips below the 0.7400 level. The second breakout level is only five to six pips below 0.7400. Getting long this close to major resistance is a high-risk entry. The entry below the "00" is too high-risk. In situations like this, I've discussed waiting for confirmation by seeing if 0.7405 trades (thus assuming considerably slippage) or looking at the longer-term time frames for an opportunity. The longer-term charts such as Figure 22.3 had momentum setups of their own and the breakout was climbing all across the board.

The Swissy broke down on the 30-minute chart at 3:00 A.M. this morning with confirmation. (See Figure 22.4.) The setup was poised just above the 1.3200 level, which means that—for future reference—you have a couple of choices. First, and most obviously, you can pass on the trade. Second, you can park a sell stop at 1.3195, which would qualify the break below 1.3200. And third, you could use the lowest two of the uptrend lines to play the breakdown. The AUD/USD and USD/CHF are a lot alike this morning.

I can add the 30-minute EUR/USD to the list. (See Figure 22.5.) The breakout at 4:00 A.M. on the euro blew through multiple downtrend lines with MACD histogram confirmation. It occurred below the 1.1900 level so the "00" issue doesn't present itself here.

I've outlined three pairs with similar setups this morning, and I do this to make a point. Each of these pairs has given a second level at which an entry is available. Before you start thinking that these "gifts" are the best entry, please think again. Yes,

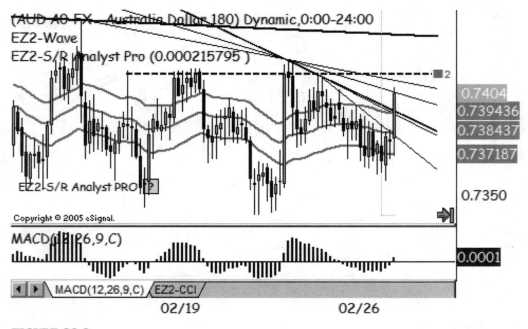

FIGURE 22.3

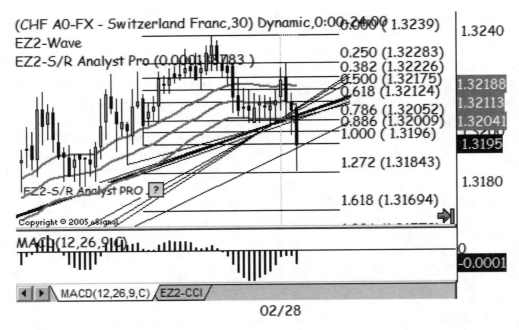

FIGURE 22.4

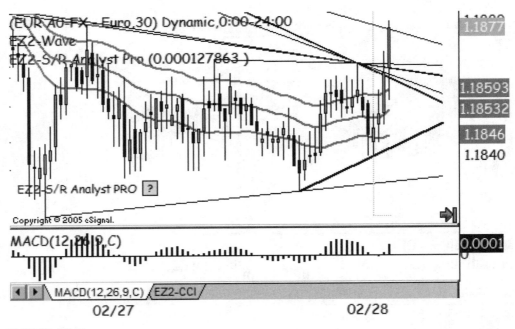

FIGURE 22.5

sometimes they follow through; but other times they do not. One thing I must make clear here: The entry must be valid on its own merit. In other words, if the Wave has changed its reading or prices have hit a profit target from the initial entry opportunity, you have a strong reason *not* to take the trade. *Do you remember when I described trading as "assuming and managing risk"?* Now it's a matter of how much risk you are willing to assume.

Bottom line: **A good entry makes for an easier trade.** I know that's no news flash, but it's amazing how quickly we forget this when we miss a trade. Chasing an entry, a late entry, or a just plain bad entry increases the difficulty of an already difficult game. It's the difference between stepping into the ring with a heavyweight and facing an amateur in the ring. Sure, you *could* win against either one, but you know which one is more likely to beat you up.

My objective throughout this book comes to a head here. I don't simply want to present a book that is a collection of canned setups that you must memorize or do's and do not's that you must follow. These won't *ever* make you a successful trader. I've given you the very tools that I use day in and day out. These are classic and time-tested tools like trend lines, moving averages, MACD, support/resistance, and market psychology. We've discussed the questions you should ask yourself before and during the trade. You must learn to make decisions yourself using these tools and asking the right questions as I have outlined. The risk that one trader is willing to assume is not always what is right for another.

As we get closer to 8:00 A.M. I see that most of the shorter-term intraday charts are still moving way in front of the hot zone and the longer-term charts have not moved enough to register a near-term setup. I think back on what set up much, much earlier this morning and I realize that I am probably going to be reduced to reacting to the movement of the hot zone or chasing a trade, neither of which I am wired or willing to do. So it's time to look for some pullbacks and bounces and see if I can't find a correction to capture! I'll have to park some limits and see if prices go my way.

The pullback on the EUR/USD in Figures 22.6 and 22.7 is showing me support not only at the Wave (my personal preference for swing entry) but also at the 0.500 Fibonacci level at 1.1868. This offers me two great reasons to enter long within the context of this morning's uptrend in the euro. This is a living, breathing example of a trade with multiple confirmation!

The setup on the EUR/USD now that we have the pullback is straightforward, which is the beauty of a swing setup. The stop-loss (save the 60-second stop we will use just before the hot zone) will be set just below the lowest line of the Wave at the "50" pip level. The initial profit targets will be 1.1882 (two pips beyond the minor "80" pip psychological level), then the full retracement at 1.1896 (four pips below 1.1900).

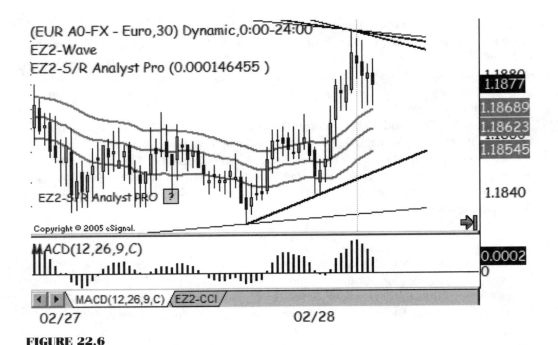

FIGURE 22.6

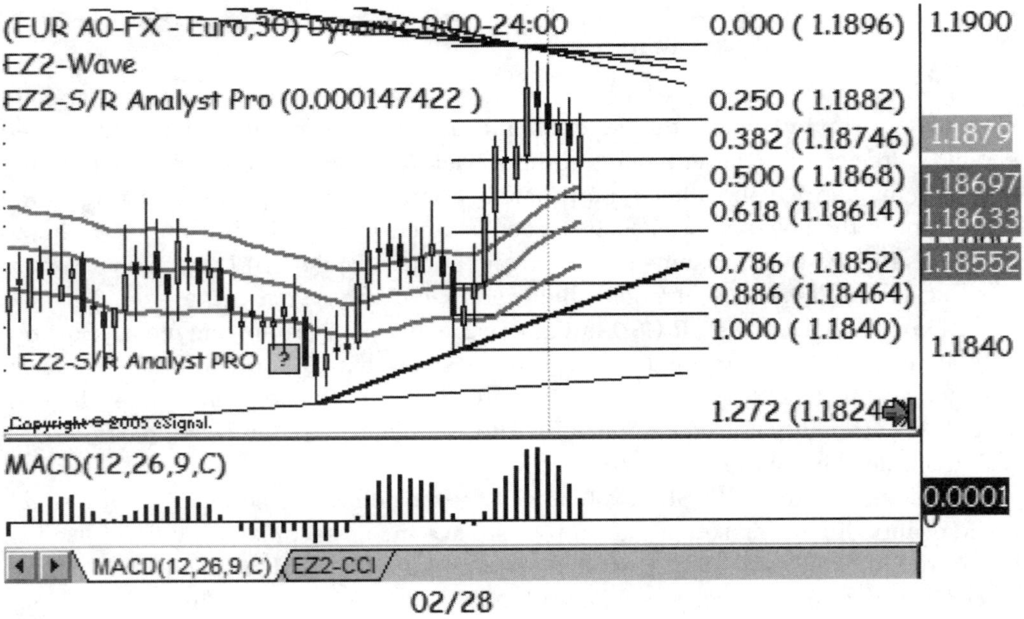

FIGURE 22.7

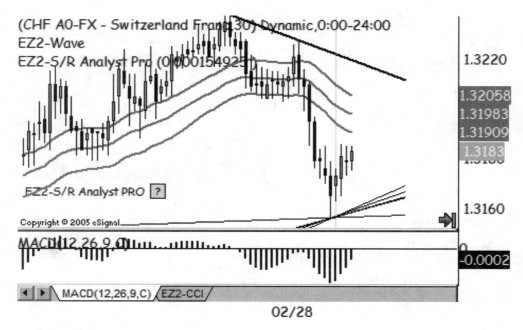

FIGURE 22.8

The chart of the USD/CHF (Figure 22.8) is bouncing, as we should expect after looking at the charts of the euro. In Figure 22.9 the bounce touches the bottom line of the Wave but falls just short of the 0.500 Fibonacci level at 1.3192—it's still a valid entry and only three pips from the 0.500 so it's certainly a very strong resistance level. And it is eight pips below the 1.3200 level, which does position this entry short below significant resistance. Support awaits at 1.3174 (the 0.250 Fibonacci level) and then at the full retracement at 1.3156. Notice that we're forgoing the 0.382 at 1.3183 because it's within the 10-to-12-pip cushion. *Forgoing this level does mean that it is not valid resistance; it's a profit consideration because taking profit within 10 to 12 pips does not make sense considering that we're paying the spread.*

The follow-through was right at the hot zone, like clockwork! (See Figures 22.10 and 22.11.)

The movement from this hot zone, coupled with the fact that most setups confirmed earlier this morning and the fact that I don't want to take on too many positions before noon on Friday—this is a great point to wrap up my morning! *And you do remember why trading after noon on Friday is not a good idea, right?* After noon on Friday the only market open is the U.S. market. London has closed and there will be no Asian session opening in six hours. It's the weekend! You've worked hard this week. *Go enjoy it.*

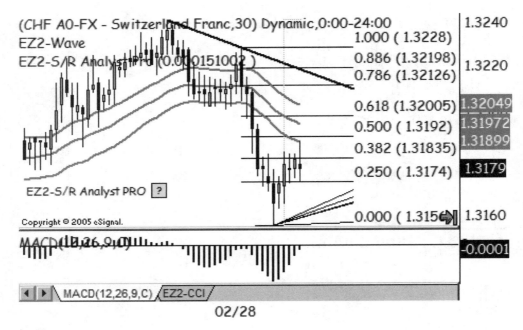

FIGURE 22.9

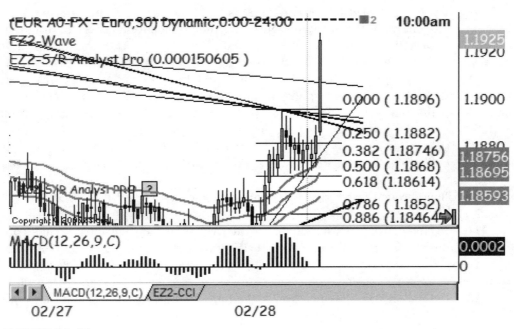

FIGURE 22.10

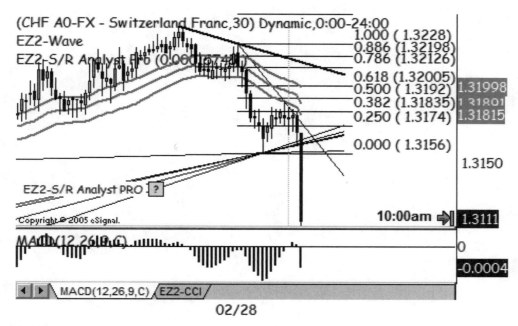

FIGURE 22.11

Wednesday, March 1st

It's the first day of March. It's just after 7 A.M. EST and I'm listening to CNBC commentators discussing Google. Since the first of the year, this stock has been increasingly volatile and gapping frequently. The organized march upwards since going public has transitioned into an Internet bubble burst–like distribution market cycle. I have been telling my students and fellow traders who have asked me about my opinion of "GOOG" that it's a speculative stock. With the run-up this stock has seen, it's not a matter of what I or anyone else thinks of Google's value. I mean really, is it worth $450 a share? It's not my job as a trader to decide this or, frankly, to really care. I trust the price action and I keep an eye on the Wave. We've seen a 100-point sell-off in this stock since the end of January. I was just e-mailing a student the other day what I felt was psychologically going on in this stock, and this can apply to any market that has seen a run-up like Google has. When a stock does nothing but continue upward with very little correction, as Google has done, the slightest bit of bad news can shake the will of the public to continue buying. When you get to the peaks that we saw in late 2005 and early 2006, any bad news can make so-called investors who bought the stock at the heights—*without really knowing why they did in the first place*—run for the hills fast! The selling that occurs at these heights is especially volatile because most times, buyers at these levels did not have a plan when they bought, other than they would like to see prices go higher. They usually leveraged, especially with a stock this expensive. So the panic is not an organized line to the exit door. It's an all-out frenzy, trampling anyone to the exit door. In fact, you'll notice that selling can often happen this way because the decision to sell usually is something that sounds like "Ooh! I made money! Get me out now!" or it sounds like "Aah! I'm losing money! Get me out now!" My friends, what more proof do we need to convince us that market action reflects the most basic aspects of human psychology?

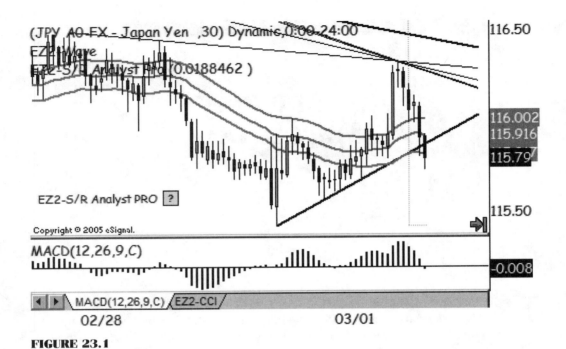

FIGURE 23.1

Let's take a look at what's on my radar this morning. The first one I want to discuss is the 30-minute yen, shown in Figure 23.1.

The setup looks decent enough, right? The Wave has very recently come out of transition and leveled out to a three o'clock direction so we know right off the bat that it's a little "aggro." *No problem, though, just as long as we are aware of this.* However, I wanted to take a moment to bring up a concept that we first discussed at the beginning of the month. On February 1st I introduced the movie analogy and the habit of rewinding the charts as you set up a potential trade. It's something that you must exercise every day. Let's do this with the yen because I want to make sure that you do this with every setup. I want to bookend this lesson by an examination of the rewind practice here at the end of the month and nearing the close of our time together in my trading room. If I go about rewinding this chart just two hours before the 8:30 A.M. EST breakdown, I can see that prices were rallying. (See Figure 23.2.)

The question you should be asking yourself is: Where did this rally begin? It's pretty likely that the last three o'clock Wave yielded a long entry earlier this morning. And let's keep in mind that we're not looking to punish ourselves for trades we missed. We're just catching up on the movie as it played earlier in the trading day.

Looking at the 3:30 A.M. EST chart in Figure 23.3 I can see that the prior move was a breakout to the upside. And two hours before that, at 1:30 A.M., the very first signal of the breakout long was triggered with MACD histogram confirmation. What this allows

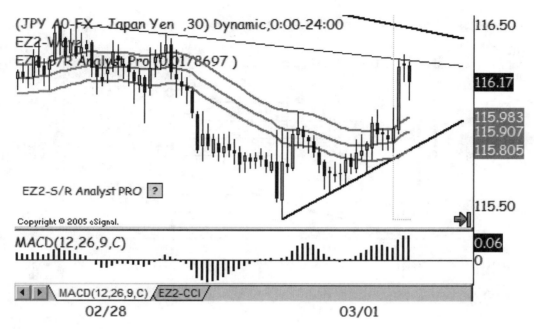

FIGURE 23.2

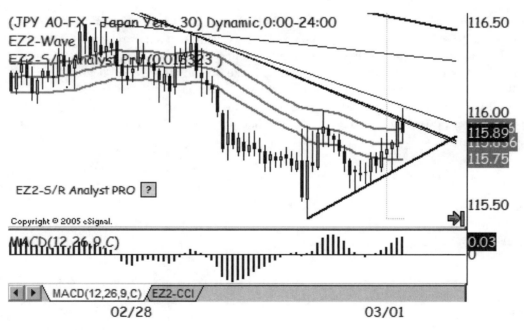

FIGURE 23.3

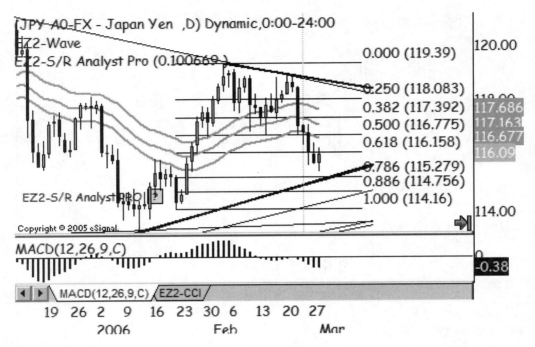

FIGURE 23.4

me to see is all the price action and setups that occurred while I was not watching the market. This doesn't necessarily make the subsequent setups less relevant. The goal is simply to see (1) what has happened in my absence and (2) where prices have been and how the current setup formed. Please don't make this any more complicated than that. *We're just rewinding the movie to catch the stuff we missed.*

By the way, I am (trailing) stopped out on the daily chart of the yen (Figure 23.4) as prices pop up through the resistance of what was my initial profit target, now resistance, at 116.15.

Thursday, March 2nd

Today is a really light day if not practically an off day for me. I'm rereading the very manuscript that's to become to book you're now holding in your hands. It's amazing to me when I think about the fact that what I am typing into my laptop is going to be in hardcover by this summer. So I am trying to squeeze in some last-minute charts, distinctions, and edits because my deadline is a mere five days away. But that doesn't mean the markets weren't moving. As part of what I do teaching, I hold two webinars a week. I am conducting two of those because I am covering for my usual evening chat presenter, Ed. So I will be doing one webinar at 3:00 P.M. and the second at 7:00 P.M.

At the 3:00 P.M. presentation, one of my students brought a chart to my attention. It was a cross rate that I typically would not be watching for myself. But as I always say to all my students, *this stuff works on any market and any time frame.*

The chart is of the GBP/JPY (the British pound/Japanese yen) on a 30-minute time frame. The Wave was traveling at a perfectly flat three o'clock angle and prices were inside a balanced, symmetrical triangle. We discussed this chart after 3:30 P.M. EST and we all agreed that once Tokyo opened we'd see some action. I recommended that he revisit the chart closer to 6:00 P.M. to 7:00 P.M. this evening, and that if the triangle broke out with confirmation before this time to go ahead and take the trade but that the follow-through would most likely happen when Tokyo opens. Look, I'm not clairvoyant; it's just a matter of attention and who's awake. At 3:00 P.M. the only market that's open is the U.S. market and in an hour it will close. After that there's the "black hole" between the U.S. close and the Sydney open, which is followed by the Tokyo open.

You'll notice in Figure 24.1 that I set up the trade for a potential breakout to the upside; that's only because the MACD histogram is above the zero line. Don't expect a breakout or breakdown ever. But you know if you're looking at a three o'clock Wave that the MACD histogram must confirm the direction of the potential move. So you can set up the side of the trade that is currently confirmed even though the price trigger hasn't

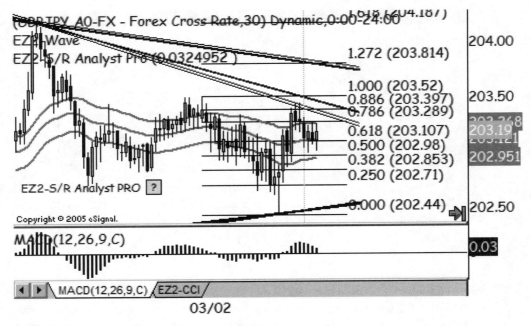

FIGURE 24.1

occurred. Since the lines and levels are on the chart, the setup is easier to recognize. The breakout is not a static level when you are playing downtrend and uptrend lines because they continue to tighten as prices continue trading. But it's not difficult to project an approximate breakout as long as you are staying within a few candles of current prices. If not, you will have to check back from time to time to verify not only the continued tightening but also the MACD histogram confirmation. The stop-loss level is going to be decided by using support and there is plenty of it. The breakout candle low or the preceding low is a good point to reference in deciding where the trade is no longer valid. In this case that would be all the way down at the other side of this triangle, the uptrend. That's too much heat for me to consider for a 30-minute time frame chart setup. The lines of the Wave are lining up with the Fibonacci levels, which is great secondary confirmation of the validity of the support they will represent. So I can consider the 0.618 or the 0.500. The 0.786 will be too close to the actual breakout and will actually be better used as a secondary confirmation to the breakout itself. Also, do not forget the "00" pip level at 203.00. (See Figure 24.2.)

At the 7:00 P.M. webinar, that same student mentioned the trade because he took it at the breakout just before the evening's chat. It ran up to the 1.886 Fibonacci level and reversed there. The last time I checked, and by the way it's 12:08 A.M. Friday morning, prices were still hovering around the 1.272 Fibonacci level. So it did sell off from the highs and is now battling with the 204.00 psychological number—that was a profit target on the trip up. It's pretty likely that prices will bounce between the resistance at 204.00

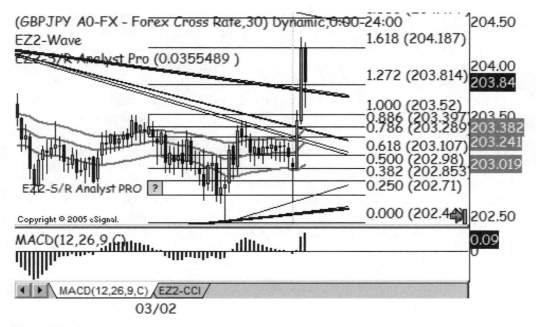

FIGURE 24.2

and the 1.272 Fibonacci level, which is now support at 203.81, just a pip above the "80" minor psychological level. This breakout is also another opportunity for me to point out that you must take your predetermined profit targets. When prices broke to the upside, the targets were the Fibonacci resistance levels. In fact, these levels, the 1.000 and 1.272, lined up with psychological levels. So we're looking at the 203.52 and 203.81 levels before we even get long.

Remember that we have a cushion of 10 to 12 pips from the breakout level (do not confuse this with your actual executed entry price) to the first target. We also will apply this cushion from profit target to profit target. This means that if the first resistance level is within 10 to 12 pips of your entry long (the reverse goes for your short), then you can skip that level in terms of placing a profit target order. The exception to this rule is the "00" psychological levels; you should enter in front of them, anyway.

I also had a great discussion about mind-set at the 7:00 P.M. presentation. A trader's mind-set revolves around confidence. The three Rs concept of *recognize, react, repeat* is where my mind-set comes from. The first step is education; it always has been and always will be. Without education there is no recognizing. The act of recognizing a chart setup starts with taking a clock angle reading of the Wave, then drawing support, resistance, and trend lines, and finally finding psychological numbers and Fibonacci levels. This takes practice, and eventually you will be able to recognize the setups within this framework. Once you have confidence in your ability to recognize the setups and once you have confidence in you chart work, then reaction comes naturally because you are just waiting for the chance to put this good chart work to use. The ability to repeat only comes from reacting over and over again and seeing that your trading plan is guiding you in the right direction. And I am definitely not talking about just profitable trades! Following a trading plan means disciplining yourself not to chase an entry, obeying your stop-loss level, and exiting at your predetermined profit targets. You do this often enough and you will begin trading from confidence. You do that and "repeat" comes all by itself. It's a natural progression that builds upon itself, but it must start with education, with an understandable trading approach. This is such an important point to understand so I'll include the chat I mentioned earlier in the CD-ROM so you can watch and listen to that presentation.

Friday, March 3rd

We're winding down to the final few days. As I think about this I realize that it's going to be a little strange not "talking to myself" after a month of doing just that. It's been great sharing this with you; I even find that it has allowed me to see nuances that at one time were so ingrained in me that they happened on a subconscious level. I just got trained to look for the charts to set up in a certain way and then reacted to what I saw. I have to say that these past 30 or so days of deconstructing this process have been my chance not only to share with you what I do but also to improve the process. Certainly observing something can change the very thing observed, and knowing all eyes are on me, so to speak, did change what I do. I have to say it added a certain degree of depth and detail to my observations. I didn't want to miss a chance to point out a distinction or nuance. I wanted to make sure that the setups I took could be reconstructed by you—that the process could become a learned behavior and therefore repeatable. It went back to the three Rs that I have believed to be the cornerstone of productive trading approach: *Recognize, react, repeat.*

It's benefited me in ways I'm probably just now beginning to acknowledge. I've always said my students have been my best teachers, and it keeps coming back to that, doesn't it? What you get in life is equal to what you give. I believe that. So let's keep meeting like this for a little while longer. Head on over to www.thirtydaysoftrading.com. I look forward to seeing you there. I hope you've enjoyed this as much as I have enjoyed sharing this with you. I never want to take your time for granted, so I appreciate your time and thank you.

There are just three ideas I want you to keep in mind now that you've sat beside me for a month. (1) There is no one trading approach that is right for everyone. (2) No one trading approach will capture all the market breakouts, breakdowns, and swings. And finally: (3) More is not better. Better is better! Having more tools, more indicators, more studies, and more strategies is not going to make anyone successful.

I've met and been influenced by some great traders. I've spent a lot of time studying not so much their tools but their mind-sets. If you've had a chance to watch or sit beside successful traders for any length of time you will notice right from the start that their approach is usually remarkably straightforward. Never confuse simple with simplistic, my friend. You'll also notice that successful traders know what works for them. They are not going to try to put your approach down just to make theirs seem better. In fact, they are rarely going to mention their approach unless invited to do so. They're quiet and humble about their success and enjoy the fruits of their labor without rubbing someone's face in it. They are also usually not concerned with the latest and greatest in the trading business. They are not tempted by these new tools and toys.

Let me tell you a funny story; in fact, unfortunately, I see this over and over again. I'll leave the names out (and I was not one of them) but you can rest assured it has happened to most traders who speak at any one of the International Traders or Forex Trading Expos. I enjoy the expos. In fact, Tim Bourquin, whom I think the world of, is one of the founders of the original Forex Trading Expo. The expos are great fun and one of the few chances to meet and listen to great traders in a relaxed, educational setting. I speak at the expos a couple of times a year and enjoy meeting and helping other traders. But let me tell you about the stupidest thing I see at every one of these shows: A few attendees in the crowd will approach a speaker after the presentation to tell them all about *their* own approach. And I mean go into great depth and detail about what they use and even, occasionally, how great their approach is.

Now really, does anyone think in their wildest dreams that a successful trader really cares what it is that you are doing at your trading desk? Do you think that's why they traveled all this way to make a presentation? It's nuts! When I have the chance to meet a trader I respect, I shut up! I *listen*. I may ask some specific questions, but it will be about *their* approach, not mine! I want to make the most of every minute I have to listen to their thoughts and ideas. I can't for the life of me figure this one out, and let me tell you why I think this is not only stupid but the symptom of a larger problem. It's human nature to want to impress others by acting like a trader with some market prowess. Let me tell you this, though: *Successful* traders do not do this. The good ones don't go to expos or speak in public to stroke their egos! They go because they want to share what has worked for them. It's our job as students of the game of trading to listen! Remember that next time you go to an expo (not that you are one of those annoying people). Great traders are consummate students. Even after they have learned what they need to know in order to succeed at trading, they are always learning new things outside of trading. They know that an active mind is a sharp mind and that idle fingers get stuck in your nose.

Online trading of forex, futures, and stocks is here to stay. In fact, just this past January, online trading/investing (in stocks) increased 30 percent to 40 percent. *So if you think you've missed the boat, think again.* I don't mean day trading, either—that is too limiting an approach. I do mean active trading and active investing. We're not going to limit a trade to a day. The time it takes should not matter. Follow your plan. Trade what you see on your charts.

All right then, you are now armed with all the strategies, setups, and trading screens that you need for trying this stuff out. We're going to embark on the last week of trading together, so it's time to starting thinking about how you will put these strategies to work. Open up your charts! Give it a go. Practice, practice, practice. See how the setups shape up on your charts. Give hot zones the respect they demand. And be sure to come visit me at www.thirtydaysoftrading.com for more daily insight.

Now back to the markets: Here's what's on my radar for this morning.

The daily chart of the Aussie is finally starting to level out. (See Figure 25.1.) I say "finally" because the Wave never traveled downward steeply enough to generate a four to six o'clock Wave and thus never allowed me to try to set up a swing entry. There's no telling where the Aussie will go from here, but it's on my radar and I will revisit it daily.

Let's see what's going on on the intraday charts. The 30- and 60-minute charts have my attention this morning. It's just a few minutes after nine o'clock EST and I have a choice to make, courtesy of the Aussie. (See Figures 25.2 and 25.3.)

These charts have similar setups and both are breaking down through uptrend lines, but only the 60-minute chart has a negative reading on the MACD histogram. It has been treading water, meaning that it is switching between a positive and a negative reading, but currently it's below the zero line (−0.000008). That alone can confirm this momentum breakdown. I'm going to mark this entry as an aggressive entry because of this. (If

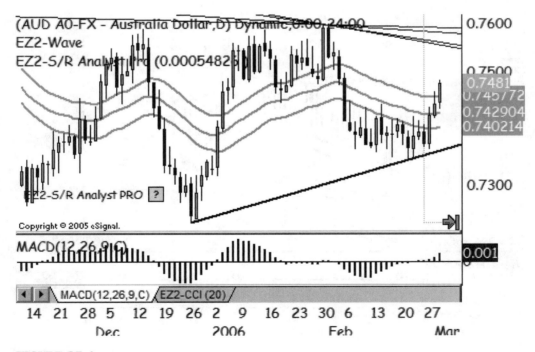

FIGURE 25.1

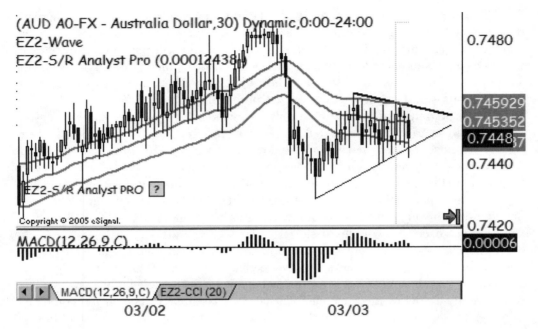

FIGURE 25.2

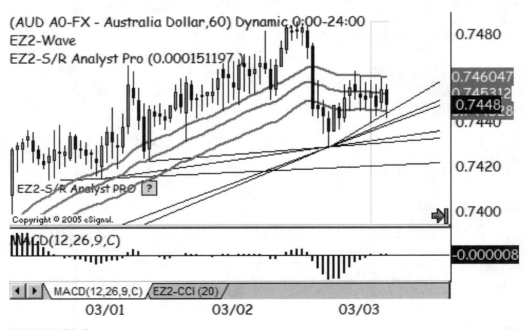

FIGURE 25.3

you're wondering why I do this, it will allow me to review my trading notes from time to time and see how these more aggressive setups followed through.) I'm not exactly crazy about the MACD histogram on this chart. Notice how it's been bobbing above and below the zero line? I acknowledge it's a little aggro and I'll keep a tight leash on the trade and trade only two lots. I'll look for the closest *valid* stop-loss level. My entry short is at 0.7443, and I'll place my stop-loss just above the middle line of the Wave at 0.7455. My profit targets will follow the support levels that my Fibonacci levels have laid out for me. I see that prices are bouncing off the 0.618 Fibonacci. The level outside my 10-to-12-pip cushion is the full 1.000 retracement at 0.7429, then the 1.272 Fibonacci level at 0.7419. I'll place two limit orders to exit one lot at each profit target level. (See Figure 25.4.)

The Canadian dollar is next on my scan, by virtue of my alphabetical quote window. I have conflicting confirmations on the 30- and 60-minute charts. The 30-minute is confirming short while the 60-minute has a strong, positive MACD histogram. As I have mentioned in prior days, when in this situation always go with the longer-term chart. (See Figure 25.5.)

The 60-minute is still presenting me with a dilemma, and it seems that I am destined today to enter aggro trades. One of my rules, I should say guidelines, is to avoid momentum setups where prices have broken both support and resistance. Notice how the 9:00 A.M. candle has a low that broke down through the uptrend line and also the downtrend line? Even though the MACD histogram never confirmed the short, prices ranged wide

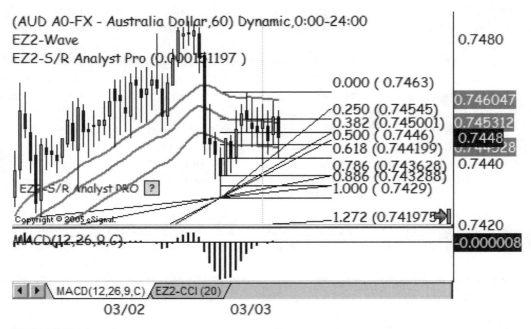

FIGURE 25.4

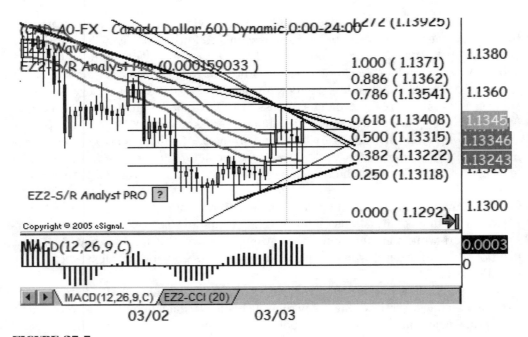

FIGURE 25.5

enough to trigger a break . . . so it's an aggressive entry long at 1.1344, and that means I will have to keep an eye on the "50" pip. The first upside target is the 0.786 Fibonacci level at 1.1254, which is inside the cushion so we'll look to the 1.1362. It's time to park the target, and I'll be using a 60-second stop. Don't forget that all this is setting up as I am heading into three hot zones; the first is the Consumer Confidence number at 9:50 A.M. and then the Institute for Supply Management (ISM) number at 10:00 A.M.—between 9:50 A.M. and 10:00 A.M. will be one big hot zone.

I'm quickly running out of time to scan the rest of the majors, so I'm going to scan the Swissy, euro, pound, and yen so that I can position myself before the volatility begins. It is especially important to have your profit targets (limit order) proactively placed in the market before the hot zone. Many times the breakouts that happen so quickly will reverse just as quickly. Be proactive!

The Swissy, euro, and pound are a pass: There is no clear Wave reading or I am waiting for a correction to set up a swing entry. The yen, however, has a setup on the 180-minute chart. (See Figure 25.6.) The Wave is sideways, and downtrend lines that are coming down on current prices are establishing a nice breakout level that I will watch. I can place a proactive buy order here because the MACD histogram not only is positive but has been above the zero line for many days. The breakout level is right at 116.50 so I will give this major psychological level five pips to show me it's not short-term resistance. Waiting for prices to get beyond the psychological number by five pips is far from

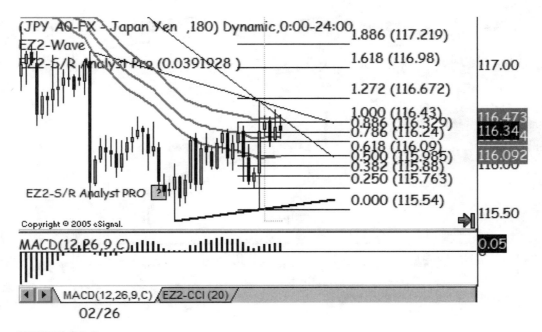

FIGURE 25.6

a sure thing, but I wait to see whether prices have enough buying momentum behind the move to merit a climb. With a 116.55 entry long, my first profit target could be the 1.272 at 116.67, but that's right on the 10-to-12-pip cushion, so we'll move that out to the 116.80 minor psychological level. By the way, the 10-to-12-pip cushion is a guideline and not a rule; it is your choice. *But I do stick with it.* So the "80" minor psychological pip level it is. There seems to be a good amount of support just below the 0.786 Fibonacci level. In fact, a recent low was at 116.17, and while the trade is technically valid until the bottom of the triangle is taken out (the uptrend line) I will choose either this 116.17 low or the bottom line of the Wave, which is lining up with the 0.618 Fibonacci. *It's all about recognizing support and resistance!* I'm going to go with the 116.17 and also figure that the minor "20" level will kick in a little help from the support side as well.

The Aussie broke down during the 9:30 A.M. candle but really didn't tank on the Consumer Confidence number, which is not totally unexpected as the U.S. dollar was already weak and the number just seemed to pause the selling of the past four or five candles. Of course that was a good sign for my trades this morning. (See Figure 25.7.)

The candle formed on the 30-minute chart was a classic stall or "pause" candle. It was a doji: tall wicks and small body. Many traders will consider it a reversal candle. This is key because any commonly known charting tool in the market, especially a candle that is as widely known and as easy to recognize as a doji, will create a market reaction. Notice that we have also matched an earlier low at 89.50 (major psychological number!) that was established yesterday at 6:30 P.M. So why am I happy? Consider that

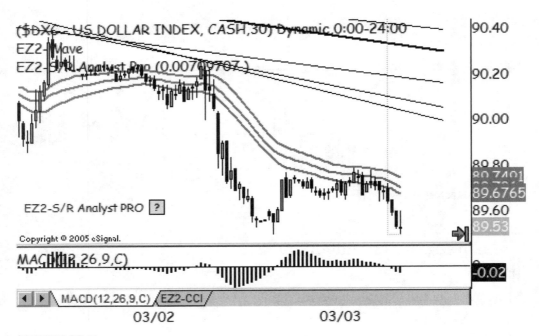

FIGURE 25.7

the Aussie has an inverse relationship with the U.S. dollar and if my Aussie short is to follow through, I want to see at least some strength in the dollar. My Canadian dollar buy will move with the U.S. dollar, so this pause is a positive in that aspect as well. The same goes with my yen entry long—it will move in most part with the U.S. dollar. The Canadian dollar and yen do not move with the dollar tick for tick like the Swissy, but there is a strong correlation there nonetheless. Notice that I don't hedge my positions. I am looking at basically six (seven if you include the kiwi) ways to trade the U.S. dollar. All my positions this morning are contingent on strength in the U.S. dollar, and I've got a major psychological number and support level at 89.50 with a doji. *What more can a girl ask for?* My bets are placed and it's time to take a deep breath and sip some tea. It's time to emotionally disconnect from what's going to happen. My 60-second stops are a manual order entry. My profit targets are in place. That's all I can do. And just like that it's 10:00 A.M. All the charts are moving as the volatility does not disappoint.

The Aussie nails the 1.272 Fibonacci with the candle wick on the sell-off (Figure 25.8) and starts bouncing from the low, leaving a long wick below the body of the candle. This is exactly why I park my profit target orders. Chances are that without that limit (you can use a stop order as well) I would not have been able to grab the price and get the execution. Imagine trying to grab three of these kinds of moves.

Looking at the Canadian dollar chart in Figure 25.9, I see the 0.886 Fibonacci was hit and even though prices pulled back some, I have taken half of my position

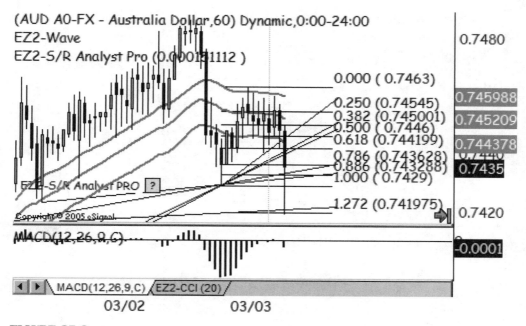

FIGURE 25.8

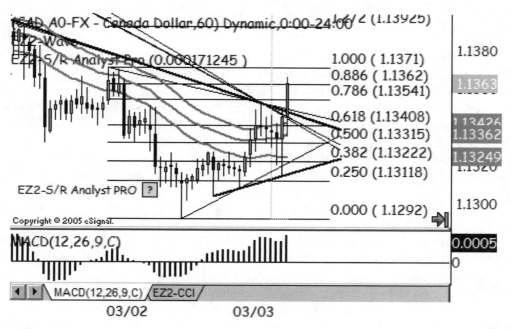

FIGURE 25.9

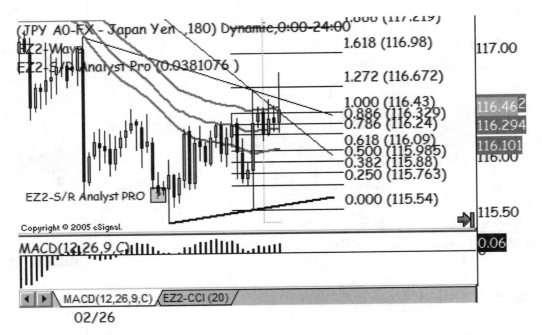

FIGURE 25.10

off the table, which is to say that I had two lots and now I have one. I would like to see the 1.000 Fibonacci hit and I will wait to see if there's enough push to get prices up there.

The yen is also moving up with the U.S. dollar. (See Figure 25.10.) And how do I love those psychological numbers? Let me count the ways! However, prices never got above the "80" pip and I didn't get my exit and fill. I have to put in my stop as 60 seconds has elapsed. The subsequent pullback was sharp but less than 10 pips from my initial entry long. My stop is just below the 0.786 Fibonacci level of 116.24 so I'll use 116.20. *Two out of three ain't too shabby.* The pullbacks start coming across the board as the U.S. dollar also begins to pull back and trade lower. So just like the U.S. dollar propelled my trades at 10:00 A.M. by the ISM number, the dollar is now retracing as the fundamentals are being absorbed by the trading and investing public. (See Figure 25.11.)

As this continues I am trailing stopped out of my AUD/USD and USD/CAD positions. (See Figures 25.12 and 25.13.)

That concludes my morning, and since it's Friday I figure this is as good a place as any to call it a day. It was a light morning of trading since most of the entries were aggressive momentum trades and because of that I kept the positions small. Remember I want to keep my eye on the clock because London is winding down for the day and by noon the participation is limited to the U.S. markets. I'll keep my OCO order in the USD/JPY and see what happens before the markets close this evening.

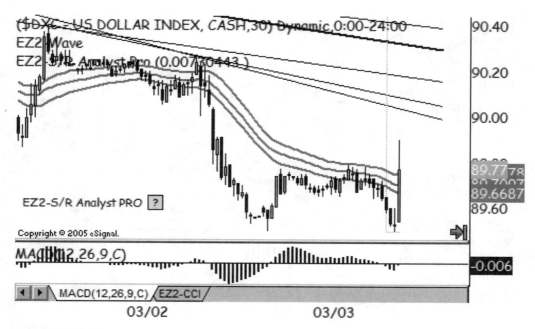

FIGURE 25.11

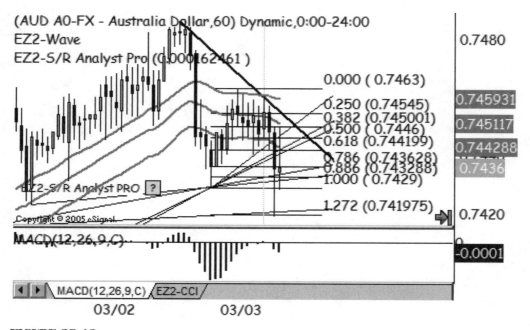

FIGURE 25.12

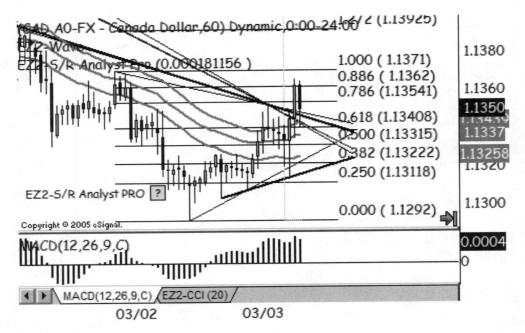

FIGURE 25.13

Sunday, March 5th

I took a quick look at the 180-minute yen Sunday afternoon. (See Figure 26.1.) It is trading in a range, which is not too unusual since Sydney and Tokyo are opening for the first time this week. Although Sydney represents the official open of a new week, it's London that will hold the major participation. Sydney can offer some insight, especially as Tokyo, Hong Kong, and Singapore begin to overlap.

The MACD histogram is still well above the zero line and as prices have continued sideways the Wave is still heading at three o'clock. I'm still long from 116.55, which isn't too far from current prices.

FIGURE 26.1

Monday, March 6th

The morning starts with a bang. Remember my position in the yen? Well, it has gone crazy overnight. (See Figure 27.1.)

I exit immediately since it's beyond my initial profit target, and then some. With just two lots in this trade, I take both off the table at 117.20, which is where prices were at that time. I suppose I could have managed this one from where prices were but

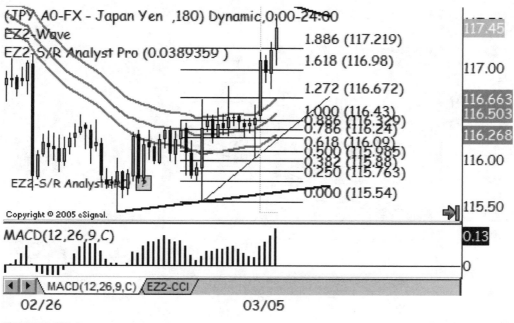

FIGURE 27.1

since it was all a gift above my original profit target of 116.80, my follow-my-trading-plan mind-set kicked in. It's wired into me now.

This is a great way to start the morning, but it's early and it's time to refocus and not let this go to my head. So here's what's on my radar this Monday morning. It's just after seven o'clock.

I hope by now I have dispelled the myth that you must get up at 2:00 A.M. EST to trade the forex, because if you noticed none of these days started earlier than (I think) 4:30 A.M. If you can get up earlier, great—you'll be able to capitalize on more trading action!

The Aussie pair that was so good to me Friday is breaking down this morning. Looking at the chart (Figure 27.2), I can see that the market has been weak since before 5:00 A.M. I want to spend just a few extra moments discussing this breakdown. We also have a hot zone at 10:00 A.M. with the Factory Orders release.

Notice that the first of many pierces occurred earlier this morning. The clearest was during the 5:00 A.M. candle. The subsequent candles stayed within the range of the breakdown level and made a low of 0.7427. This level, while support, was within the 10-to-12-pip cushion. *My rule is that once a profit target is hit, second-chance entries are*

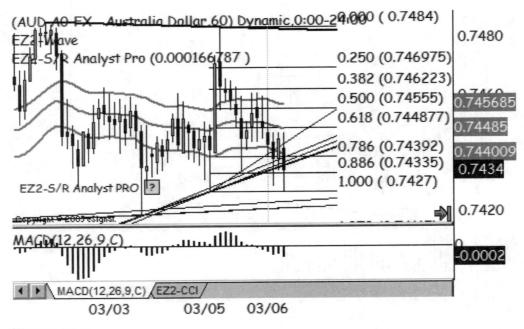

FIGURE 27.2

no longer valid. Here we see that is not the case and the entry is certainly valid. However, if the price has reached the initial profit target and then given us a second-chance entry, then we would not take the trade.

Now that we have that out of the way, I'm short from 0.7434. My stop-loss is just above the 0.618 Fibonacci level and the Wave at 0.7455. I'm going to use the psychological number's resistance since the Fibonacci and Wave are only two pips below the "50" pip level. The profit targets are out of the visual range of my chart, but my first profit target is the 1.272 Fibonacci extension, which is just 11 pips from the 0.7400 level. If and when we get below 0.7400 there is further support at the 1.618 at 0.7391 and the 1.886 at 0.7376. And don't forget, I've been keeping an eye on the daily chart of the Aussie as well—while it's still trading sideways within a triangle pattern.

The Swissy has confirmed a breakout on the 60-minute chart. (See Figure 27.3.) The Wave is sideways, and prices are coming out from the middle of the triangle pattern. Only one thing keeps me from entering right now, the 1.3000 level.

Since the trade is confirmed, I will park a buy order at 1.3005. This will present one problem, which is that if I had gotten long at the initial trend line break, I would be placing an initial profit target at 1.3010. But since I am getting long at 1.3005, it makes no sense for me to take five pips off the table. I will have to acknowledge that this level will be potential resistance but I will not park a limit order there. Instead I will use the 1.3026 level, which is the 1.000 Fibonacci; then I will look to the "50" pip level as my

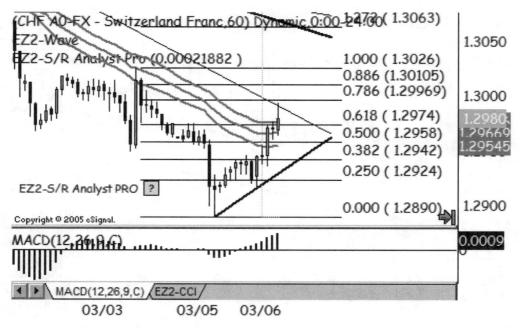

FIGURE 27.3

next target. The triangle is a tight one and of course the uptrend line is the point at which is the buy becomes invalid. That represents a large loss for a limited gain, though, so I will use the next best level, the bottom line of the Wave, which is also below the 0.500 Fibonacci, for multiple confirmation. If prices move in my direction I have now given myself a choice: keep the stop-loss at the 0.500 Fibonacci level or trail it with the Wave. By the way, and I really can't say this enough:

The process of determining your stop-loss starts with asking yourself where the trade is no longer valid.

You can adjust and make decisions from that level, like I just did. In this example you do have some other (and closer) choices—for example, the 0.618 Fibonacci level and the middle line of the Wave. It's your choice, but remember that the less wiggle room you give the trade within the range of where the trade is no longer valid, the more likely you are to get stopped out prematurely.

The next pair that I notice is the pound. I'm going with the 60-minute chart as the Wave is established at three o'clock and the MACD histogram has been negative for some time. (See Figure 27.4.)

The way the pound on the 60-minute chart climbed up did not leave any usable last major moves. Because I will need downside support levels I must find a last major move that is an uptrend. I will have to go with pivot points and psychological numbers. (See Figure 27.5.)

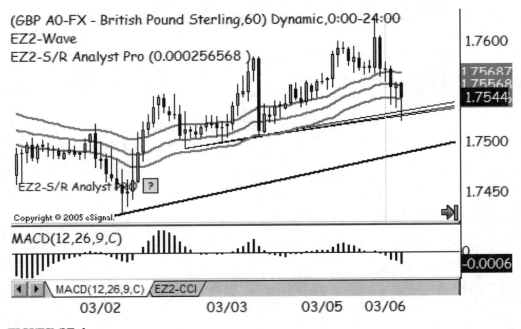

FIGURE 27.4

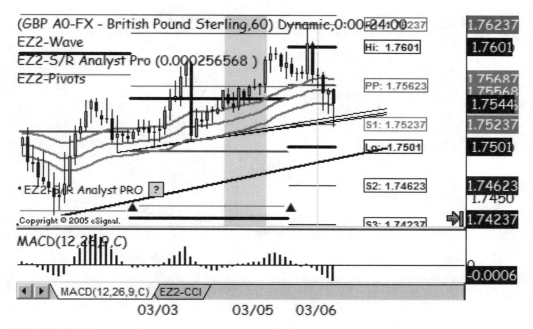

FIGURE 27.5

The setup on the pound has confirmed and pulled back—so if you want to get short on the pullback it's not an issue of an invalid second-chance entry or entering before confirmation; neither is the case here. If you want to short the pound as it comes back down through the uptrend line, that's fine, too. I'm going to get short here at 1.7544. The first profit target is the 1.7500 psychological number, which you'll notice is also the "Lo" level of the pivot point. Of course the order will be at 1.7505. *But you already knew that, didn't you?* The stop-loss level I am focusing in on is the pivot point or the top line of the Wave.

The actual pivot point, "PP," is the line in the sand according to pivot point theory. That "PP" level is where the market determines strength or weakness. Above the "PP," prices are considered strong and below they are considered weak. I'll use this to my advantage as well as the top line of the Wave at 1.7568 and place my stop 1.7570. This is a one-sided pattern as there is no downtrend line or horizontal resistance level in place to complete a symmetrical or asymmetrical triangle.

Right now I'm short the pound, waiting to go long in the Swissy, and short the Aussie. Notice that again all three setups are contingent upon a strong U.S. dollar. I haven't hedged against myself. I am typically very conscious of doing this. I want you to be aware of the U.S. dollar. This means that I pull up a chart of the U.S. Dollar Index Cash (symbol $DXC) on my eSignal (Figure 27.6). For those of you interested in trading the U.S. dollar, you can do that with the U.S. Dollar Index futures contract (Figure 27.7).

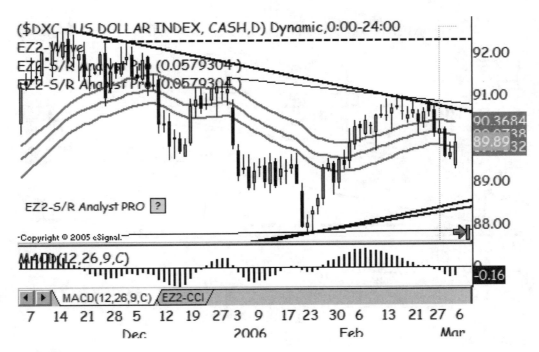

FIGURE 27.6

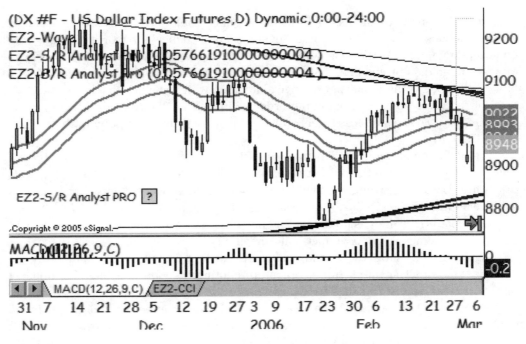

FIGURE 27.7

So you see, there is certainly a way to trade the U.S. dollar directly; it's done with the U.S. Dollar Index futures contract. *I don't want to go off on a tangent here, but the fact is that the entries and exits that have been executed and outlined in this book can be applied to forex, futures, and yes! stocks, too.*

It's not quite 10:00 A.M. and my 0.7434 short on the Aussie is following through to the downside in front of the hot zone, which further confirms my position; but it's the 10:00 A.M. candle that accelerates the drop. Right away I am hitting my initial profit target at 0.7411 at the 1.272 Fibonacci level. (See Figure 27.8.)

My order gets filled in the Swissy as I am watching the psychological number get taken out. (See Figure 27.9.)

The range on the Swissy is not so severe that I am in immediate fear of getting stopped out, but it's close. I really would have liked to have seen the 1.3000 price level become support rather than a resistance level. I've got my eye on the 0.500 Fibonacci level and the bottom line of the Wave. Again, if you are wondering why these levels are the best considerations for a stop-loss, look at the chart. It's not my decision—it's the chart telling me where support is waiting! When we initially were breaking out earlier, I made the decision to wait for the 1.3000 to be broken to the upside. That's just plain common sense and prudent. In fact, if you flip back to the 10:00 A.M. chart of the Swissy (Figure 27.3) showing our initial setup of the trade, you'll see that the breakout candle that was piercing the downtrend line had been trading through the top and middle line of the Wave as well as the 0.618 Fibonacci. This shows me (and you) that prices really didn't respect these levels as support. Does that make sense?

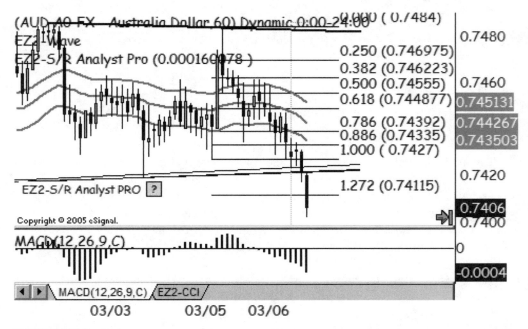

FIGURE 27.8

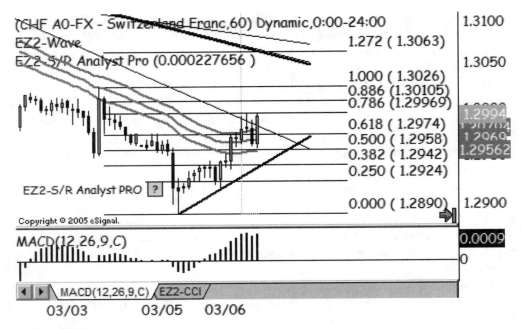

FIGURE 27.9

Here's another easy decision: If this represents too much risk for your liking or your account, don't take the trade! That's your right, and only you can make that decision. It doesn't matter what I think is a reasonable risk. It only matters what you are comfortable with.

The 10:00 A.M. candle on the pound hit the 1.7501 level with little hesitation. (See Figure 27.10.) Since I am already exiting half my position at the 1.7505 level, I am out before the psychological number support and slight bounce.

The next candle is a strange one for the Aussie and I get trailing stopped out just after prices hit the 0.7399 level and bounce. I'm out at the 1.272 Fibonacci extension of 0.7411 (my trailing stop once prices established themselves below this profit target). I wasn't planning on using 0.7405 as my second profit target since I had just peeled out at 0.7411. I was, however, hoping that prices would break the "00" pip and head down to 0.7391, which is the 1.618 Fibonacci extension. But it was not meant to be, and I am certainly not complaining.

The Swissy is still moving sideways. (See Figure 27.11.) The 10:00 A.M. hot zone seems to have s-l-o-w-l-y pushed prices up to the 1.3010 level, which is now resistance as I (and Fibonacci!) expected. Boredom is no reason to exit a trade, so I will watch it. My stop is in place as is my profit target so there is no need to get restless here.

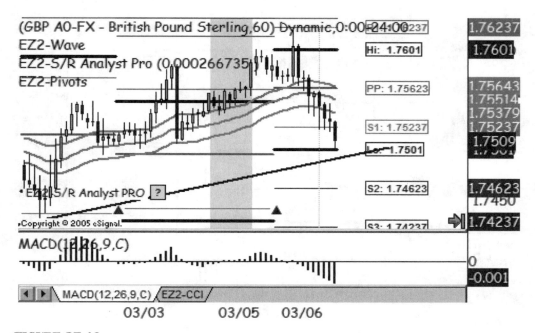

FIGURE 27.10

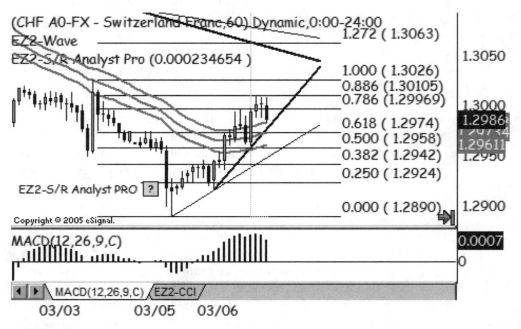

FIGURE 27.11

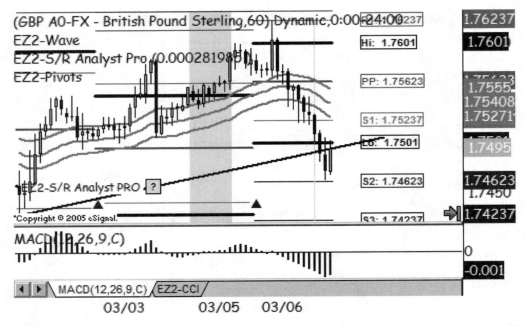

FIGURE 27.12

The pound, however, did bounce and I am trailing stopped out as prices bounced back above 1.7500. Prices never did get to the "S2" level, but in fact fell just short of it with a low of 1.7464. Two lousy pips, *but that's just the way it goes sometimes.* (See Figure 27.12.)

Now all my attention is on my only open position, the Swissy. (See Figure 27.13.)

Let's finish this morning with two charts: The daily chart of the GBP/USD (Figure 27.14) is looking promising because with the continued weakness in this pair, there's a potential breakdown from a triangle pattern that has been forming for some time now with a nice flat Wave. At this moment, the MACD histogram is not cooperating, though, so I cannot place a proactive order and will have to watch this one. This is a two-sided pattern, so even though the pound is weak, there's certainly a chance that it could break to the upside as well.

The 60-minute chart of the euro (Figure 27.15) is breaking down and it's well after 11:00 A.M., which means London is closing and I'm just over a half hour from closing things down here in my office. Remember, after lunchtime the Europe/U.S. overlap narrows down to U.S. participation. But the setup is pretty good here on this chart: three o'clock Wave, really negative MACD histogram, and multiple uptrend line breakdown, and it's all occurring just below the 1.2000 level. If this was happening at 2:00 P.M. it would be iffy for me, but since it's about 11:25 A.M. I give this one a green light. Now remember, this is also in line with my earlier trades this morning. This move, too, relies on U.S. dollar strength just as my current open position in the Swissy does, so I'm not

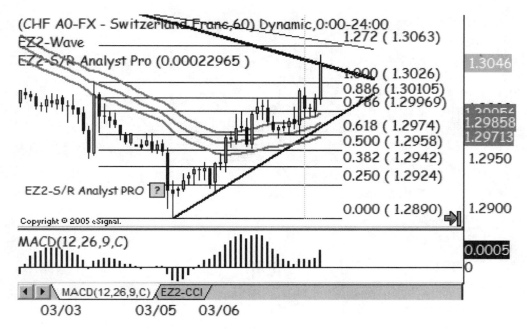

FIGURE 27.13

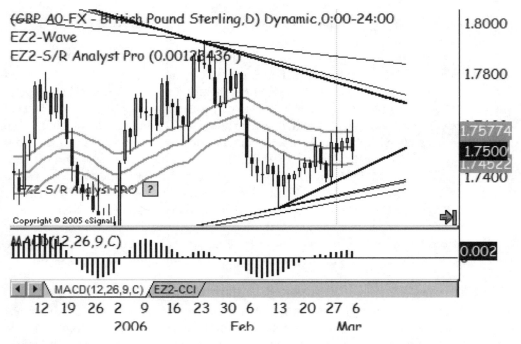

FIGURE 27.14

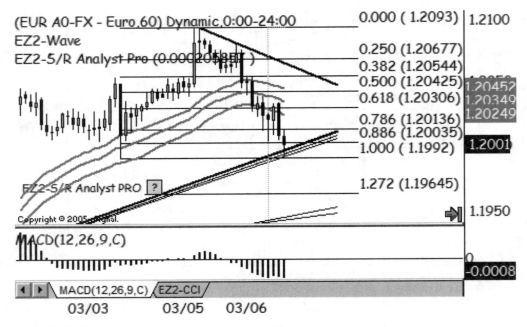

FIGURE 27.15

hedging myself in any way with this euro short. In fact, I'm pretty sure that this move may be exactly what my Swissy long needs.

The entry short just happens to also be as prices are hitting the 1.000 Fibonacci level; my fill is 1.1994. I suppose I could have waited for this level to break and perhaps even should have—but with the 1.2000 level overhead I feel certain that this break below the "00" pip level will keep prices heading downward, *just maybe not as swiftly as I would like!* The breakdown candle high is also at the 0.786 Fibonacci level, but that's a pretty tight resistance level and too close to current prices. The trade is technically valid until the downtrend line is broken to the upside, but that's way up at 1.2055 and I am not going to give this entry that much room. It's a 60-minute chart and this entry is close to my closing time so I don't see any need to give it much more wiggle room than the top line of the Wave and the 0.500 Fibonacci level. It's a good compromise as well as multiple confirmation of resistance just above the 1.2040 price level. I could also use the middle line of the Wave, but it's not as solid a level as the 0.500 Fibonacci/top Wave line combo. Besides, I will chase prices down with a tighter stop if and when prices do continue lower.

As the day progresses both the Swissy and now the euro are just meandering around, not hitting their respective stop-loss levels nor their profit targets: *boring but definitely still confirmed trades.* My profit target in the euro is the 1.272 Fibonacci level at 1.1964. I OCO my stop and profit targets in the euro and call it a day. I'll keep an eye on these as I come in and out of my office but with my OCOs in place. I am not going to worry. Whether I am staring at the Swissy and euro or not they're just going to do their thing. Besides, what is it that they say about waiting for a pot of water to boil?

If you want to know just how important conditional orders are to me, then think about this: Not until after 11:00 P.M. EST does the Swissy finally take out 1.3026 and the euro slices through 1.1964. Prices stayed well above the bottom line of the Wave and the 0.500 Fibonacci level on the Swissy. And while the euro did trade as high as 1.2025 it was well below the middle and top lines of the Wave.

How do I love thee, my OCOs, if/thens, and if/then OCOs? Let me count the ways! I truly would not even dream of trading forex without these order types. **Good night!**

Tuesday, March 7th

Other than the Non-Farm Productivity revision this morning, we're looking at a light day of hot zones. No problem. We'll get to focus on strictly price action—and that suits me just fine.

For no other reason than for a change of pace, I will start with the kiwi today. Let me mention that the kiwi broke down yesterday—early. *Too early for me.* These are both charts from Monday at about 4:00 A.M. This way as you look at Tuesday's action in the kiwi you can see what we are dealing with.

The view of the 60-minute chart in Figure 28.1 is the 4:00 A.M. breakdown, which if you were up was nice. With a proactive order you certainly could have parked a sell stop. The breakdown happened quickly and I believe a proactive order would have been your best, if not your only, choice. But take a look at the 240-minute chart in Figure 28.2.

The 240 shows a breakdown that was subtle enough to register a break and allow a manual order entry. This was a midnight candle, however, and it's a four-hour chart. Certainly with the MACD histogram in place, a proactive order would have been a good choice here as well. So let's see where the kiwi is *this* morning. (See Figure 28.3.)

It's long gone. As we move on to the yen I do want to mention something. Depending upon the time zone you live in, or if you are a night owl, you can focus on certain pairs. Remember that pairs like the kiwi, Aussie, and yen are perfectly suited for evening to early morning trading, specifically 7:00 P.M. to 4:00 A.M. EST. Always ask yourself "who's awake?"

The yen is still flying from earlier this week. Remember what prices were doing on the 5th and then Monday, the 6th? (See Figure 28.4.)

The only thing we can do here is watch and wait for a pullback since the Wave is climbing up at between twelve and two o'clock. If there is going to be an opportunity for a pullback or even a leveling out of the Wave, I'll be keeping an eye on the 30- and 60-minute charts.

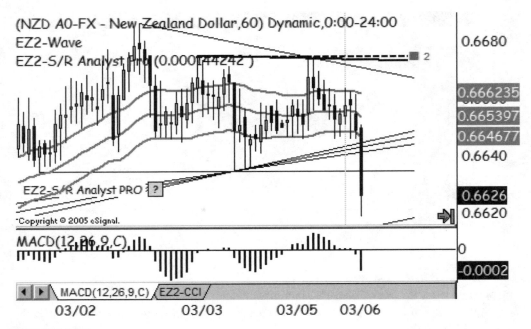

FIGURE 28.1

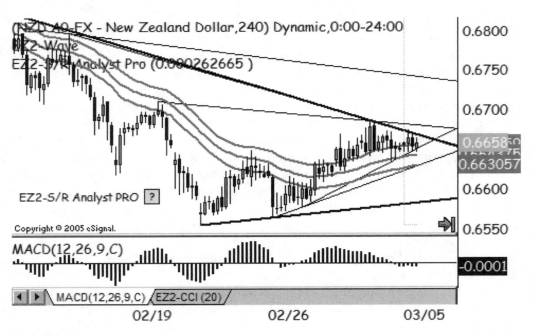

FIGURE 28.2

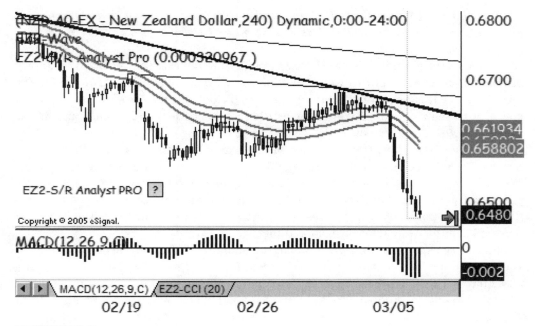

FIGURE 28.3

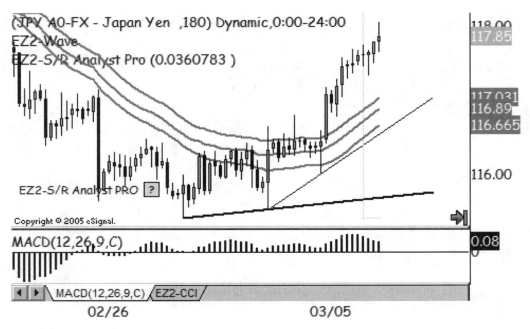

FIGURE 28.4

By the way, I have time today since we're not counting down to a hot zone this morning, and I think that it's just as important to discuss charts that are not on my radar and the reasons why.

Intraday, the pound is also following through from the prior day's sell-off and really has shown no intention of slowing down or bouncing just yet. (See Figure 28.5.) The Wave is firmly traveling at between four and six o'clock and we have to just be patient and wait to see if a bounce will occur or whether prices will find a range and let the Wave settle to a three o'clock angle.

The end-of-day chart is almost enough to make me want to push the "Sell" button. *Almost.* Prices have broken down through the support we were monitoring, but with no MACD histogram confirmation. (See Figure 28.6.) I have to tell you that this does happen from time to time but I will not hold a grudge nor will I break this momentum confirmation rule. For as often as it saves me from a bad entry, I will forgive it the few, scant times it keeps me from entering a good trade.

Since prices have settled (for now) at the support of a lower uptrend line and the Wave is still moving sideways at three o'clock, I can still look for a shorting opportunity. I have to keep in mind, however, this is not the first sign of weakness and if prices are going to continue downward I still need a good push down. It's not going to be as great a short as what could have been—but I will eagerly wait for a chance to short this chart all the same. And after such a large sell-off today (the high of the range is 1.7509

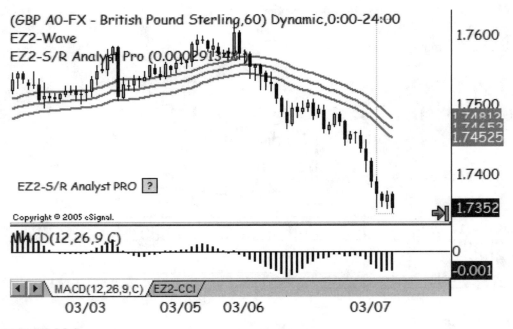

FIGURE 28.5

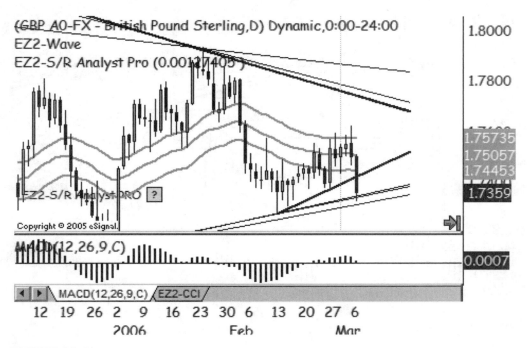

FIGURE 28.6

and the low is 1.7330) I would not be surprised to see that market bounce a little on some profit taking. So I will wait for the MACD histogram to confirm. In the meanwhile, Figure 28.7 shows the chart setup with Fibonacci levels. If we do get a confirmed break there are two levels that will be support as prices head down. First we'll have to deal with the 1.7300 (major psychological) level and then the 1.618 Fibonacci level at 1.7281, which is just one pip above the minor "80" pip psychological level. There's good near-term resistance at the 1.272 Fibonacci level and also the bottom line of the Wave, but the middle line of the Wave would probably offer the *best combination* of resistance as well as sufficient wiggle room because it is the high of the breakdown candle we have today.

So far we have looked at charts that are not confirming much today, but we've also been able to establish some setups that we could see bear fruit in the near future. It's easy to forget about these setups, especially when it could be many hours or even days before we see a confirmed entry. So I use sticky notes to remind me or, if you use a daily planner (I do!), then just jot the setups on your planner pages and keep carrying them over until they confirm or until the setups are no longer valid.

You already know how the euro and Swissy waited until almost midnight when they hit my initial profit targets. Let's see where they are this morning.

The euro has found support for now at the 1.886 Fibonacci level, which for

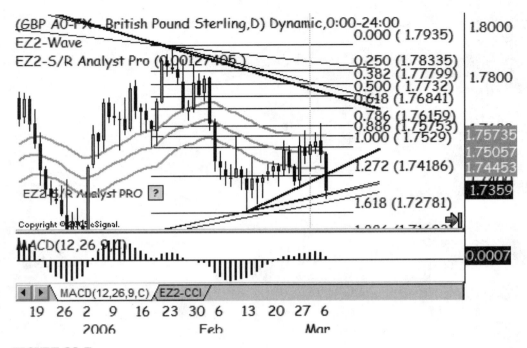

FIGURE 28.7

anyone who had stayed short in the position from yesterday past the 1.618 Fibonacci profit target (I did not) would be another profit target as the short followed through. (See Figure 28.8.)

At this point all I can do is wait and see if prices correct into the Wave—and that's only valid as long as the Wave heads down at four to six o'clock.

As I continue my now seemingly futile exercise of finding a setup to trade this morning, I see from the chart in Figure 28.9 that the Swissy is trading higher from the earlier breakout and the wait-and-see game will continue, as I want either a correction or a leveling out of the Wave to establish a new trading setup. I'm patient. Prices are trading at the 1.618 Fibonacci level, which would be the next profit target above my initial profit target of the 1.272 Fibonacci level if I were still in the market. That brings me to a thought I don't believe we have discussed yet these past 20-something days.

I hope you'll notice that even as laid-back as I am taking our walk through the charts this morning, I'm not focusing on the fact there's nothing to trade and I'm not upset because I exited certain trades that continued in my direction. Some traders might chase entries or beat themselves up for getting out too soon. I'm not worried about any of that. I'm just taking the market's pulse. I'm not going to force anything, and I'm not looking for a reason to trade. On days like this, there's no reason that I can't look to the E-mini S&P 500 at 9:30 A.M. EST or even end-of-day charts of commodity futures and

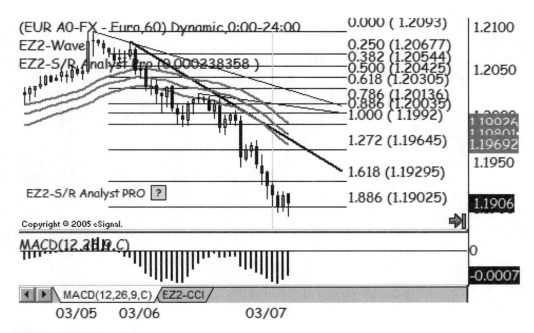

FIGURE 28.8

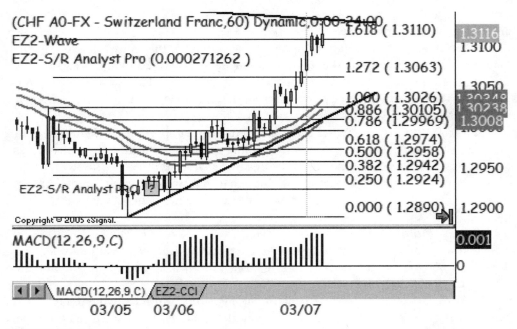

FIGURE 28.9

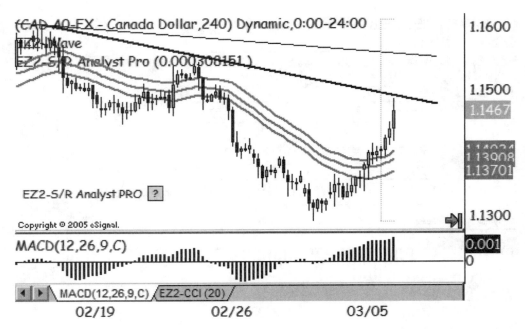

FIGURE 28.10

stocks. There's always something else I can look at, and this is exactly why traders should not limit themselves to one market. Once you know how to read charts, any liquid market is your playground!

Let's see what the Canadian dollar and Aussie are up to this morning. The Canadian dollar had been selling off on the daily chart since the 24th of February. Prices recently leveled off at the 1.1300 level and rallied. (See Figure 28.10.) There was no setup for a buy on the daily, but the intraday charts are all in rally mode as well so it's a matter of a pullback or a Wave that levels out to set up an entry.

After 6:00 A.M. EST the Aussie broke down through support on the 60-minute chart. (See Figure 28.11.) The Wave was already heading down at a four to six o'clock angle, so on this chart I'm actually looking for a bounce to get short; thus there's no trade here.

But the daily chart has broken down through 0.7367, which is the uptrend of a large triangle pattern. (See Figure 28.12.) A three o'clock Wave has been in place for about six to seven candles.

Nice, eh? But did I mention any confirmation? Take a look! The MACD histogram is above the zero line. The breakdown is not confirmed! I *never* break this rule. And I know it's said "you should never say never." But I mean it: I *never* trade a momentum break without MACD histogram confirmation.

All six majors plus the New Zealand dollar: no setups. No tragedy here. I'll keep an eye on that pound, though. It's early and I think the weather is just about right to grab a book and head over to the beach. That's a wrap!

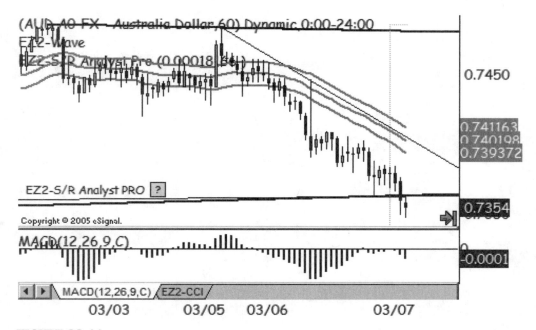

FIGURE 28.11

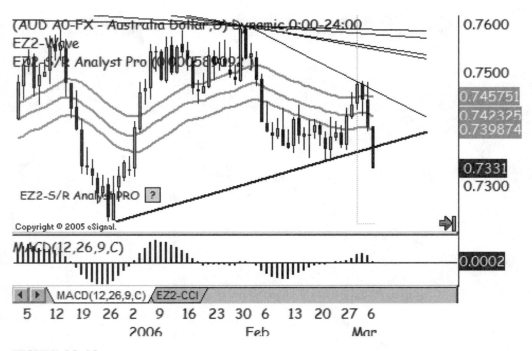

FIGURE 28.12

Wednesday, March 8th

I slept in too late this morning. Late even for me. I've been particularly exhausted these past few days. I'm starting to work off all the "creative pounds" of writing two books almost back to back. It's amazing, but I have discovered that sitting behind a laptop typing furiously does not burn too many calories! I've gotten back into the gym and have been training like a machine. Side effects: soreness, cravings for Myoplex, and sleeping for 10 hours. Moderation has never been my strong suit. I'm almost unreasonable in my expectations. I've always thought of trading as an extreme sport. And if you've done it for any length of time, you know it's true.

Since I'm counting down to the Crude Inventories release at 10:30 A.M. EST, that makes me think of the Canadian dollar. So let's check what it is up to on the 30- and 60-minute charts. Since I have slept the morning away, I'm not going to be surprised if I have missed some intraday opportunities. Scrolling back on my charts I can see that the Canadian dollar had a confirmed break to the upside earlier this morning, about 5:00 A.M. EST. (See Figure 29.1.) The triangle pattern had two downtrend lines. The lower of the two broke at 4:00 A.M. but did not have MACD histogram confirmation.

Remember that this break to the upside precedes the Crude Inventories number by more than five hours. The Crude Inventories number effect is basically because the Canadian dollar is what is called a commodity currency. Canada is the ninth largest exporter of crude oil, so this number affects the Canadian economy and thus the Canadian dollar. But beyond all that, it's really no more than a hot zone that is especially targeted to the Canadian dollar. A commodity currency is a currency of a country whose economy is strongly correlated with the price fluctuations of a specific commodity, like crude oil in this example. In my experience this type of relationship is limited mainly to the Canadian dollar, the Aussie, and the kiwi among the major pairs. The Aussie and kiwi are strongly correlated to precious metals, gold in particular.

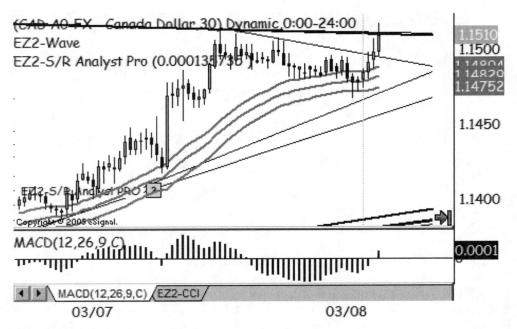

FIGURE 29.1

So let's see what else is on my radar. It's almost 7:00 A.M. The euro is moving sideways but there's no clear setup in any of my intraday charts. Looking at the daily chart (Figure 29.2), I can see the larger triangle that prices are moving within. This may take time, but I will be patient and watch this chart. Right now notice that the MACD histogram is positive. If I wanted to, this would allow me to place a proactive buy stop. But prices are far from a break so I'm not going to get ahead of myself. I do, however, want *you* to start thinking about proactive order placement. And you can do this with a simple limit order for entry or you can get more sophisticated and use an if/then OCO conditional order and put the whole trade on autopilot.

Let's take a look at the Swissy. (See Figure 29.3.) I like to check on the euro and the Swissy one after the other because of their strong and opposite correlation with regard to the U.S. dollar. Strength in one means almost immediate weakness in the other. The Swissy is also trading within a large triangle, and whichever way the euro breaks, the Swissy will move in the opposite direction.

I seem to be on a roll with the daily chart setups—the yen also is setting up nicely within a triangle pattern. I have to tell you that when I see patterns like these with their flat three o'clock Waves they have my attention. Daily charts, above all the other time frames, are the most relevant.

Intraday many of the pairs are trading within narrow triangles, but it's the end-of-day charts that look, by far, the best. It has been another flat and inactive day. It's certainly

FIGURE 29.2

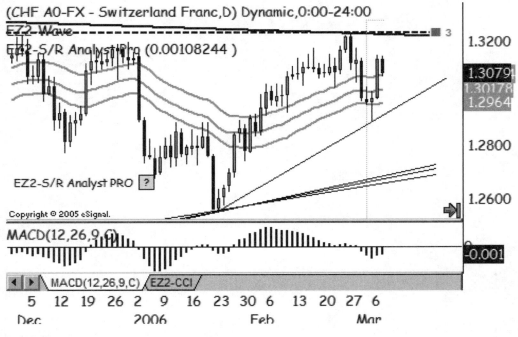

FIGURE 29.3

not that I am trying to make a point, but since the market has given me the opportunity to do so—don't feel like you have to trade every day. If setups are not there, move on. With Initial Claims and Trade Balance tomorrow at 8:30 A.M. EST we should see many of these consolidations break.

Well, it's time to hit the gym. I've been heading over there after the morning's trading for about 90 minutes of exercise. I've found it's a great way to get out of the office after noon.

Thursday, March 9th

There are major hot zones coming today. I didn't want to get to the party late so I'm up early—*early for me, anyway.* It's 4:17 A.M. and I'm trying to get as much Earl Grey tea into my system as possible. Maybe I'm overcompensating for my late arrival to my office yesterday. Let's see what's on my radar this morning. I'm counting down to the 8:30 A.M. hot zone.

I'm starting with the EUR/USD this morning. The 30-minute has leveled out in front of a hot zone—that's a nice plus. (See Figure 30.1.)

Here's what I *don't* like about the setup, though. The Wave is traveling sideways, but it's doing so in a bumpy way. See how it's not flat and smooth. It's trying but it's not there yet. I want to point this out because when it comes to 30- and also 60-minute charts I'm fairly rigid about this point. I'll cut the longer-term charts like the 240 and daily some slack on this but not the 30 and 60. *There are just far too many setups on short-term intraday charts, so I choose to cherry-pick! And whether you want to call this selectivity cherry-picking or sniper trading, the point is that you are looking for the best setup and the best opportunity.*

Since we know the Wave is trying to level out, we can look to the 60-minute chart. That's why we track five time frames. Each is relevant in its own right and each has nuances that may make it a better chart to trade off of. The 60-minute gives me a much cleaner setup and a flatter Wave. (See Figure 30.2.)

The MACD histogram is flat now but it's not yet 5:00 A.M. and I'll keep an eye on this chart to see if it breaks. I am not likely to take a break*down*, though, because the breakdown level is so close to 1.1900, which could leave prices with very little room to run. But I will make the final decision when I see the actual price and direction of the break.

Let's move on to the Swissy. Since I already know that the 60-minute EUR/USD is moving sideways, it's no surprise that the USD/CHF is doing the same thing. Of course,

219

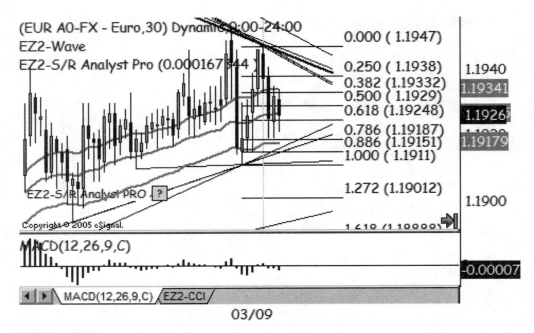

FIGURE 30.1

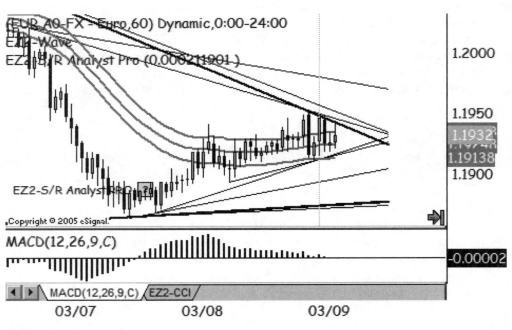

FIGURE 30.2

this does not preclude me from looking at the other four time frames, which I do and it's the 60-minute that has the best setup. (See Figure 30.3.)

Did you notice that the 2:00 A.M. and 3:00 A.M. candles both broke the support of the uptrend line? They did so without MACD histogram confirmation, though, so they are not valid entries.

You've probably noticed that on hot zone days I will usually focus on 30- and 60-minute charts. It's not that the 180 and 240 are not considered, however, because of the volatility of hot zones; it seems that my shorter-time-frame charts just position themselves better in front of reports. They also allow me to take advantage of the shorter-term profit targets they offer, which again is better suited to pre–hot zone trades.

The GBP/USD is actually triggering a buy four hours in front of the hot zone. As a rule, unless there's enough room for prices to run a bit before hitting significant support or resistance, it makes no sense to enter the trade. The pound is setting up within about 20 pips of the 1.7400 level, which is resistance. The breakout level is just below 1.7380, which doesn't leave much room for prices to run before hitting the 1.7395 level, where we would have to take initial profits off the table. It's up to you, but I don't see why I should take this trade—not only because of the limited upside but also because the pound trade will be very similar to the potential euro trade, so I'm not going to miss the move in the U.S. dollar if it happens.

That doesn't mean that the pound has nothing to offer this morning. In fact, it is setting up a potential swing short entry. This potential entry is setting up on the longest-term intraday chart, the 240. (See Figure 30.4.)

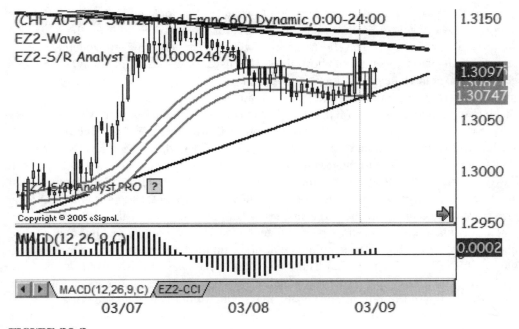

FIGURE 30.3

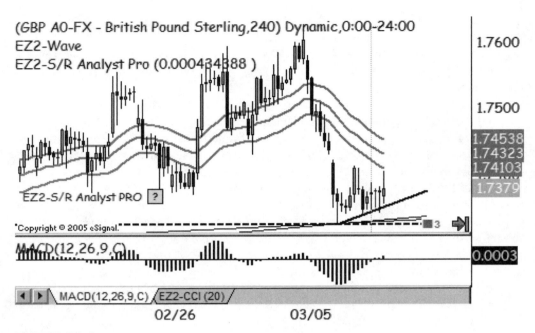

FIGURE 30.4

The Wave is heading down at between four and six o'clock, and while the sideways action of the prior dozen candles has taken some of the sharp angle from the Wave, it's still within a swing setup. The short currently will be triggered at 1.7410, which is a problem as I won't short this market above the 1.7400 psychological number. Maybe as prices continue this will change. If it does not, here's how I will play it: Once the trigger price is hit, whatever the bottom line of the Wave is reading at the time, I will then wait for prices to dip back from below the 1.7400 level, 1.7395 to be exact, and it's at that price I will enter the short. So prices must hit the Wave and then I will wait to enter if prices reach 1.7395. This will allow me to wait and see if a swing trade is triggered, and then I can wait for the 1.7400 level to be broken to the downside before I get short. The middle or top line of the Wave will be the stop-loss, and the initial profit target will be the horizontal support level at 1.7326. By the way, you've surely noticed by now that horizontal support and resistance levels are not common in the forex market. I am particular about the variance I allow when drawing a horizontal support or resistance level. By variance I mean the difference in pips between the hits or touch points that make up the level. In this example, the three hits are 1.7326, 1.7327, and 1.7326. That's a one-pip variance, which makes for a solid support level. The greater the variance, the softer the support or resistance level. I will typically use a three-to-five-pip variance as the maximum for horizontal levels.

I'm still well ahead of the hot zone and have three potential entries. If the trade is confirmed I will be sure to enter proactive trades, especially in examples like the swing entry on the pound. I will have to revisit these charts to make sure the trade setup is still valid and the trigger price is up-to-date.

The USD/JPY has already confirmed a short on its 60-minute chart and I am not going to chase this trade, but let me share the view regardless because it was a good setup. (See Figure 30.5.)

The stop-loss will require some significant wiggle room because of the volatility of the breakdown. The breakdown high is 117.88 and near the top line of the Wave. Notice that this is also a one-sided pattern because there is no downtrend line. The 0.500 Fibonacci level is just above the top line of the Wave and will offer enough wiggle room; it also is nine pips from the 118.00 psychological level. The two initial profit targets are the 1.272 and 1.618 Fibonacci levels. Let me mention a few things about the last major move I used here. It is certainly the last, and there's no doubt that the move was major. However, it's right on the edge of consisting of enough candles to merit a move that I would draw a Fibonacci series from. It is a total of three candles, which is the minimum. So it is valid, but I just want to be sure that we have the minimum criterion understood because this move is right at that minimum number of candles.

Both the 30- and 60-minute charts of the Canadian dollar are traveling sideways with three o'clock Waves. However, it's the 60-minute chart that is setting up a short and actually has confirmed through three uptrend lines and with MACD histogram confirmation. (See Figure 30.6.) The 1.1535 breakdown price does allow for potentially 30 pips of room to run until the 1.1500 level. The Wave has not been at a three o'clock angle for

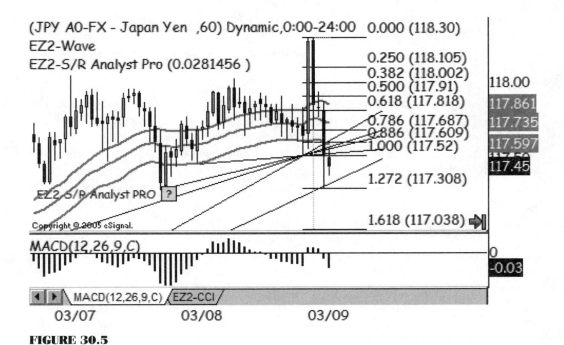

FIGURE 30.5

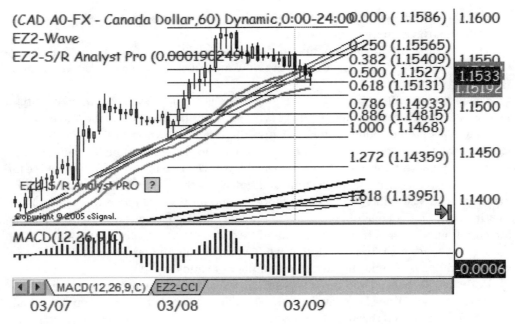

FIGURE 30.6

much more than four candles. You could say that this Wave is in the last stages of transition so this entry is aggressive. The other aspect of this trade is that I'm not quite sure where the U.S. dollar is heading. I'm looking at sideways markets in the euro and Swissy so there's no insight coming from those highly correlated U.S. dollar pairs quite yet.

This is also a one-sided pattern, so I will look to near-term resistance and also the 0.250 Fibonacci level as stop-loss choices. I think I will go with the 1.1556 Fibonacci 0.250 level as it will allow me to position myself above the near-term highs and the 1.1550 psychological number. It's not a great deal of risk, either, at about 20 pips. I'm going to look to the 1.1505 level as my profit target. We're looking at about a 1:1 risk-to-reward ratio. I haven't spent a lot of time on this facet of the setup. Although we have discussed the fact that if a trade represents too much risk for you or your account you should not take the trade, I haven't discussed what a good balance is. I will often take 1:1 or even 1:1$\frac{1}{2}$ risk-to-reward ratios. You may read that you should focus on 1:2 and 1:3 or even 1:4 risk-to-reward ratios, but I have to tell you, those ratios are rarely found when you use the charts to determine stop-loss and profit targets. Most of those high ratios are based on fixed pip and percentage setups, and for that matter this type of approach could allow you to manufacture any risk-to-reward ratio you'd like!

The AUD/USD took off earlier during the Asian session (which centers on Tokyo), and currently there's not a setup that will allow me to hop on. The 30- and 60-minute charts are already moving higher above breakout levels. The 180 and 240 aren't really setting up anything according to the action. In fact, the move higher seems to be slowing the downtrend the Aussie had been in and is leveling out the Wave. If you recall, we also have a daily chart breakdown of the Aussie that was not confirmed by the MACD histogram, and right about now that's looking like a great nontrade!

As we approach the hot zone, I'm short the 60-minute Canadian dollar, I'm waiting on a bounce to get short the 240-minute pound, and I'm watching for a break on the 60-minute euro and Swissy.

During the 7:00 A.M. candle the euro makes its subtle move to the downside by trading through the two minor uptrend lines. The MACD histogram went negative during the previous candle, so the trade is a confirmed short. (See Figure 30.7.)

Notice that I used pivot points here, as I don't feel there is a clean "last major move" from which I can draw a Fibonacci series. The breakdown is also confirming through the pivot point (PP), which is great secondary confirmation. The first support level to the downside is 1.1900, which means that the 1.1905 level would be the first profit target. If you recall, I had already made my mind up concerning the short side of this setup: It was not one I was likely to take because of the limited profit potential. It's a valid setup but one I am choosing to pass up. Besides, don't forget I have the Swissy that I am watching as well, and with some weakness in the euro I should be seeing some strength in the Swissy.

The reaction came some 15 minutes or so later as the Swissy broke the resistance of multiple downtrend lines after 7:30 A.M. with MACD histogram confirmation. (See Figure 30.8.) The break also occurred above the 1.3100 psychological level, which alone

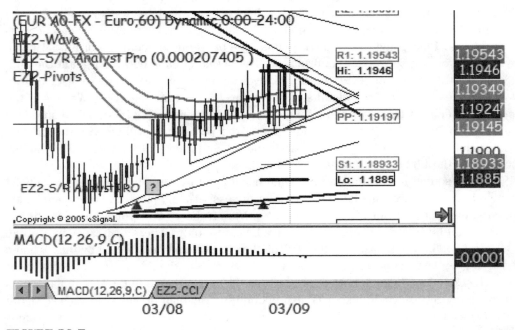

FIGURE 30.7

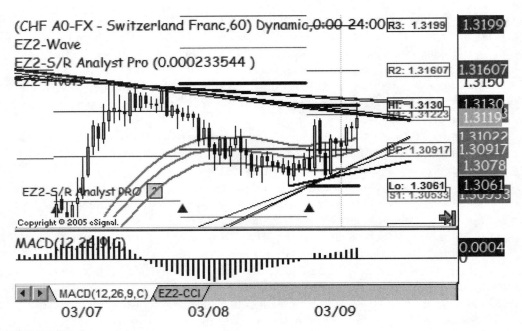

FIGURE 30.8

makes this trade a better entry than the one I passed up in the euro. Also consider that both trades relied on strength in the U.S. dollar.

Just like on the euro, I couldn't find a valid last major move to draw a Fibonacci series from so I am going to use pivot points. The breakout is occurring at the R1 level, which is excellent secondary confirmation. The breakout candle low is right at the middle line of the Wave and below the 1.3100 level, so one choice would be to place a stop-loss five pips below the middle line of the Wave. The bottom line of the Wave is at the point at which the trade would no longer be valid and this would be the ideal stop-loss price. It's only 13 pips from the middle line of the Wave and I will go with this choice. The initial profit target is 1.3160, which is the R2, and then I'll look to 1.3195, which is just below the 1.3200 "00" pip level and the R3.

Here's something to think about when using pivot points: They're good for only 24 hours. Since they are calculated upon the prior session's high, low, and close, each new session brings new levels. *So we're on a deadline.* If these pivot point–based profit targets are not hit before the next session, we have to look to where resistance is waiting. But the 1.3195 level is based on the "00" pip level and won't be affected by this. We just have to keep an eye on the initial profit target, which is at the R2.

The Canadian dollar is not cooperating, as the very strength in the U.S. dollar that is carrying my Swissy trade higher is also taking the Canadian dollar with it. (See Figure 30.9.) Since I had entered the USD/CAD much earlier than the USD/CHF, these two trades are hedging one another. I don't like that and since the U.S. dollar looks to be gaining

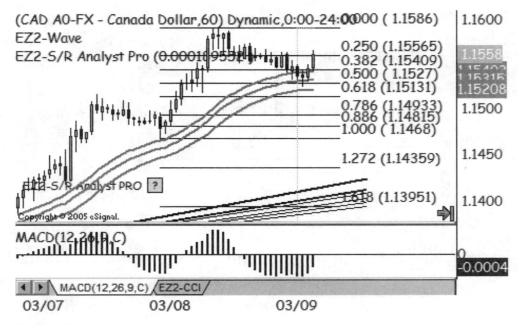

FIGURE 30.9

some strength I am not only hitting my stop-loss on the Canadian dollar at 1.1556, but I see that the 30-minute Canadian dollar is setting up a confirmed trade. (See Figure 30.10.)

Here's where you have to trust your charts and set your setups. One chart of the very same pair is stopping me out for a loss and I'm looking to jump into the same pair . . . but on another time frame. This is not something that is going to necessarily feel good or natural until you have proved these setups to yourself. And frankly, it's just going to take time and experience as you learn to recognize, react, and repeat.

The setup on the 30-minute is triggered at the same time I am being stopped out of the 60-minute. The Wave is flat and prices are taking out what looks like three downtrend lines as well as the 1.1550 "50" pip level as well as the 0.500 Fibonacci level, which makes for great multiple confirmation of this entry long.

This entry is still over an hour in front of the hot zone. My stop-loss is going to be best placed at either the 0.786 Fibonacci or the bottom line of the Wave. I am not going to hold on to this entry long all the way down to the 1.000 level and the uptrend line. While that does represent the point at which the trade will no longer be valid, I will cheat up from there because that just represents more risk than I want to take on. The first two profit targets will be the 0.250 Fibonacci level (notice that the 0.382 is within the 10-to-12-pip cushion) and then the 0.000 level at 1.1586.

As the hot zone becomes imminent, the prices begin the typical prerelease fluctuations. The pound hits the bottom line of the Wave just in front of the reports. (See

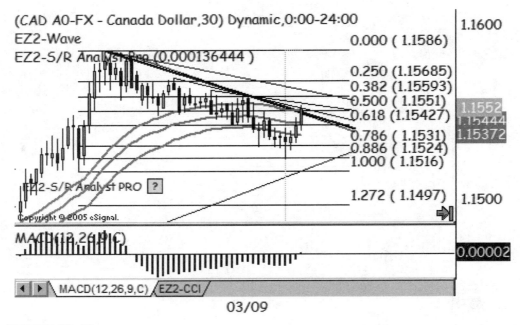

FIGURE 30.10

Figure 30.11.) However, this is not my execution level. Remember that I am waiting for prices to (1) touch the bottom line of the Wave and then (2) drop back down below the "00" pip level. As soon as we hit 1.7410 (the high of the candle was 1.7412) I place a sell stop order at 1.7395. I used a stop order because I do not want to get filled unless 1.7395 trades. If I were to use a limit order here then I would get filled immediately because the order assumes I will take price improvement. That is not what I want here.

Prices head lower and my 1.7395 stop order gets hit. Do you know the best thing about swing trading with the Wave? Deciding on your stop is as easy as choosing which Wave to use. Either will work for this trade; it's a matter of how much wiggle room you want to allow in the trade. Of course, the point at which this trade is no longer valid is above the top line of the Wave. The initial profit target is the horizontal support level at 1.7326.

It's 8:30 A.M. EST and the hot zone does not fail to inject some excitement! The Canadian dollar slices up through 1.1586 with very little problem. (See Figure 30.12.) The high of the candle is 1.1597, just short of the "00" pip level. I trail my stop up to protect profits to the 1.1586 level. Beyond the "00" I will use psychological levels, and the minor "20" will be my next target. If prices can get established above the "00" I will trail my stop up to 1.1597.

The Swissy traded as high as 1.3132 and is starting to pull back. It's nowhere near the 1.3160 that is my initial profit target. Since the volatility of the hot zone is fading, it'll

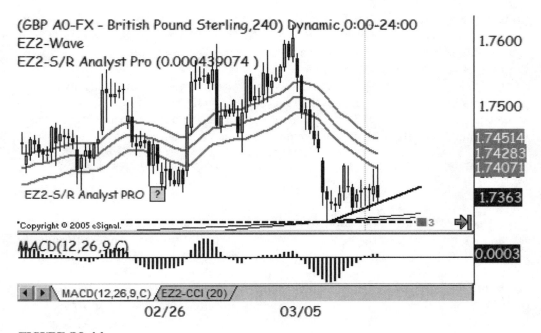

FIGURE 30.11

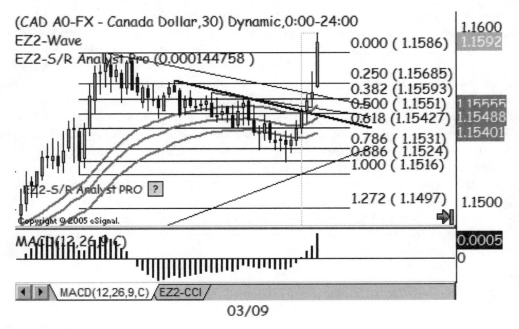

FIGURE 30.12

probably take some time for the market to find a reason to move. My stop-loss is in place, as is my limit order for my profit target. Now I just have to sit back and wait. The same goes for the pound. I'll have to revisit the chart every four hours to stay on top of the stop-loss since I am using the Wave.

I don't know about you, but I'm exhausted. This was an active morning. My contingent orders are in place so I am covered regardless of whether prices move in my favor or they don't. There's no need to be chained to your desk and held hostage by the market. That makes me think about the two most common questions I get:

1. Raghee, don't you have to get up at two o'clock in the morning to trade?
2. Raghee, do you sit in front of your computer all day?

These are certainly valid concerns from people who are learning to be successful traders. It's interesting, though. Most people sit in front of their computers for a large percentage of the day regardless of their job, yet somehow they think this is an unreasonable burden when trading. Let me say that if you've read this far you absolutely know that I treasure and enjoy sleeping. I rarely am in my office before 5:00 A.M. and it's pretty common that I am gearing up to trade sometime around 6:30 A.M. to 7:00 A.M. There's absolutely no need to get up at 2:00 A.M. If you can and do, fantastic—you are going to increase the number of setups you see because in effect you are increasing your trading day and including London.

The second question is particularly amusing because trading is a career and thus a job. If you have to be present to make money, you have a job. Trades won't make themselves, and your money gets put to work only when you make it do so. I don't mind having a job and I know that means that I will have to put in the hours in my office. Some people think that trading is an easy way to make a lot of money. That couldn't be further from the truth. But I am not by any means staring at my PC all day. I want to be at my desk during the good market overlap between London and New York, and once London closes, I want to end my day. If I have positions, conditional orders take care of the execution so I don't have to be at my desk all day. For almost every day over the past month, I haven't traded past noon—on a few occasions I have managed a position in the evening or looked at the Sydney, Tokyo, Hong Kong/Singapore overlap. It's the best overlap for evening setups and to get a pulse of a fresh trading day.

So there you go. These are the real-world examples of what you can do with practice and some experience. This isn't easy and I don't want it to look like I'm making it seem effortless. Where I am now is certainly after years and years of long days and weekends studying. *But then again, I didn't have someone to teach me and share their experiences with me . . . for, say, 30 days.*

A Follow-Up and the Wave/CCI Setup

We've made it through a month of trading together! I wanted to share all my setups with trades in my first book and show how I use them in this one. It's obvious to you by now that my main source of setups is momentum trades. This is not to say that I do not like swing trading. However, my definition of swing trading involves first recognizing a trend (using the Wave) and then waiting for a correction within the trend that will allow me to enter. It's my definition of a correction that prohibits my entering swings more often. This is a point that I want to make clear because if *you* are personally comfortable with shallower retracements—unlike my preference for the typically larger correction to the Wave—then you will certainly have more chances to enter on a pullback or bounce.

Remember that a swing trade is valid as long as it is trading below a four to six o'clock Wave (downtrend) or above a twelve to two o'clock Wave (uptrend). This means that if you enter swings on a shallow correction, your stop is still the line of the Wave that is opposite to the trend (i.e., the top line of the Wave in a downtrend or the bottom line of the Wave in an uptrend). Let me add, though, that momentum trading will get you in on the ground floor of a potential trend. Again, think back to the four market cycles.

By the way, if you are wondering what I use to confirm swing trades (like the way I confirm momentum trades with the MACD histogram), the only confirmation necessary is that the Wave is heading in the correct clock angle at the time of the entry and that prices touch whatever correction price you are waiting for, whether that be a Wave line, a Fibonacci level, or a pivot level.

Notice that all the lines and levels have one thing in common: They are all different ways of identifying support and resistance. Be sure to park a limit order at these levels! It will allow you to have an order that will execute as soon as prices trade into your swing entry target. It is just as easy to park a proactive order when swing trading as it is when you are momentum trading; part of the trade setup is identifying exactly what price defines a pullback or bounce, and that (as long as the Wave is still traveling at a swing trading clock angle) is your limit order price.

Another setup that I did not employ throughout this book, because I frankly do not use it often, is the Wave/CCI entry. Like all my other trading types, the market environment and the way I enter the trade are what differentiate one type from another. The Wave/CCI is no exception. This style fills a very particular niche. However, it seems that I did not make this clear when I first introduced this entry in one tiny chapter of my first book, *Forex Trading for Maximum Profit*, endearingly named by one of my students the "little brown book."

Because it is a very simple entry to set up and is totally indicator based, the Wave/CCI garnered a following that I never imagined it would. Most of you by now may already know of my (now comical) introduction to the commodity channel index (CCI). It was literally over a decade ago when I traded commodity futures, and please keep in mind that I was in college and didn't have much access to outside trading material! I (quite naturally!) assumed that if one traded commodity futures one should also use the commodity channel index. Not until later did I get my hands on a book that explained the calculation and use, but by then I had been using +100 and –100 readings as on/off confirmations for some time. But I digress. The Wave/CCI setup is geared toward those Wave readings that are like rolling hills. Rolling hills have a habit of not giving the Wave enough time to travel sideways at the three o'clock angle and set up a momentum trade. It is also appropriate for those (more aggressive) momentum trades where the Wave will not level out to a three o'clock angle but does tend to stay within a two to four o'clock angle.

There are two sections of the euro chart in Figure C.1 that I have highlighted with a square and a circle. The section within the square is a good momentum trading Wave. Notice that it's at a flat three o'clock angle. Now take a look at the section within the circle. See how the Wave tried to get flat but never spent enough time going sideways to set up a momentum trading Wave? I have dropped a vertical line down the candle that broke down through the Wave so that you could see the triggering event. Here's the way this works. When prices cross down through all three lines of the Wave and the CCI is reading at least a –100, then the short entry is confirmed. Figure C.2 shows a Wave/CCI setup in the Canadian dollar.

There are two highlighted circles on the daily chart of the yen. (See Figure C.3.) Each is a section of the Wave that began a transition but never leveled out enough to register a flat, sideways Wave. It is precisely these breakouts and breakdowns that the Wave/CCI can help set up. Just as swing and momentum entries are best applied to very specific Wave clock angle readings, so is the Wave/CCI entry. Don't let the ease of this setup lull you into frequent and incorrect setups. These setups work on any time frame—just as the swing and momentum setups do—but it is vital that you begin all setups with a clock reading. It really is as simple as this:

Twelve to two o'clock Wave = swing trading

Two to four o'clock Wave = Wave/CCI trading or aggressive momentum trading

Three o'clock Wave = momentum trading

Four to six o'clock Wave = swing trading

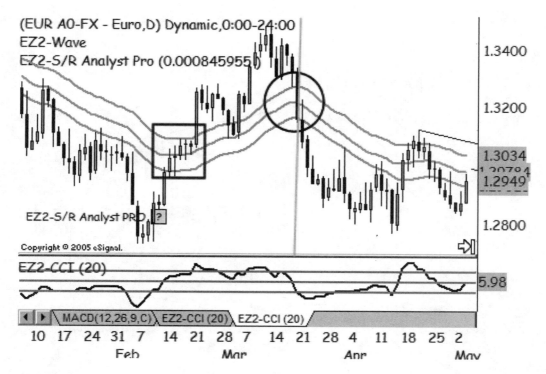

FIGURE C.1

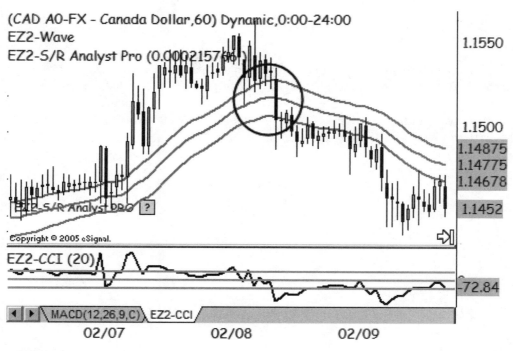

FIGURE C.2

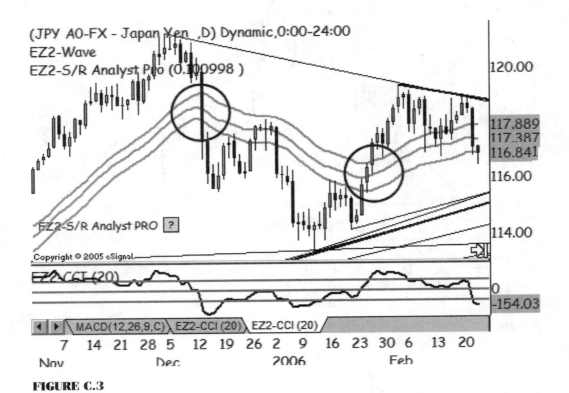

FIGURE C.3

The goal is to have an entry style that is appropriate for all market cycles, which is to say that once you have taken a Wave reading you know what type of setup to look for. And I know I said it 30 days ago when we started this adventure together, and it's just as important that we end the adventure with it now: Start all your analysis with the Wave.

Conversation with Raghee Horner

Interview by Linus K. Ahnis

I t's Sunday afternoon when I call Linus. I haven't spoken with him in some time or as often as I would like because things have been so busy. I tell him that I have almost finished writing my second book. He tells me "Great!" and asks, "What's left?" I say, "An interview with you." Just like that, Linus is standing on my doorstep a week later so that we can sit in my home office and talk. Two cups of Earl Grey tea later we're talking about the markets, hot zones, the popularity and growth of the forex, the Wave, my love of commodity futures, China, India, guitars, fishing, trading psychology, and more.

Linus: Thank you for asking me back for another interview. I reviewed many of the e-mails that you forwarded to me. I think I see some very common questions and some very uncommon ones as well! I also read over the manuscript you sent. This book seems to be more personal. It has an up-close feel to it. Was that your intention?

Raghee: I think that traders at some point have read all the "how to" books they're going to read, and frankly so have I. I wanted to present a "here's how I do it" book and the reality of trading. And I have to mention I was very inspired by a great book by Tony Oz called *The Stock Trader*. In fact, it's funny how small the world is. I have never met Tony but I am friends with Tim Bourquin and am a huge fan of the Forex Trading Expos. And Tim was one of the people who originally challenged Tony Oz to write a book and share the insight of trading over the course of a month. After reading that book, I decided if I was ever lucky enough to write a book, I would write one like that in the futures or forex market. You know, I don't think I have the "best" trading methodology but it's what's best for me. And that's what I wanted to share with the reader. So yes, it is a personal look at my trading style and process.

Linus: It looks like you've taken up playing the guitar. There must be two or three of them here in your office! You know I play the Dobro. Is this what you do in between trades nowadays?

Raghee: You know, it is a great release and allows me to relax in between decision levels. It goes back to a quote I included in the first book where Tiger Woods refers to relaxing and "smelling the roses" in between shots. I think that's also appropriate for trading. Too often we get too close and attached to every tick, pip, point. We need to relax and realize that once a trade is in play you work with what you see and the trading plan you developed for that trade. For me the charts allow me to relax because there are specific price points—I call them decision levels—that I need to react to. Outside of that, I am just waiting for my price, whether that is an entry, stop-loss, or one of my profit targets.

Linus: Yes, I can see your office is set up to be comfortable and relaxed. Is that a Jimmy Buffett CD you have on?

Raghee: Yeah, you busted me. I have CNBC muted on this TV [*Raghee points to a small TV on her desk*] and if there's a baseball game on, it will go on this TV [*she points to the big screen hanging on the wall on the other side of the room*]. But mainly I will listen to music. My college roommate got me into Buffett—it's great music to trade by.

Linus: I really enjoyed the depth at which you discussed and explained the Wave and clock angle in this book. Why did you decide to spend so much time on the explanation?

Raghee: Frankly, I don't think I got it across well enough in my first attempt. It's such an important part of my analysis—probably the most important—and I wanted to be sure that I got that idea across to the reader. I still get so many questions about what it is, how to put it on charts, and how to read it. So it was obvious to me that my familiarity with this tool led to my making too many assumptions about how easy it is to use. Actually, it is very simple to use, but only after you know the guidelines. I am thankful that I am getting this chance to write a second book! One of the most popular chapters in my first book was one I was this close to leaving out. It was the one on the Wave and CCI entry trigger. And I went into greater detail on when to use it here. When the Wave travels in a sideways direction but is not flat enough to be a three o'clock, the Wave/CCI entry trigger is ideal.

Linus: Another aspect of the book that I found very helpful was the depth in which you discussed order execution and what you referred to as "proactive orders." After scanning through some of the hundreds and hundreds of e-mails you received since your first book was published, it seems there is a lot of confusion about how to execute and manage trades.

Raghee: You know, that's absolutely correct and I think it goes back to assumptions I made. Order execution is something that I think far too few traders really have a grasp of. Now, what's funny is that I spent a lot of time understanding order entry with my very first broker, John. This was back when I traded predominantly commodity futures over the course of many months—and by the way this was before the Internet, and orders were placed over the phone. I think this helped me a lot because I got instant feedback and I was lucky to have a broker who cared. I mean brokers often get a bad rap. I have to say that John was instrumental in building a foundation of my understanding of order entry. The other factor was that during the go-go days of the Internet bubble, I took some already good order entry skills and took them to the next level when learning how to control my own order flow, placing my orders through different ECNs, and so on. So it really was an evolution and there are certainly nuances that I still learn today.

There really are four aspects of trading. And really this is just common sense, but like my father used to say: Common sense isn't that common.

First is the most obvious. You need a way to determine how to enter and exit a market. So obviously the first thing all traders must focus on is the methodology you will be using. This includes how to enter the market, how to determine your stop-loss, and finally where your profit targets are. So this includes trade management as well.

The second aspect of trading I think most traders must understand is trading psychology. This is a particularly popular topic among traders and for good reason!

However, one of my main issues with the books that are out there—mind you, written by some very brilliant people—is that many are not written by traders. So my issue is how can someone who doesn't trade help me with what I am going through? Well, there are certainly arguments for why they can, but I think that has led to my second issue with trading psychology, which is that we're told how we *should* be . . . how we *should* behave. Yes, fear and greed rule the market but they also rule human beings as well. I don't know anyone who can shut their emotions off. We actually would serve ourselves much better by working with our natural makeup. But to do that we must first recognize what that makeup, that profile, is. Traders are told how they should react but we hardly ever are given any insight on how to work within our natural tendencies and strengths. And by the way, that's something I am working on.

As for proactive orders, that's part of the third aspect of trading: understanding order execution—when to trade at the market, when to use limit orders, when to use stops to enter, and when to use stop-loss orders. I mean it's not all that complicated once you understand the pieces, how the orders themselves work. I was really surprised by the number of e-mails I got, so that's another reason I went into detail about how to bridge that chasm between the charting platform and the trading platform. Without that all the greatest chart work in the world is—without being too harsh—worthless. Who cares that the charts set up a great buy if there's no order to allow a trader to profit from what the chart shows?

The fourth aspect is one that you will need an attorney and accountant to help with, and that is how to organize a trading structure, to treat your trading as a business.

Linus: Okay, let's shift gears a little. Tell me more about your relationship with TradeDirectFX.com. I know you have been trading through that platform for many years, but you haven't seemed to have discussed brokerages in depth before. What's changed?

Raghee: TradeDirectFX.com is the brokerage I am working with and it's a complete brokerage that will allow me to get independent, full-functioning charts to traders through eSignal's forex charts. It has nothing to do with the Elliott wave study that eSignal forex is best known for, but it does utilize the charting, which means that the Wave, all my Fibonacci levels, all the studies I use, and more can be replicated. One of the other issues I had with people who read my book and articles and attended my webinars was that they wanted to know how they could put certain studies on their charts—namely, the Wave and the multiple Fibonacci levels I use. I am also offering the *Raghee Report* through the site. So there's really a whole host of tools I am making available there for clients that I couldn't do through other brokerages. On top of membership to receive the *Raghee Report,* there will be client-only online seminar events, special discounts, articles, and more. I will also be able to offer managed accounts this fall through TradeDirectFX.

Certainly the most important decision for me is the trading platform. TradeDirectFX has the exact same platform I use daily. The other reason was because I discuss and use conditional orders very frequently. So I needed a platform that offers these types of orders and flexibility. There are some other perks as well—tools that I use personally. But the best way to check all that out would be to visit TradeDirectFX.com. I have online videos there as well as articles. I am very proud of the content that we make available there. So I guess being able to handpick the tools that will be offered, I am finally happy with what I can offer traders. I am also very happy and comfortable with the fact that TradeDirectFX is an introducing broker to Gain Capital Group.

Linus: So it seems that it was a situation where you got literally dozens of e-mails concerning this. I saw at least that many in the ones you forwarded to me. In fact, that seems to be a common thread through this book. It reads like you had many of the questions from readers and traders in mind as you wrote. Is that what happened?

Raghee: Yes, the order execution aspect was just one thing I had in the back of my mind. I think you're right. I did have these questions in the back of my mind and issues that I wanted to make sure that I not only addressed but solved. In a lot of ways, I learned a lot about my own trading from the first book. I had to ask and answer questions that I could then apply to how to make the strategies follow my three Rs: *recognize, react, repeat.* This means that any time I could, I did my best to remove the subjectivity from the tools and decisions. I've always said that teaching forces you to deconstruct your trading approach to the pieces, decisions, distinctions, nuances; you break it down to things that you really don't even consciously think about any longer. The *Thirty Days of Forex Trading* idea was a way that I would be less likely to miss the small pieces because the reader is seeing what goes on before, during, and after my trades. Each chapter is a lesson in the price action of that day. There are also certain things that I wanted to be sure I got across in the book. I mean I could have listed these as "tips" but it is much more powerful when people see these things at work.

Linus: Could you list them for me? How about five "tips"?

Raghee: Ahh, I knew you were going to ask me that! Okay, five. Let's start with opinions. Everyone has opinions, but what counts are the charts. I have spent years trying not to have opinions about where I think the market is going. I really don't care where the market goes, just as long as it moves! I really don't have a bias. There's no reason to enter the market with some sort of preconceived notion of where I think the market is going because if I do that, I am involving my ego. And there's no room for ego in a trade. Sometimes I get an e-mail from someone saying that "So and so thinks that the market is overbought" and I'll ask who "so and so" is. Often it's someone on CNBC and one time I remember it was a blog! So I replied, "It's one voice and a single voice at that! Unless it's a world leader or CEO or the FOMC—you get my point—who cares what a blog or interview on CNBC said?" Trust the charts.

Speaking of trusting the charts, I think a lot of people fall off that wagon because they get distracted. One of the main issues I had when I started trading from my home office was letting people—friends and family—know that just because I was home didn't mean that I was not working. Now it's no big deal—I have been working from home for over a decade—but in the beginning it was tough. I would get caught up in a phone call or e-mails or go out for two-hour lunches . . . well, okay, I still do the two-hour lunches, but I have learned when I can let things in and when to shut the door not only to my office but to my mind. I have learned to prioritize and communicate my schedule to the people I work with. I never schedule anything until after noon. Distractions can also be looking for opinions that agree with yours or focusing in on contrary opinions. These are dangerous distractions. In fact, as you are learning any new trading methodology, I recommend shutting all these potential distractions out because at the early stages of learning you are especially susceptible to second-guessing.

I think the next tip, or Raghee's Rule [*wink*], is to be patient. Have patience not just to wait for a setup to develop and confirm but also patience to be able to wait for the right setup and the right time. Even I find myself itching to make a trade after I haven't in some time. But activity does not equal success. This is one endeavor—trading, that is—where how hard you work or how long or how often you trade doesn't have any bearing. It's about results, that's it.

I think one rule that has been on mind is about reality, and this one goes back to how to avoid being swayed by opinions. One of the most common questions I get from people who are amazed by my use of charts is whether technical analysis is a self-fulfilling prophecy. And my answer to that is yes—and that everything is to a certain degree. Reality is based on how we perceive things. If a large number of people are perceiving things a certain way, then that perception will become reality. I think a perfect example is psychological numbers. This is the ultimate "perception becomes reality" price point on a chart. Ask yourself, why is Dow 12,000 a big deal? Is there anything magical about the 12,000 mark as it reflects on the stocks that make up this average? No. It's a whole, round number. Is 11,999 any less significant? No. But perception is reality and people react to whole, round numbers. Let me give you another example. When the Internet bubble burst, one of the easiest plays to the downside was shorting stocks that fell through 100 or 50 or 20. These were psychological support levels for no other reason than the perception of breaking down through these numbers was known widely as a negative. This "perception becomes reality" concept is the other reason that I use classic, time-tested charting tools. They are well-known and the reaction to these levels is widespread and predictable. I am not saying 100 percent of the time . . . nothing is. But by and large it is a perception that when prices fall through a support level the prices will continue lower. So it becomes reality as the reaction to the break is executed as selling. It's also why the daily chart is psychologically more relevant than, say, a 30- or 180-minute chart. I could go on and on about this "perception becomes reality" phenomenon, but I think you get my point.

Finally, I think the most important rule—and I left it for last on purpose—is to be flexible. It's a tightrope we walk when we trade . . . to try to be disciplined and follow our trading plan without deviation. But at the same time there is a tremendous amount of flexibility a trader must have: the flexibility to see a trade is no longer valid, the flexibility to be able to take a breakout trade after the prior two *breakdown* trades stopped out. This is especially important when executing your stop-loss. It's a powerful thing to have all the prices, lines, and levels on your chart pointing to one conclusion and you have all these reasons to be confident enough to take the trade. On the other hand, there's this thing we call the "stop-loss" that says "Just in case I am totally wrong I'll do this." I think this is why so many people ignore their stops: all this gearing up to take a trade that you feel will work and then having to be flexible enough to recognize and re-act to the fact that it's not working the way you planned.

Linus: You spent a lot of time discussing "hot zones." I think one question I have is: Out of all the economic reports that are released, which ones do you focus on? What are the "hottest" hot zones?

Raghee: Well, that's a huge question. Frankly, almost any report in one of the major financial centers (Sydney, Tokyo, Hong Kong, Singapore, London, New York) can move the market. The TradeDirectFX platform has an international calendar built in so I rely on this greatly. But let me get to the root of your question. Hot zones can also vary in importance. I mean there will always be emphasis on Non-Farm Payrolls and FOMC decisions on interest rates—these are the "hottest," to answer your question. But right now, housing sales and starts are big because real estate is so hot right now. Hot zones, by the way, are not just the release of the report. It's the minutes leading to, during, and one minute after the report.

Linus: Raghee, you spent time sharing things like when you took the day off or took your mother to lunch or spent the weekend fishing . . . why did you choose to do this? I've known you your whole life; I know you don't brag, almost to a fault. Why did you share this side of your life?

Raghee: I want people to have a life—the charts can be addictive! I want them to enjoy life and not be glued to a monitor all day. I say this because for about four years, that was me, 16 hours a day. And I was trading end of day! It took a toll and it burnt me out.

Also, I wanted people to see that I wasn't at my PC all day. I think that the perception is that successful traders never leave the office, that they're at it 24/7. Look, I have no illusions about what I do. I am not a hedge fund or an institutional trader. I am a private trader. It's a different world. In so many ways I am in awe of those big traders, their skill and endurance; but it's not for me. You have to be able to walk away if for no other reason than there are times in every market that are not ideal to be trading. Like the noon EST to 6:00 P.M. EST doldrums in the forex.

Linus: Tell me more about your opinion and use of indicators. You are very clear about the fact that they are (1) lagging and (2) confirmation tools. However, I have heard you discuss indicators that project price. What's the difference? Why do you use the word *project* rather than *lead*?

Raghee: The word *leading* has a connotation of an indicator knowing where prices are going, as if they are out in front of a known level or price. I know that certain momentum indicators like CCI, stochastics, and RSI are considering "leading." My question is this: How can a calculation that requires price lead price itself? Simply put, it can't. However, it can project—it's a calculated estimate or guess like most tools. I will include trend lines, support, resistance, pivot points, and Fibonacci levels as projected lines and levels.

Linus: Explain to me, because I have read many e-mails about this specifically, why do you watch multiple time frames? And also, why don't you use multiple time frame confirmation?

Raghee: It's a personal choice, and let me say I have done it both ways. There was a time when I confirmed shorter-term chart setups with the longer-term chart trend. It was what everybody did and it was in all the books at the time. Maybe I am stubborn or who knows, but I started noticing that I was missing good trades on the shorter time frames especially when they were reversals and breakouts. And I started thinking of what I have now come to call my "canary in a coal mine" theory, which is to say that the shorter-term charts will show a reversal or breakout/breakdown trade before the longer-term chart does. Now, if you were swing trading, it wouldn't apply as well because having the longer-term trend in place certainly is a nice secondary confirmation. Also, I would have to say that I am not always overly aggressive in my trading—for example, a breakout trade on the 30-minute when the longer-term charts like the 240 and daily are in firm downtrends. But a confirmed trade is a confirmed trade, and I will follow my profit targets and stop-losses regardless. So I use each chart as a stand-alone. I am not expecting a 30-minute chart to override a downtrend on a daily but certainly I can take advantage of the intraday ranges and on that 30-minute chart. In fact, I can often already be short based on the daily chart but play breakouts on the 30.

Linus: Okay, I think this is something that a lot of people will want to know after they read the book. Raghee, you almost never mention dollars and cents. You seem to talk only in pips and points. I've known you for a lot of years, and you've always done this. You've always kept score this way. Why do you do this?

Raghee: You hit the nail on the head regarding "keeping score." It *is* about keeping score. I think too many traders get fixated on making $500 a day or whatever number they settle on. I think it even boils down to single trades where someone has in their mind they want to make $100 on the trade or even not lose more than $40 on the trade. It's all nonsense. Some days you will be lucky to hit that mark and other days that mark will limit what you could have done. So it's best not to have a predetermined amount that you want to make . . . as if that has any relevance to what the market will do in the first place! So for myself, I think in pips and points and price, not in dollars. Take care of the trade and the dollars will come.

Secondarily, I have no way of knowing how small or large the reader's account may be and I don't want a small trader thinking they have to trade bigger or a larger trader thinking that they have to trade smaller or that my methodology will not translate for them. The truth is everyone has their own financial situation. The trades can be taken in any size and that's the individual's choice. I don't want to sway them or make that decision for them.

Let me use a recent example. I did 40 percent in my account last month and that was trading conservatively and part-time. Does it matter whether that account was a $10,000 or $100,000 account? I don't think so—the trades are the same. In fact, I will be sharing the returns and trades at my sites.

Linus: That's very interesting. You mention that you will continue to do this. Where can I see this?

Raghee: You'll be able to get some more logs over at www.thirtydaysoftrading.com and also www.raghee.com.

Linus: Your schedule seems full: blogging, software, writing, commentary, and of course trading. I see there must be a half-dozen Post-it notes on your desk. And a studio? What's on your schedule for the rest of the year?

Raghee: I love working on new projects! I've been developing a new site, www.ragheereport.com, and this has been a time-consuming task especially when I sit down to think about how much content is there: hours and hours of videos, daily updates, archives. It's a membership site that gives someone not only access to what I am watching and trading daily, but also educational chats, webinars, and lessons—all in multimedia playback! But you know I did find it was a great way to get away from the markets but still be involved with them at the same time. I enjoy updating the site and making it complete. I want a member to be blown away by all that is in there.

I have also been working on a clock angle degree tool for my EZ2Trade software charting collection, which is in beta testing right now. In addition, I am working on another book on investor and trader psychology (with my sister, who is a PhD in industrial organizational psychology) and also a book on commodity futures trading.

Another project has been the "Thirty Day Trader" project at www.thirtydaysof trading.com, where I am mentoring a small group of traders and putting the finishing touches on a monthlong course that includes 20 20-minute multimedia videos. Students will watch one a day so that by the end of the month they will have everything they need to become a trader. It's an ambitious project but one on which I am getting feedback from actual students so that it can be tweaked and complete.

You will also be able to see me in video updates through Forex TV (www.forextv.com). I have a studio set up in my home where I can record commentary and updates for the site. Forex TV is one of my favorite trading information sites on the Web so I am especially excited to be a part of it.

Linus: Tell me more about the commodity and psychology books.

Raghee: The psychology book is going to be unlike anything out there right now and it comes from my experiences trading and teaching as well as the fact that my sister is a PhD in psychology. She is going to bring the stats, tools, and knowledge to my mostly anecdotal experiences. I really don't want to say much more than that but I think it will finally answer a lot of the questions that traders and would-be traders have regarding why they can't trade successfully, why they can't follow their trading plans, and why their emotions so often work against them. We'll have tools and resources available that have not been available to traders before. I am also very excited to be able to write this with my sister. She is brilliant and will add dimension and expertise to the book that I could never have done on my own.

The commodity book is going to outline the way I have traded commodity futures. I started my active trading in this market, and in a lot of ways it's my first love. It's now finally gaining some recognition and airtime with China's and India's growth.

Linus: Right, I am constantly hearing about the impact of China and India when it comes to commodities. What's your opinion?

Raghee: It's all supply and demand. We're going to have more people buying more commodities and that includes grains, software, meats, and not just energy. Everyone is fixated on energy and for good reason, but there is going to be an impact on corn and wheat, and have you looked at sugar lately? Too often I see people use correlations to history or cycles, which can be useful but to relegate your decisions to just these factors would mean that you are not paying attention to the factors that could be in play now. It's like the hurricanes in Florida. Being a resident for over 20 years I can say that the last two years have been the most active by far. Is it because of a cycle? I don't know, but I do know that the Atlantic Ocean is warmer. I think that trying to rely on generalities is the easy way out because it doesn't make a person think about the current decisions, events, and factors that might really be affecting market psychology and price. Don't ignore the cycle but make sure that price levels merit it. It's the same when looking at the stock market. Sure, go ahead and listen to what's going on with the companies people are interested in, but in the end make sure that price is your trigger. Back to

China and India, though. Both of these countries are growing economic powerhouses. In fact, concerning the forex markets, the Hong Kong open is becoming a big factor, especially the Sunday open. All traders have to consider world events and markets, but forex traders live by world time zones and hot zones. Since the majors factor in another country's currency, it is necessary to understand how the U.S. dollar is affected by the other currency in each pair.

Linus: Thank you, Raghee. That was great.

Raghee: I appreciate your time, Linus.

About the CD-ROM

INTRODUCTION

This appendix provides you with information on the contents of the CD that accompanies this book.

SYSTEM REQUIREMENTS

- A computer with a processor running at 120 MHz or faster.
- At least 32 MB of total RAM installed on your computer; for best performance, we recommend at least 64 MB.
- A CD-ROM drive.

USING THE CD WITH WINDOWS

To install the items from the CD to your hard drive, follow these steps:

1. Insert the CD into your computer's CD-ROM drive.
2. The CD-ROM interface will appear. The interface provides a simple point-and-click way to explore the contents of the CD.

If the opening screen of the CD-ROM does not appear automatically, follow these steps to access the CD:

1. Click the Start button on the left end of the taskbar and then choose Run from the menu that pops up.
2. In the dialog box that appears, type *d*:\setup.exe. (If your CD-ROM drive is not drive d, fill in the appropriate letter in place of *d*.) This brings up the CD interface described in the preceding set of steps.

WHAT'S ON THE CD

The following sections provide a summary of the software and other materials you'll find on the CD.

Content

Any material from the book, including forms, slides, and lesson plans if available, are in the folder named "Media." To view the files use the interface provided.

This companion CD-ROM contains visual and audio instruction on setting up and executing successful forex trades. There are eight sessions—all can be viewed on their own and do not interact directly with the book. The files listed below require Windows Media Player. If you do not have Windows Media Player installed, you can download the software from http://www.microsoft.com/windows/windowsmedia/mp10/default.aspx. They are:

Advanced GET Charts: How to set up your charts.

Trade Direct FX: How to master order execution.

Advanced GET Chart Setups: An advanced review of setting up GET charts.

Economic Hot Zones: How to capitalize on the market reaction to economic reports.

The Wave: A detailed discussion on the Wave and the components of trade setup and follow-through.

The Trading Mindset: How to take the pulse of the market.

Live Trading Setups: How to set up your trade using profit targets and stops.

Questions and Answers: Q&A with Raghee on charts, setups, and trades.

CUSTOMER CARE

If you have trouble with the CD-ROM, please call the Wiley Product Technical Support phone number at (800) 762-2974. Outside the United States, call (317) 572-3994. You can also contact Wiley Product Technical Support at **http://support.wiley.com**. John Wiley & Sons will provide technical support only for installation and other general quality control items. For technical support on the applications themselves, consult the program's vendor or author.

To place additional orders or to request information about other Wiley products, please call (877) 762-2974.

Index

**For more information about the CD-ROM, see the
About the CD-ROM section on page 245.**

WILEY

FREE REGISTRATION

I INVITE YOU TO SAMPLE THE MANY TOOLS I OFFER TO IMPROVE YOUR BOTTOM LINE AND HELP YOU BECOME A MORE SUCCESSFUL TRADER. PLEASE REGISTER TODAY. IT'S FREE! www.raghee.com/join BECOME ONE OF THE 100s OF SUCCESSFUL TRADERS THAT ARE PART OF THE RAGHEE.COM TRADING FAMILY.

- FREE DEMO TRADING ACCOUNT
- FREE NEWSLETTER
- FREE TRIAL TO THE RAGHEE REPORT
- FREE ONLINE LIVE WEBINARS
- FREE ACCESS TO ARCHIVED EDUCATIONAL WEBINARS
- FREE AND SPECIAL OFFERS FROM OUR FOREX AFFILIATES
- FREE WEEK TRIAL TO THE RAGHEE.COM NIGHTLY LIVE FOREX TRADING AND TRAINING CHATROOM

FOUR WAYS TO JOIN!

1: GO TO: www.raghee.com/join
2: FILL IN THE POSTCARD BELOW AND DROP IT IN THE MAIL
3: CALL (877) 864-3727 AND TELL THE OPERATOR YOU WANT TO JOIN
4: FILL IN THE POSTCARD BELOW AND FAX TO: (818) 933-8999

---

* BONUS * REGISTRATION FORM

www.Raghee.com

Name _____

Address _____

City _____ State _____ Zip _____

Day Phone _____ Evening Phone _____

Email _____

DO YOU CURRENTLY TRADE?   ❑ Yes ❑ No
What Markets: ❑ Forex ❑ Stocks ❑ Futures ❑ OTHER _____

Website: www.raghee.com ▪ Email: info@raghee.com
Phone: (877) 864-3727 ▪ Fax: (818) 933-8999

Superior Management, LLC
DBA In Touch
P.O. Box 261460
Encino, CA 91426